Portrait of Humanity

Portrait of Humanity

First edition

Cover image by Michal Solarski
Introduction by Lucy Davies
Design and sequence by Daniele Roa
Text edited by Faith McAllister and
Gemma Padley
Production by Anna De Pascale

With special thanks to Shaz Madani for the design work of *Portrait of Britain* which informed the design of this book.

Images shortlisted from Portrait of Humanity 2019, created by 1854 Media in collaboration with Magnum Photos

A CIP catalogue record for this book is available from the British Library

ISBN 978-1-910566-52-7

First published in the United Kingdom in 2019 by Hoxton Mini Press

Printed and bound by: Livonia, Latvia

To order books, collector's editions and signed prints please go to: www.hoxtonminipress.com

FSC www.fsc.org
MIX
Paper from responsible sources
FSC® C002795

Portrait of Humanity

HOXTON MINI PRESS

Note from the Publisher

At Hoxton Mini Press we try to do two things: bring great photography to a wider audience and use that photography to tell stories. We hope this book does both.

The images and accompanying captions come from over 65 countries and each speaks uniquely about the human condition. We are indebted to 1854 Media and Magnum Photos for bringing this wonderful project to us.

The experience of making the book has been up and down. First we were excited, then we were worried, then we were excited again. We'd had great success working on *Portrait of Britain* with The British Journal of Photography and when their parent company, 1854, had ideas on expanding the concept and crowd-sourcing portraiture from the entire world we leapt at the chance. Then it occurred to us: would a book about the world have as much focus as a book about Britain? Could one say anything meaningful about humanity in 200 images? Would we be able to harvest stories from photographers from so many backgrounds?

Then we saw the images, and more importantly the words, and the excitement built again. I'm not going to sit here in my east London office with my Macbook Pro and claim a profound understanding of what it means to be human in the wilds of Kenya, but I am going to say that seeing these faces and reading these stories of hope, sadness, love and loss touched me. At a time of such global division I am moved by a sense of familiarity.

We hope you are touched too.

Martin Usborne
Co-founder, Hoxton Mini Press

Foreword

'It has been clear for a while that the world is at a crossroads. At an inflection point,' said Barack Obama in 2017, calling for the world to stand up for tolerance, moderation and respect for others, and noting that some countries have adopted 'an aggressive kind of nationalism' and an 'increased resentment of minority groups'.

Our intent with Portrait of Humanity was to provide an antidote to the negativity and animosity that we hear about relentlessly in mainstream media and international politics.

We wanted to utilise the undeniable power photography has in the connected world we live in, to paint a portrait of humanity – photographing the people of planet Earth and celebrating every race, religion, sex, gender, age and culture that makes up the intricate tapestry of humanity. We wanted to show the diversity of individuals, accepting that we are all uniquely different, yet the same.

'Portrait of Humanity celebrates global citizenship, at a time of great instability,' says Fiona Rogers, Chief Operating Officer at Magnum Photos, our partner, and purveyors of authentic storytelling for more than 70 years. 'As chroniclers of the world, Magnum photographers have maintained an insatiable curiosity since 1947, and, as the landscape continues to shift, we have embraced our own journey to expand and diversify our membership. We are therefore proud to be an inaugural partner on Portrait of Humanity, recognising and honouring the importance of respect and empathy.'

The response to Portrait of Humanity has made it clear that this antidote is particularly necessary today. The many media partners who have promoted the award, the galleries and museums who will be hosting a touring exhibition between September 2019 and January 2020, and the reputation of our partner Magnum Photos, have all helped to create a phenomenal public response.

The thousands of diverse images from all over the world are a testament to this. They have also made it extremely hard for our international judging panel to select the 200 images that make up this book, which is our second collaboration with Hoxton Mini Press – following Portrait of Britain in 2018 – and the first ever Portrait of Humanity book.

This award serves as a timely reminder that, despite our many differences, we are able to unite as a global community, to create one of the greatest collaborative photography exhibitions in history. Next year, in 2020, 100 commended images from this book will be exhibited on Clear Channel International digital out-of-home screens. The scale of this public exhibition will make Portrait of Humanity the most viewed exhibition in history and, we hope, play a small part in bringing people together to embrace our shared humanity and to aspire towards a society that is filled with empathy and respect for everybody.

'There is more that unites us than sets us apart'

Marc Hartog
Founder and CEO, 1854 Media

Introduction

A little boy stretches his arm forward, his body arched like a fish. The curve of his head echoes the ripples on the water's surface, which race ahead of him, unspooling toward the lake's tree-fringed far side. Shadows cast by their dense overhanging branches are murky black. The hand grasping his and anchoring him to the bank near our feet, is taut and determined.

It is a charming image, undeniably beautiful in its depth, detail, and composition. It is also brimful of allegory. We don't have to know the boy's name, or that the picture was taken in Spain, or that the water was chilly, to understand that he is feeling his way gingerly, fearful of what lies ahead, moving into an uncertain future. Because after the Stone Age and the Iron Age, the Dark Ages and the Enlightenment, the Age of Industry and the Age of Information, where are we now?

The 200 photographs presented here for Portrait of Humanity are a good place to begin – drawn from all over the world they are in effect a crowd sourcing of the climate, a map of global fears and wants, and as much a reflection of the things we have in common as the things that make us different.

In Yamal, arctic Siberia, the child of a family of Nenets reindeer herders plays with his toy car in the snow. Meanwhile, in the city of Kampala, Uganda, where there are more traders than there is space for them to trade, a savvy hairdresser sets up shop on the balcony of a building, high above the haze of pollution and red dust. Thousands of miles away, a 63-year-old Mongolian man cradles a fully-grown eagle in his arms and a child runs along an empty road to launch his kite into the gathering light of a Myanmar dawn. In Pennsylvania, seven barefoot Amish girls try not to laugh as the cow behind them delivers a torrential wee, perfectly on cue. In Hackney, east London, a boy slings his t-shirt over his head to pretend he is one of the Greek heroes he marvels at in his books of mythology. In Ouagadougou, Burkina Faso, a man so attuned to horses makes them lie down on the ground as easily as you or I would a family dog.

These other lives are probably very distant from your own. But via thoughtful compositions and the mastery of light and shadow, succesive photographs demonstrate that the same live/play/love/battle/work/eat consumes all of us. They applaud our variety. The best kindle a charge of emotion. That person isn't really there, but your brain responds as if he or she is. Because while 'Humanity' means all the living inhabitants of the earth, it also means the quality of being humane, which is really empathy, or compassion.

In 1955, the Museum of Modern Art in New York trialled something similar; an exhibition of photographs that would 'explain man to man and man to himself', as its curator, the American photographer Edward Steichen (1879-1973) explained. The Family of Man, as it was called, is now considered a landmark in the history of photography. So many people queued to see it that it went on a seven-year tour to 39 countries. The book of the show remains the museum's most popular publication ever.

When you think about it, the exhibition's popularity wasn't hugely surprising. It opened at the height of the Cold War (and when the Second World War was still an uncomfortably recent memory) and was very cleverly positioned as a sort of manifesto for peace. Moreover, Steichen had simplified the entries into eminently relatable themes (birth, death, children, education, love, work and so on), all in the name of freeze-framing 'the essential oneness of mankind... People looked at the pictures, and the people in the pictures looked back at them,' he later remarked. 'They recognised each other.'

Sixty-four years is a long time ago, though – more than two generations – and history spins on. Or does it? Because what struck me most, leafing through the images here, is how few of them would have looked out of place in Steichen's exhibition. The toxic scrap dump in Agbogbloshie, Ghana, where our unwanted phones and laptops go to die, and the man at the Mars Desert Research Station in Utah – yes. But nearly every other picture is a portrait of lives we have been living for centuries – shepherds, healers, herders and the like. I think we should be heartened by that. In a polarised, warp-speed, baffling world, that sinew of history is like the arm holding on to that tiny boy as he surges forward into the stream.

Lucy Davies
London, 2019

Portraits

Family

by Roland 'Kilimanjaro' Błażejewski

Berlin, Germany

I met this couple in Berlin. They were sitting together on the side of a street when I started a conversation with them. We talked for a long time and the man repeated, 'We are a family, we are together, we are strong' over and over. When I got up to leave I glanced back at them and took this photograph.

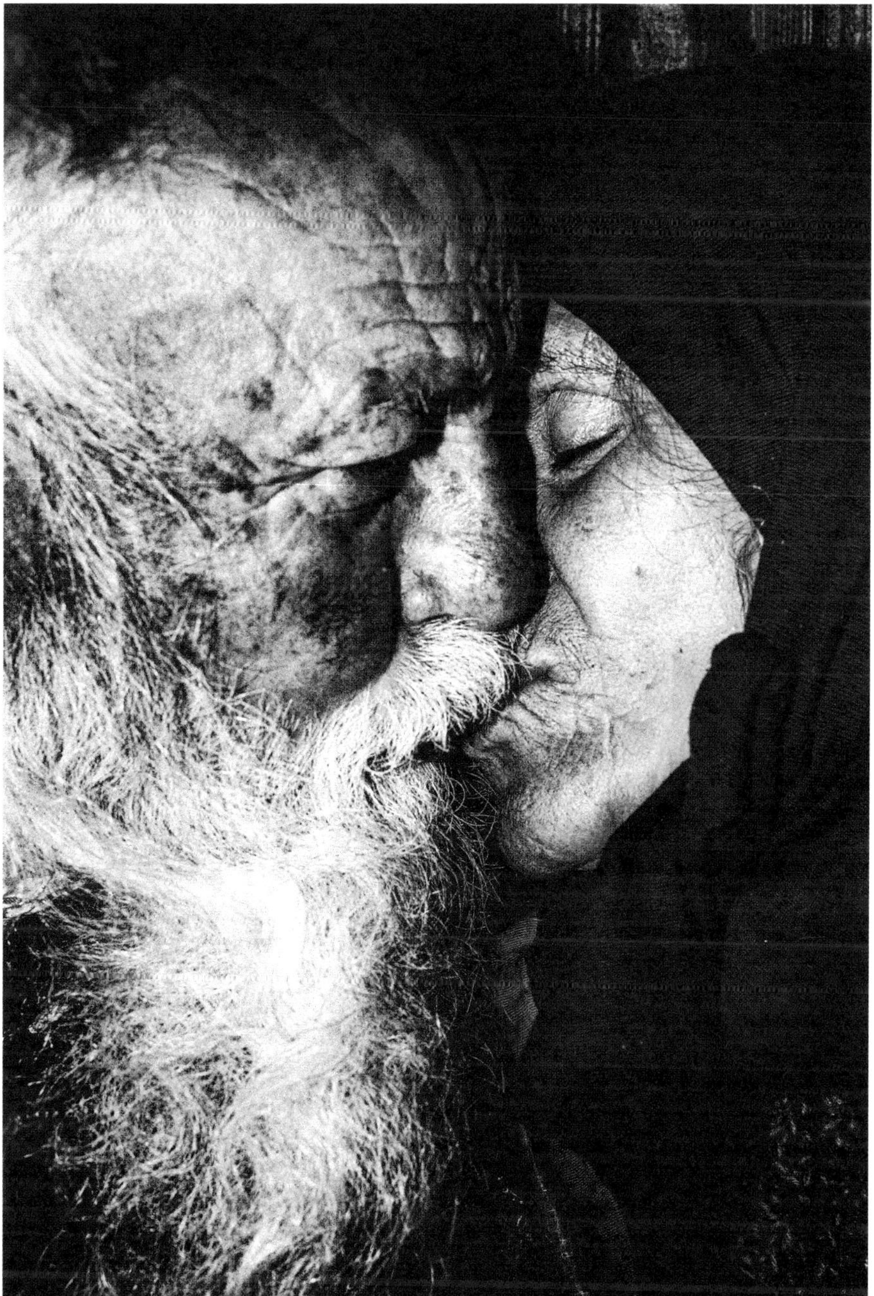

Mother and Daughter

by Bente Marei Stachowske

Mediterranean Sea, close to the Libyan coast

I joined the crew of a rescue ship as it patrolled international waters in search of refugees. This mother and baby were rescued from a rubber dinghy.

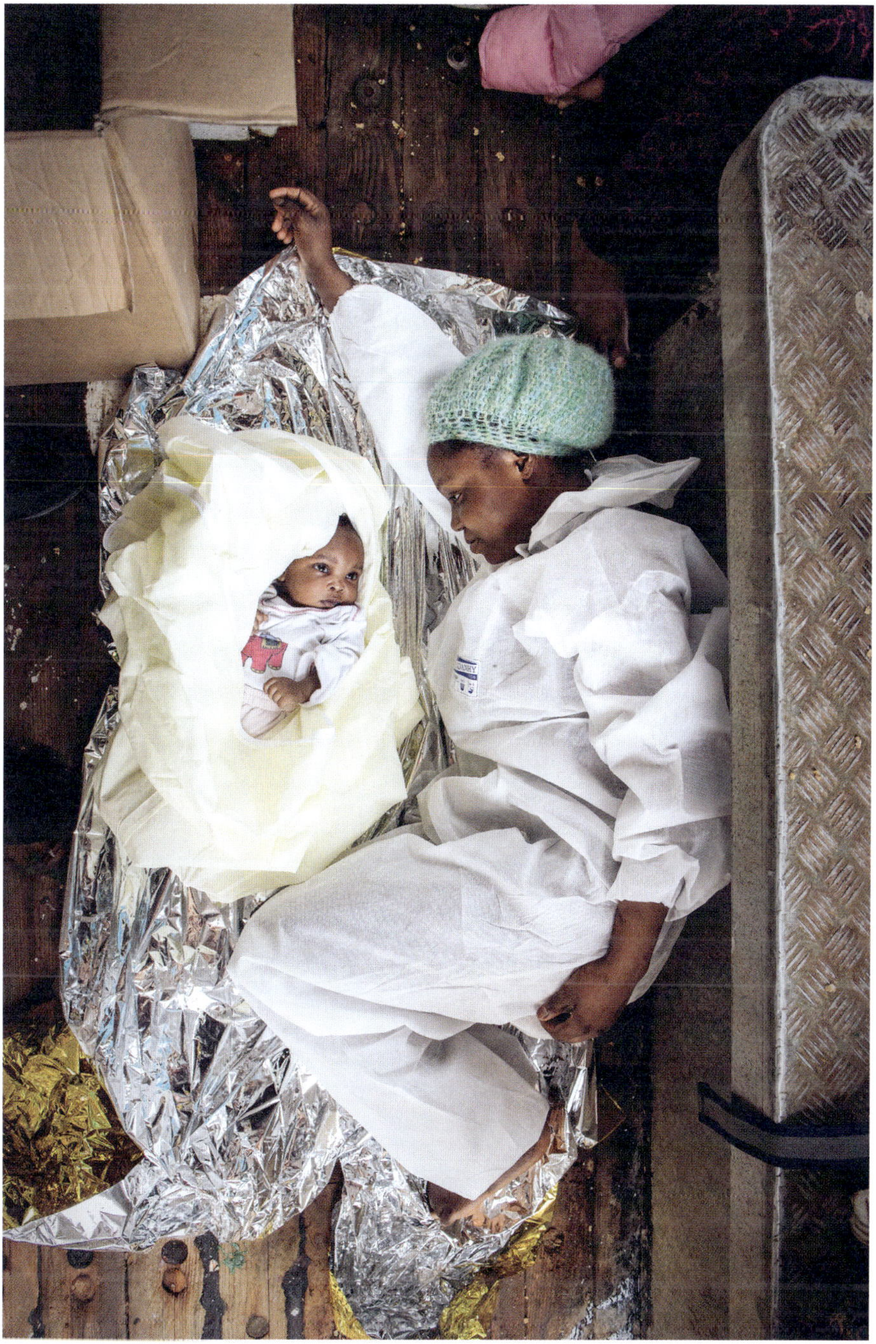

Mother and Daughter:
80 and 50 Years on Earth

by Johanna Berghorn

Valencia, Spain

There is something special about motherly love.
It has an intensity and strength I can't put into words.

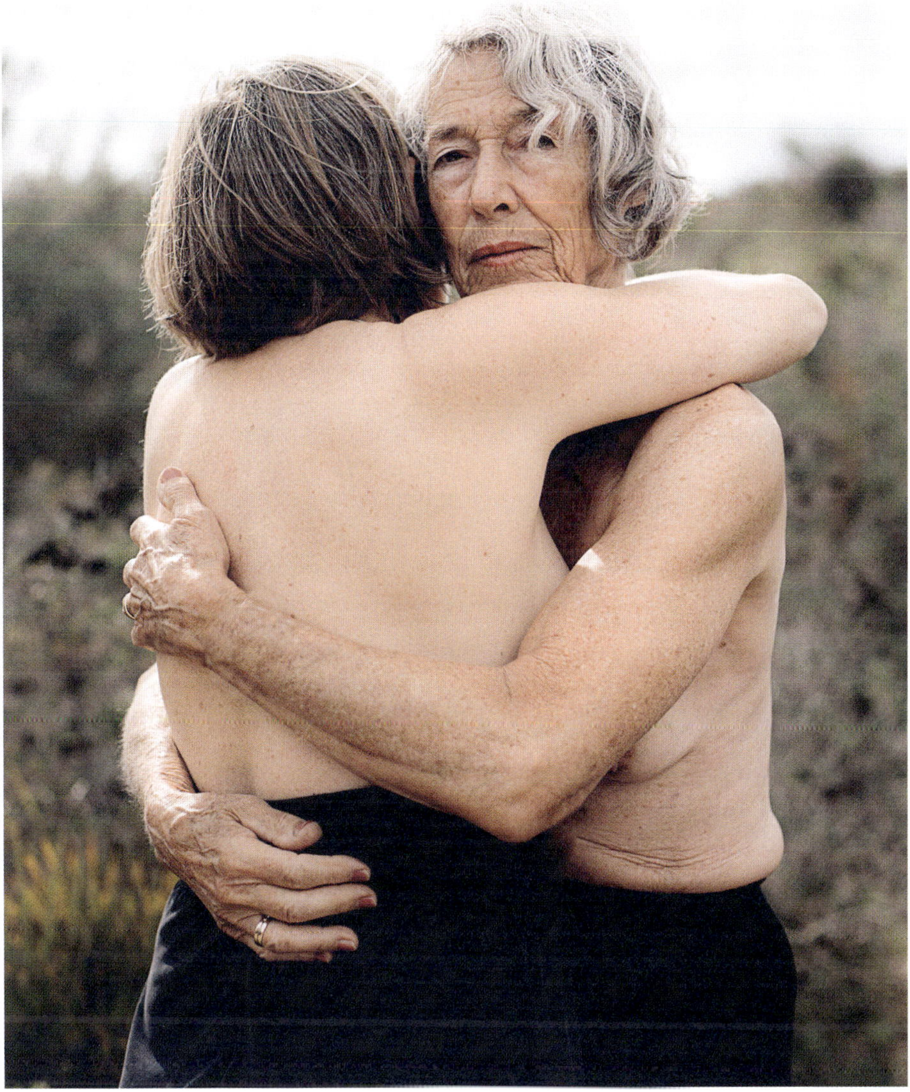

Onika

by Camila Falcão

São Paulo, Brazil

When I was photographing Onika she told me about her experience of transitioning: from the side effects of the hormonal therapy to how good it felt to have curves. But she also talked about the violence against transgender people in Brazil.

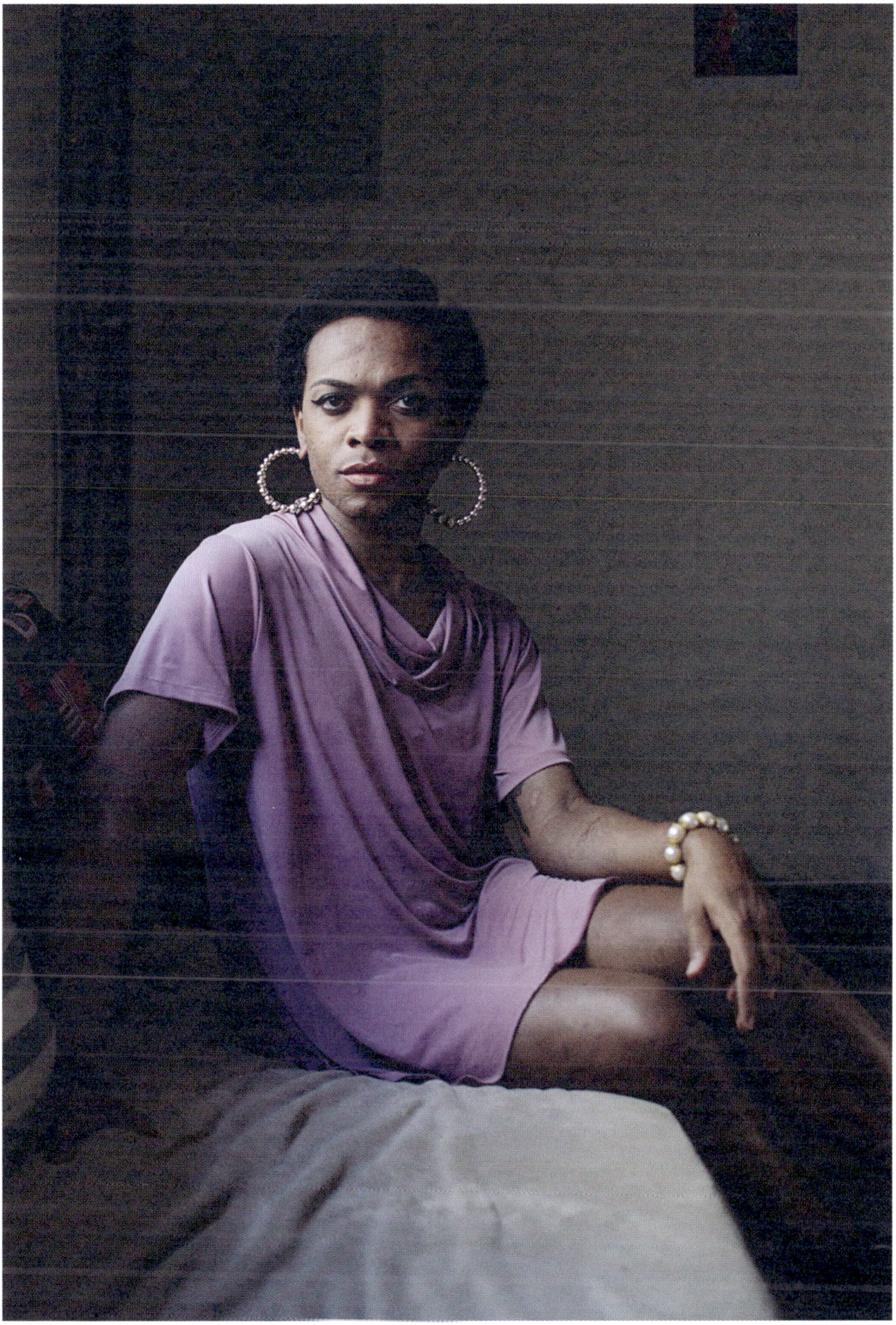

Captain America

by Charlie Kwai

Mexico City, Mexico

This Mexican boy dressed as Captain America walked unaccompanied down a street in Mexico City.

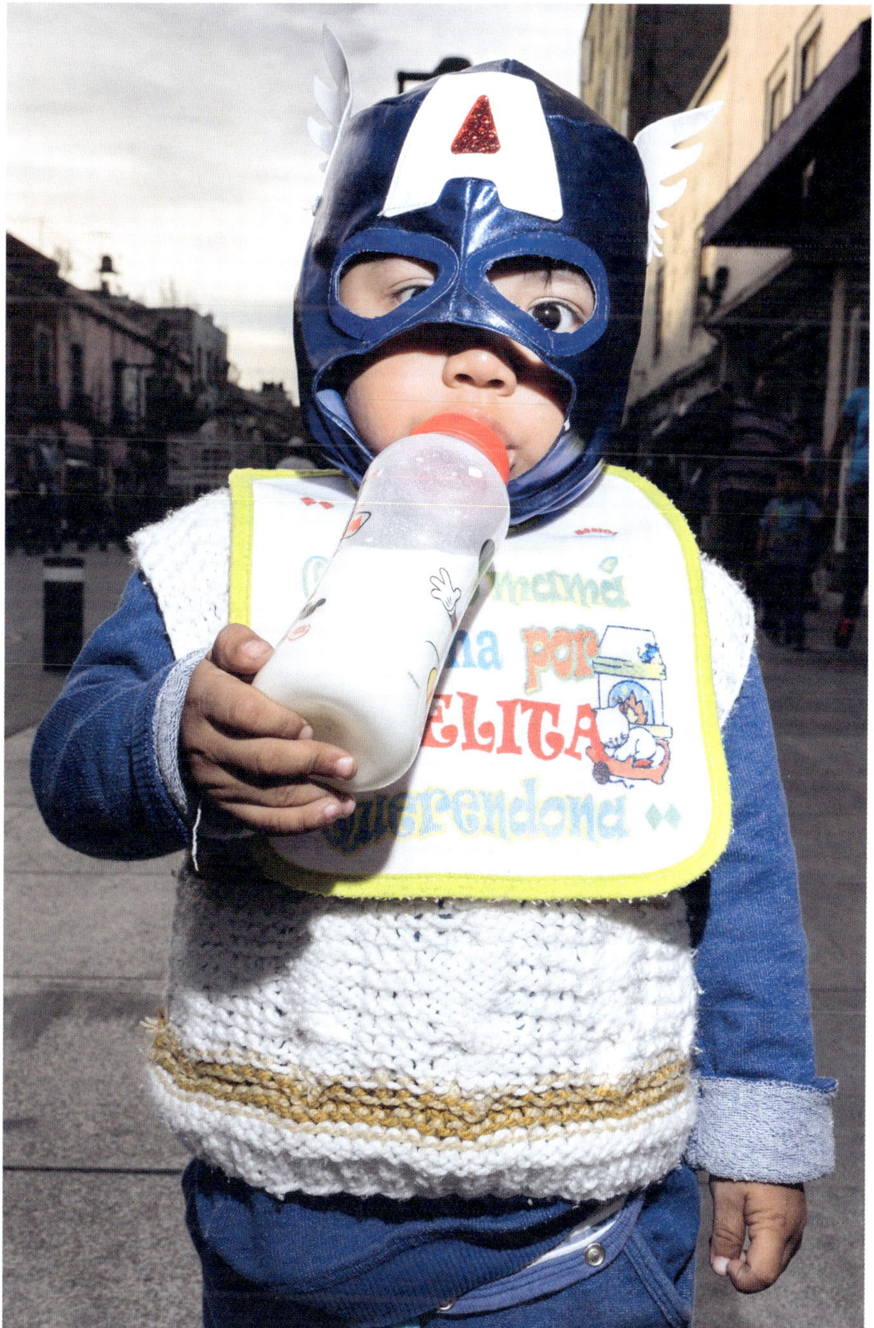
mamá
por

Coral

by Sam Robinson

London, UK

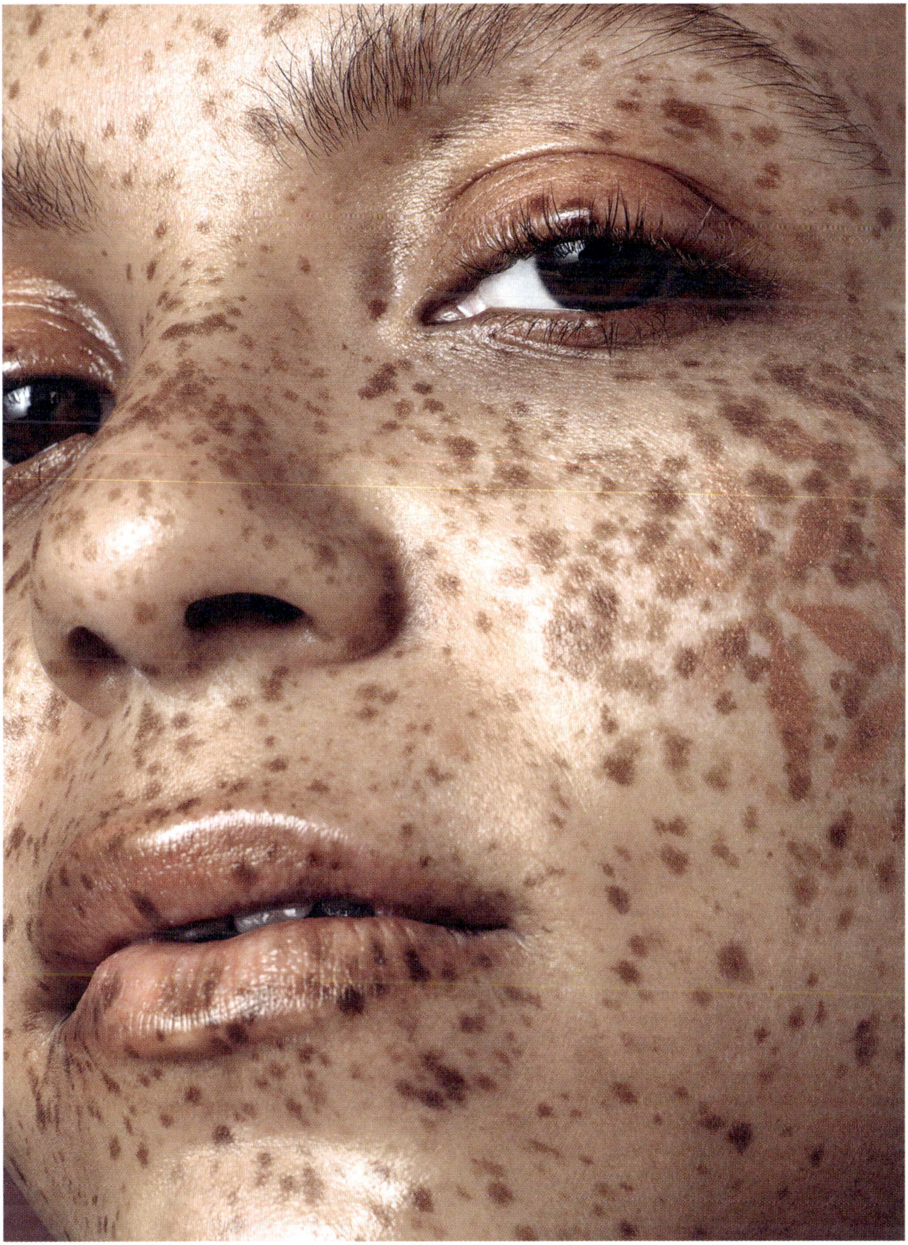

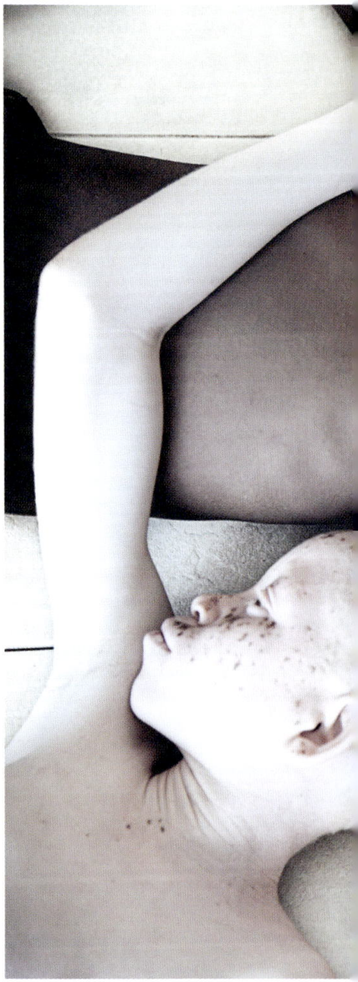

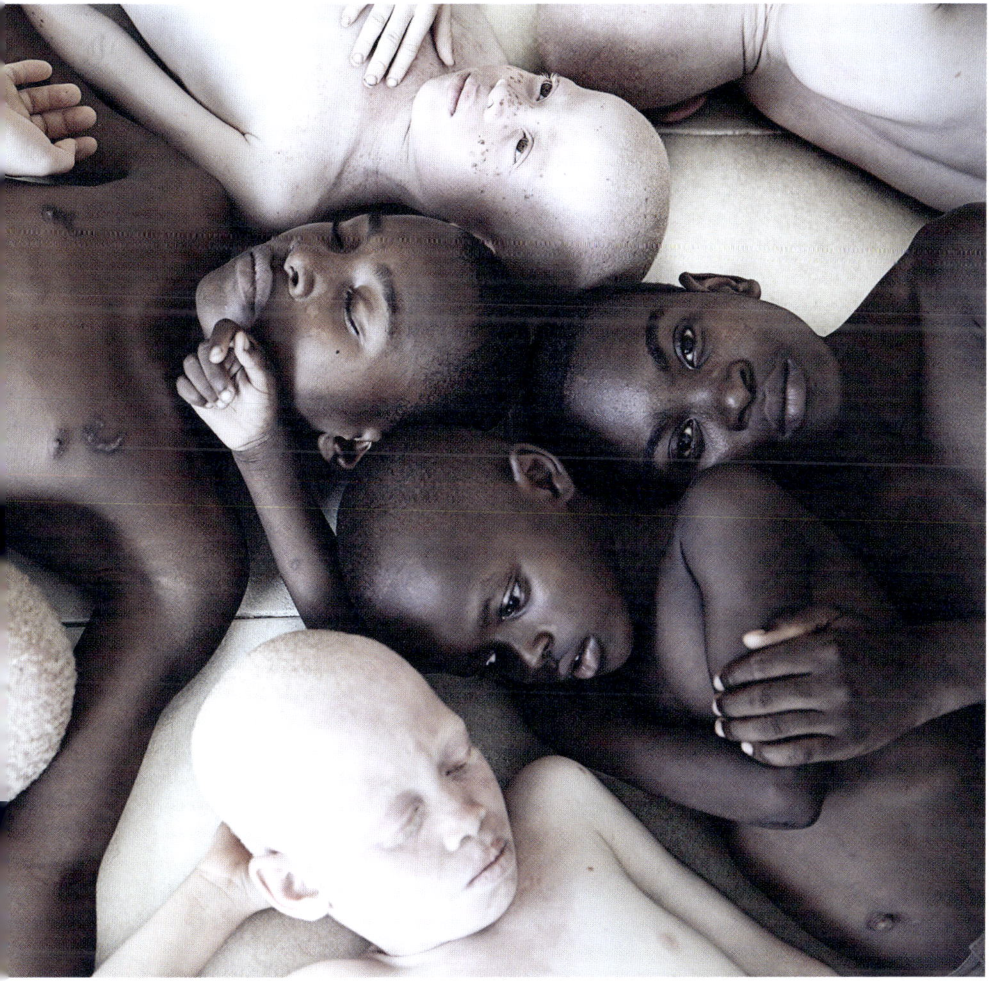

Under the Same Sun
by Marinka Masséus
Dar es Salaam, Tanzania

The superstitions surrounding albinism run deep in Tanzanian society. Many children are rejected by their families and live in camps where they are often mistreated.

Face to Faith

by Samuel Zuder

Mount Kailash, Tibet

These two friends – pilgrims – were dressed almost identically and looked like twins to me. They had travelled thousands of kilometres to worship at the holy mountain.

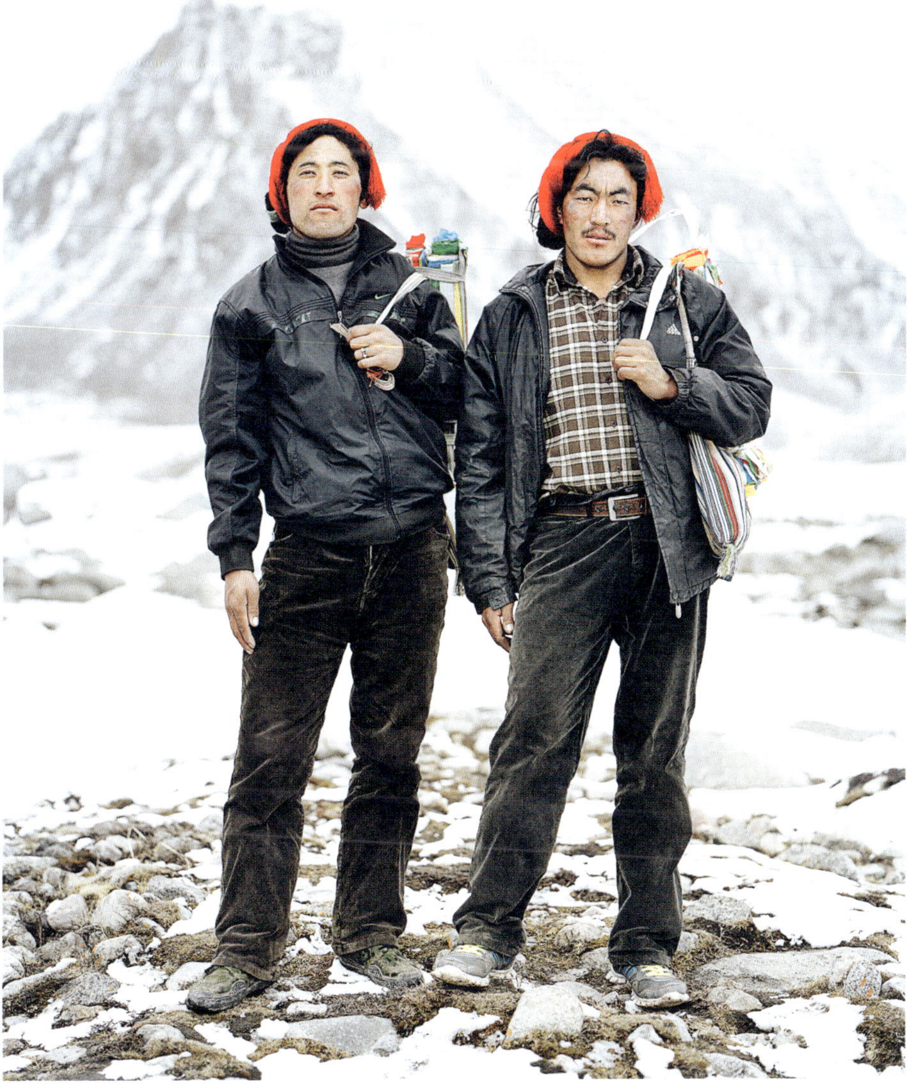

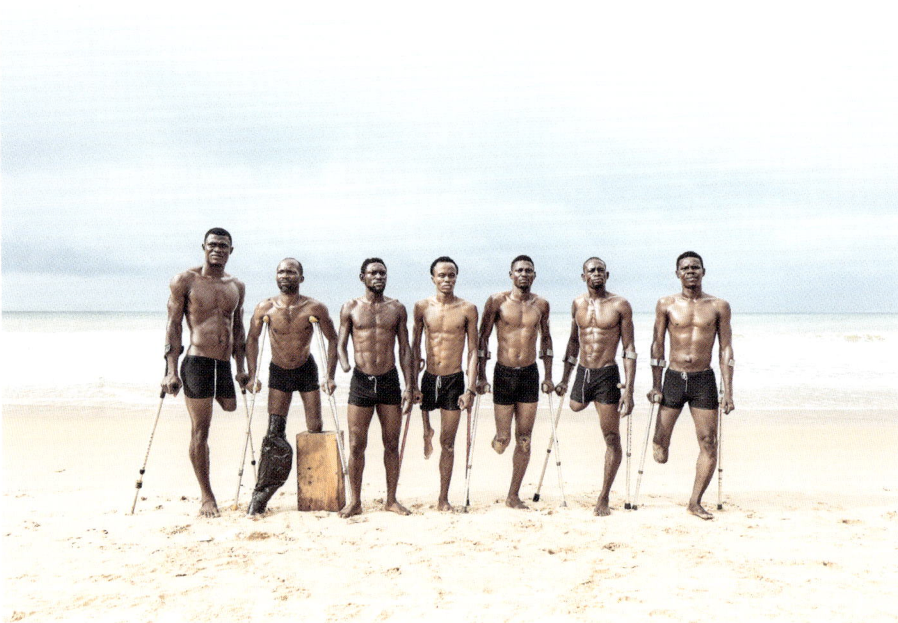

Special Eagles

by Jack Lawson

Lagos, Nigeria

Limb amputation is commonplace in Nigeria, especially among young men. Primary causes include diabetic complications and trauma, such as road accidents. One group of amputees refusing to be held back is the country's amputee football team, Special Eagles. Football has brought these men together and they share an incredible bond.

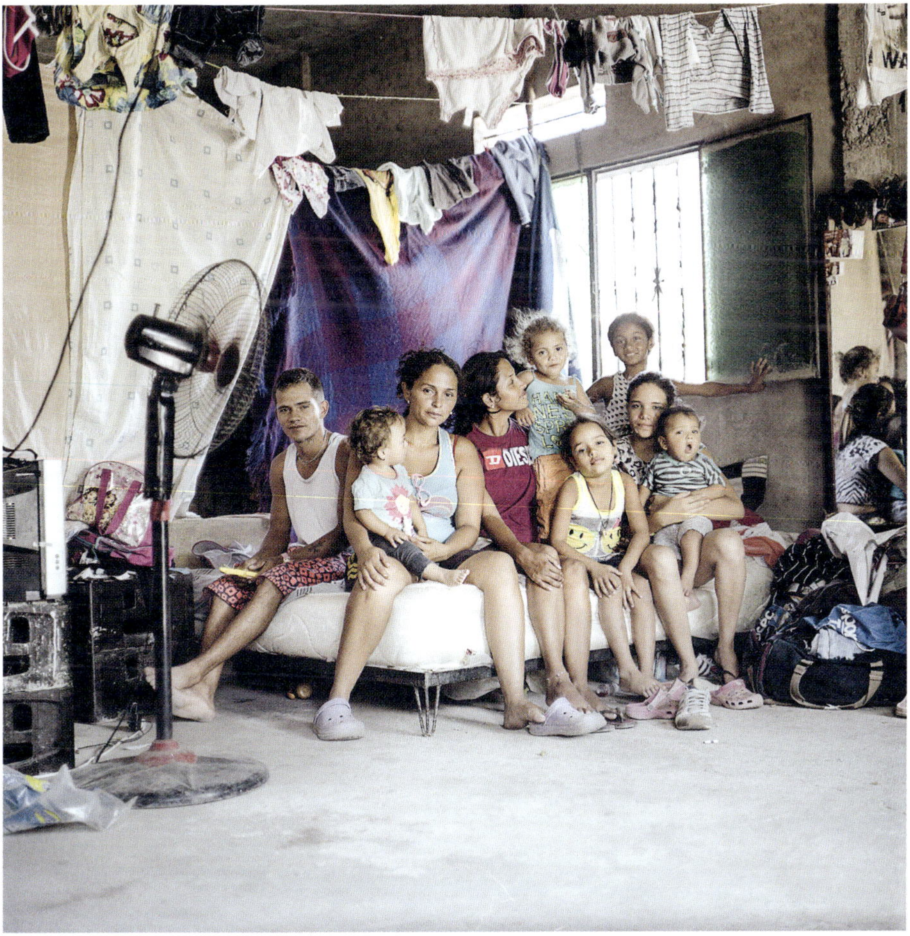

Keep Moving

by Sebastián Delgado Caicedo

Cúcuta, Colombia

In 2008, the Giraldo family fled from danger in Colombia and lived in Venezuela for seven years until they were ordered to leave. They left behind the life they had built to face an uncertain future in their home country.

You Can Post This After I Die

by Tajette O'Halloran

Boca Raton, Florida, USA

I took this photograph one evening while staying with my grandma. She was undressing from the day and I was about to hop into the shower. As I walked through her room to use her en-suite bathroom, she looked at me and said, 'Oi vey, what a figure!' She then stood next to me, shrugged, and lifted up her breasts to where they might have sat 58 years ago when she was my age. I laughed and laughed and Grandma giggled her infectious little giggle. She died on 11 March 2018 at the age of 94 and I can still hear her voice: 'Put that damn camera away!'

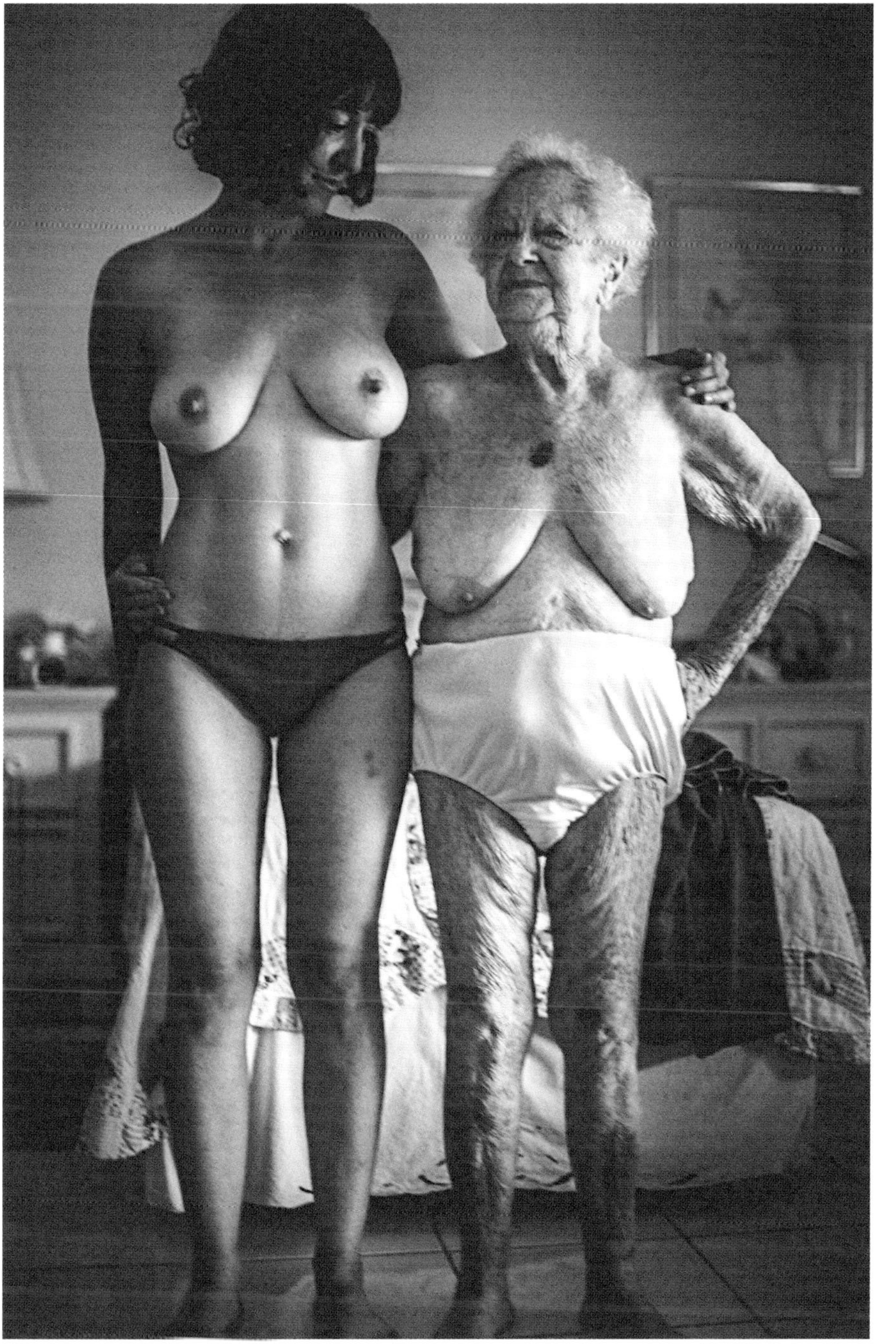

Lissy

by Anna Berry

Milton Keynes, UK

I met Lissy in a feminist group and found her to be incredibly fierce yet vulnerable. Her demeanor in this image is queenly, magnificent and unapologetic, and yet there is a sadness too.

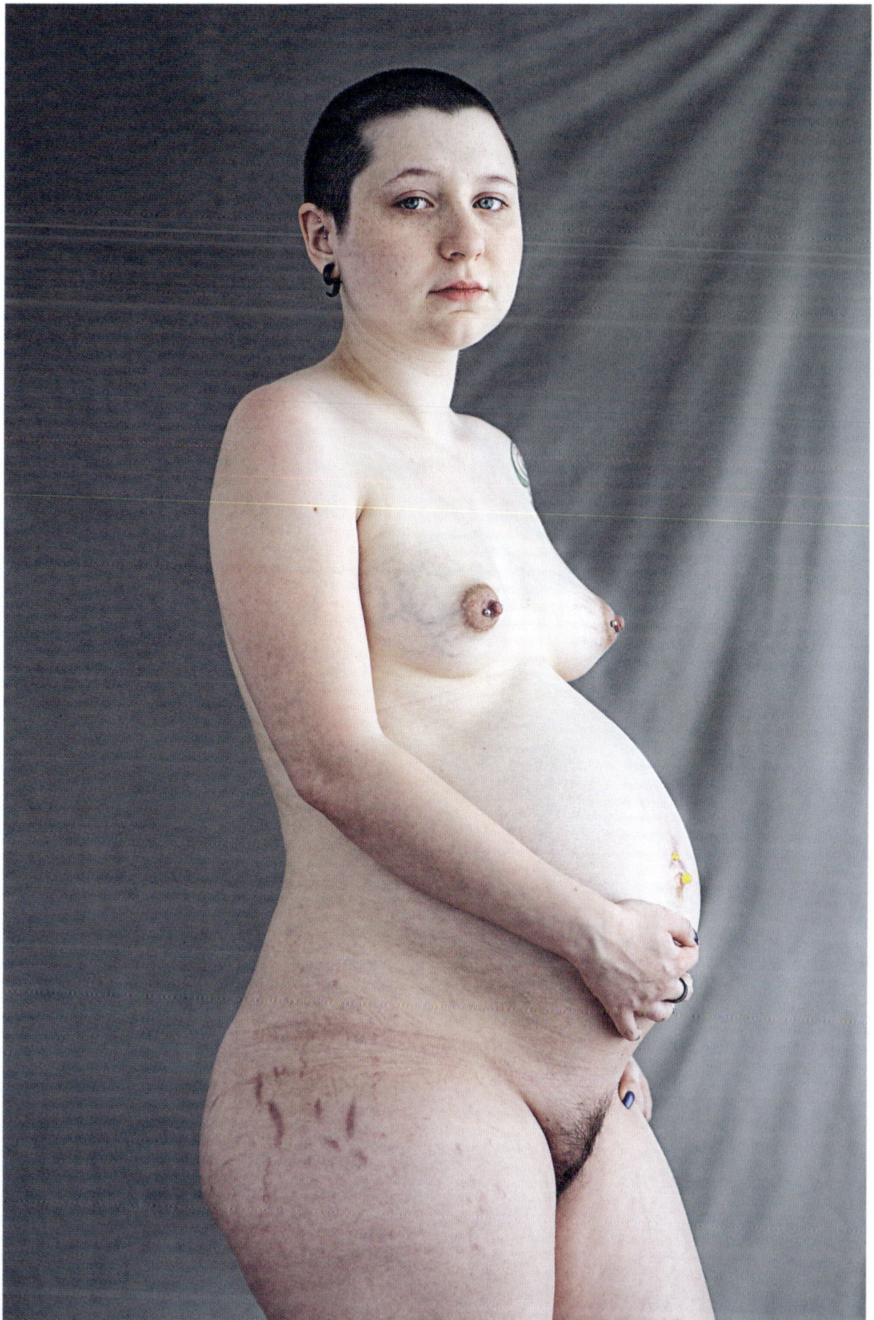

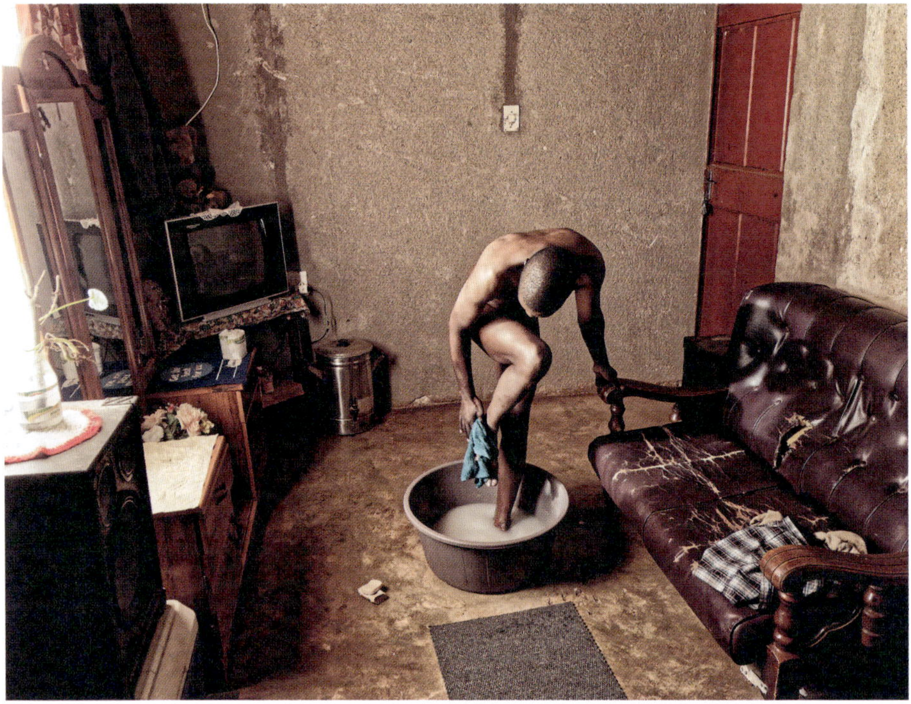

No Man's Land

by Pieter de Vos

KwaMhlanga, South Africa

Christopher has spent most of his life on the economic margins of South Africa despite his dogged pursuit of employment and stable housing. 'I was a street kid,' he said. 'The kid that grows up on the street is in no man's land.'

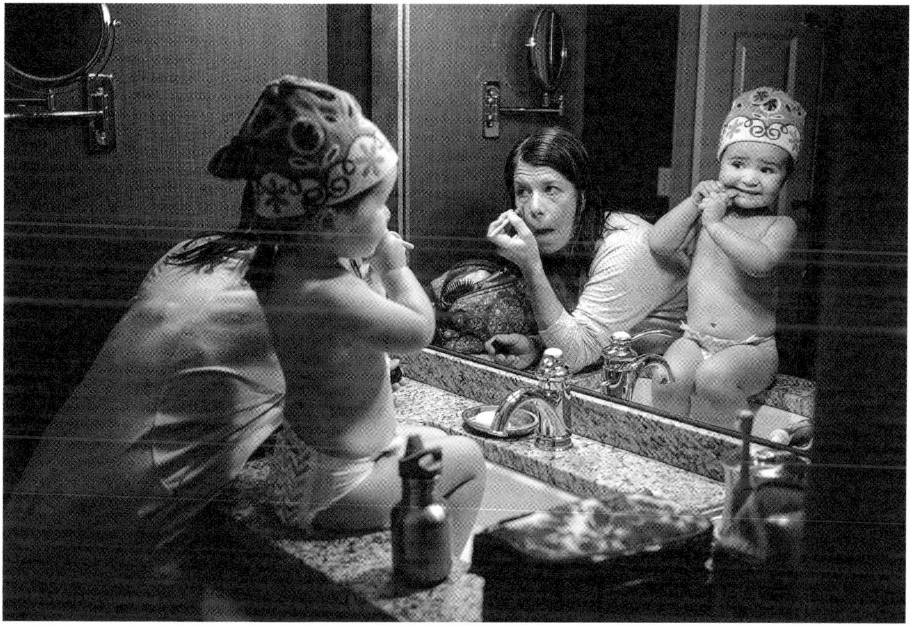

My Wife and Daughter, Hotel Bathroom
by Jeff Borkowski
Burlington, Vermont, USA

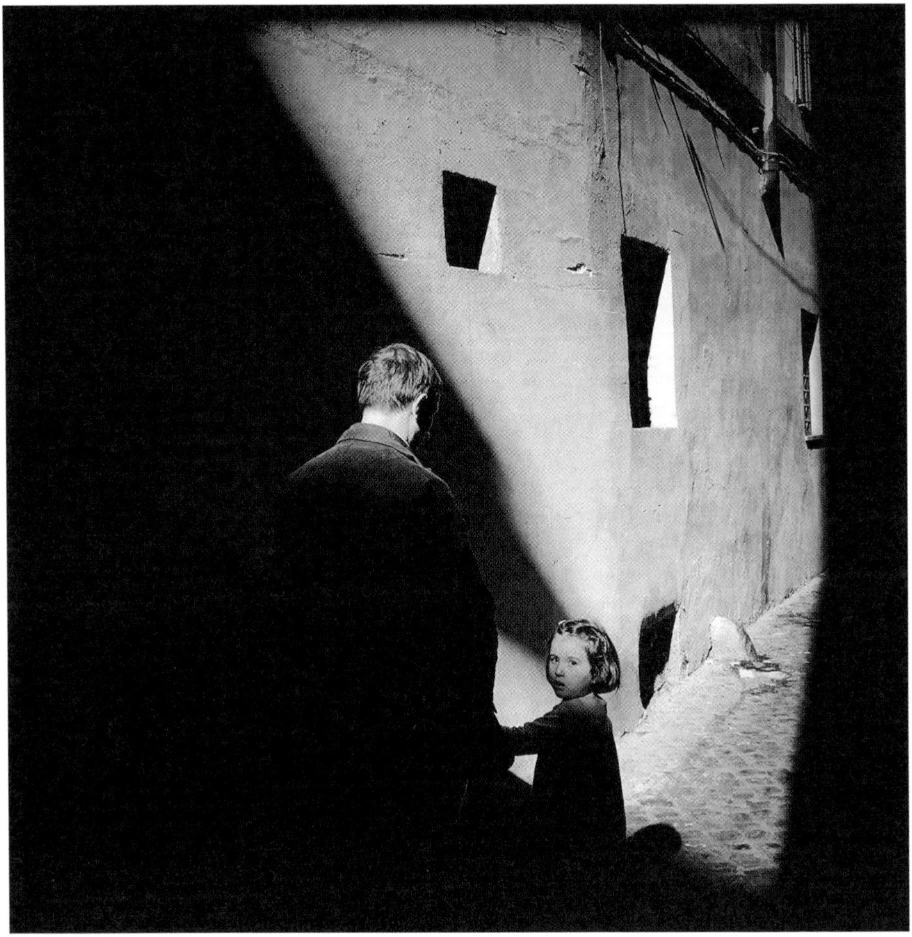

Looking Back
by Marina Sersale
Rome, Italy

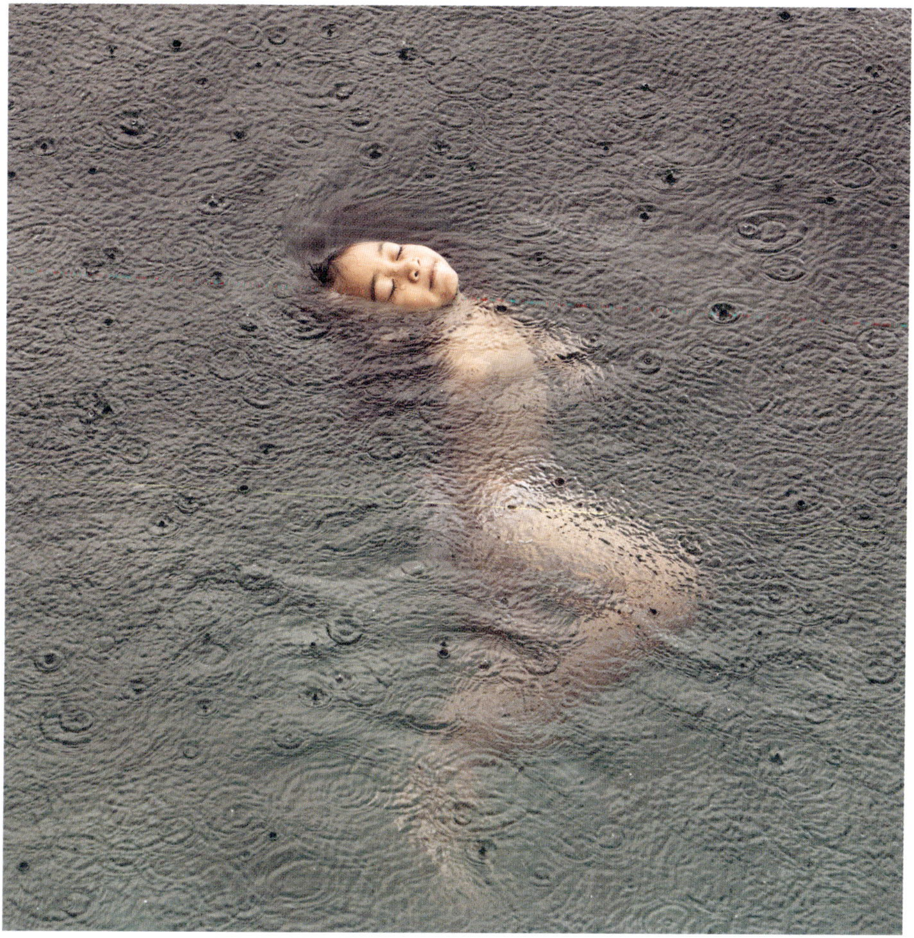

Materic Water #1
by Bruna Rotunno
Bali, Indonesia

I was looking out of the window from my hotel room that overlooked a swimming pool. No guests were swimming because of heavy rain, but suddenly this little girl leapt into the water.

Portrait of Dan

by Manon Ouimet

London, UK

Dan lost his arm and shoulder in a motorbike accident. 'Beauty is about knowing and accepting who you are,' he says. 'I would class myself as a lucky guy because I am comfortable in my own skin.'

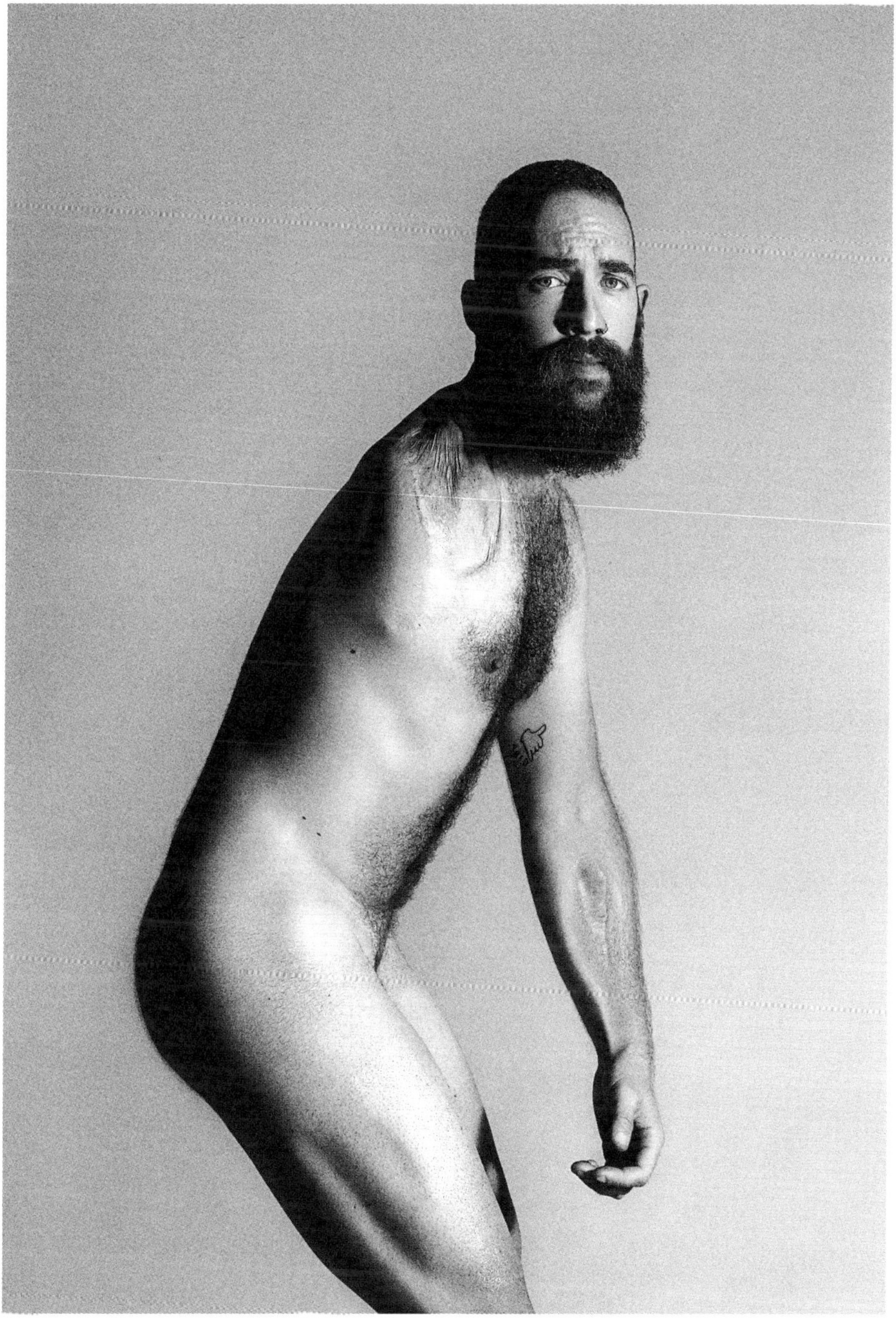

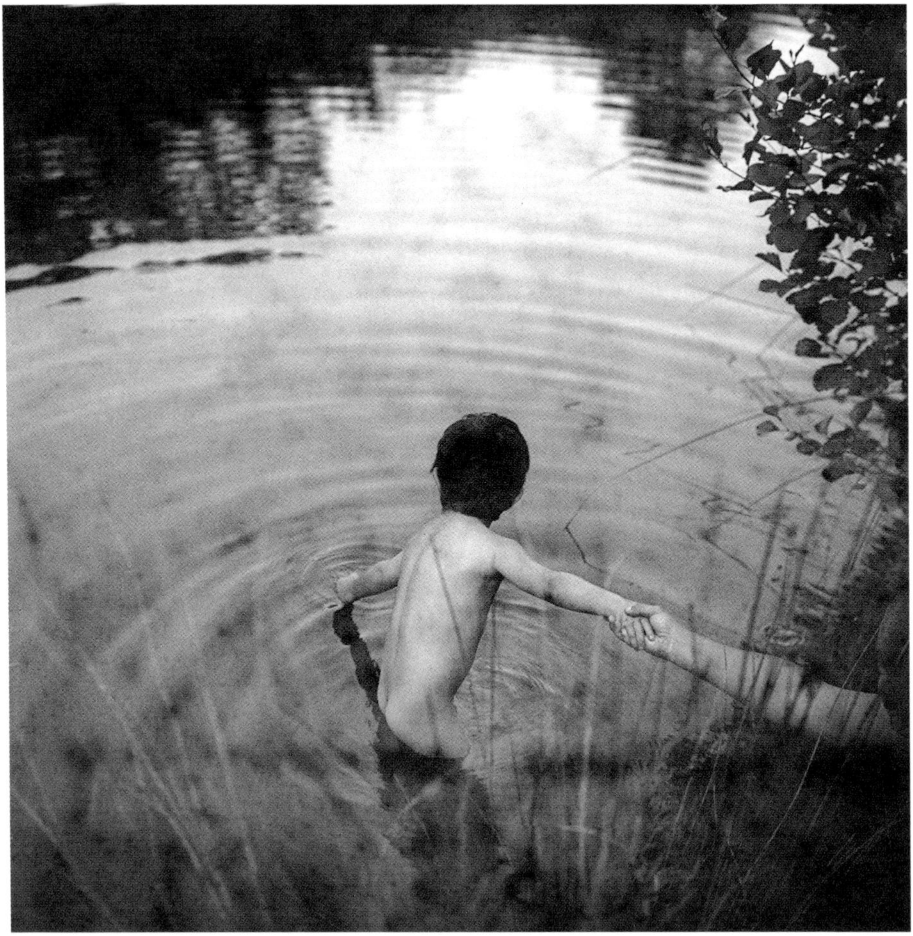

Mateo Trujillo Takes a Dip
by Álvaro Maria Gómez-Pidal
Jaén, Spain

The water was cold and Mateo was fearful
but he ventured in anyway.

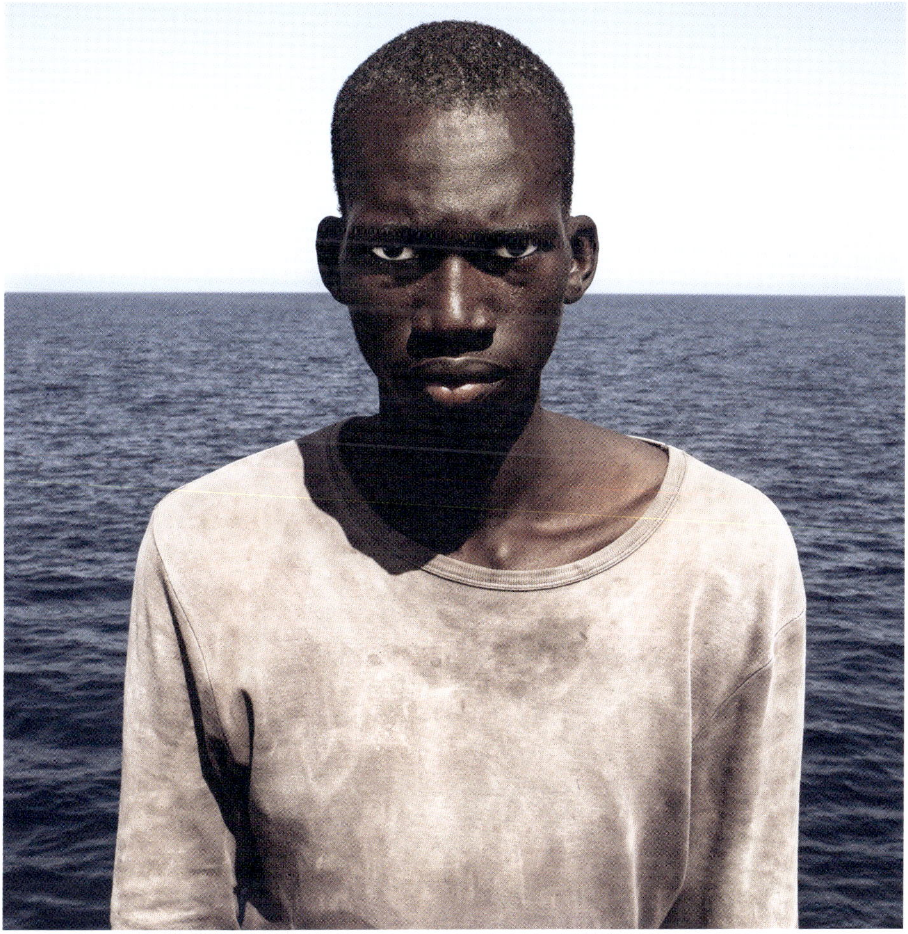

Amadou Sumaila
by Cesar Dezfuli
Mediterranean Sea, Libya

Amadou, a young Malian, moments after he and 117 fellow travellers were rescued from the sea. The boat he was on had only departed Libya a short while earlier.

Charles

by Guoman Liao

Vancouver, British Columbia, Canada

Charles is a friend who I met on a photo shoot.
He is a model and student from Kelowna, Canada.
I used the flower as a contrast to my subject, and to
show both the gentleness and masculinity of Charles.

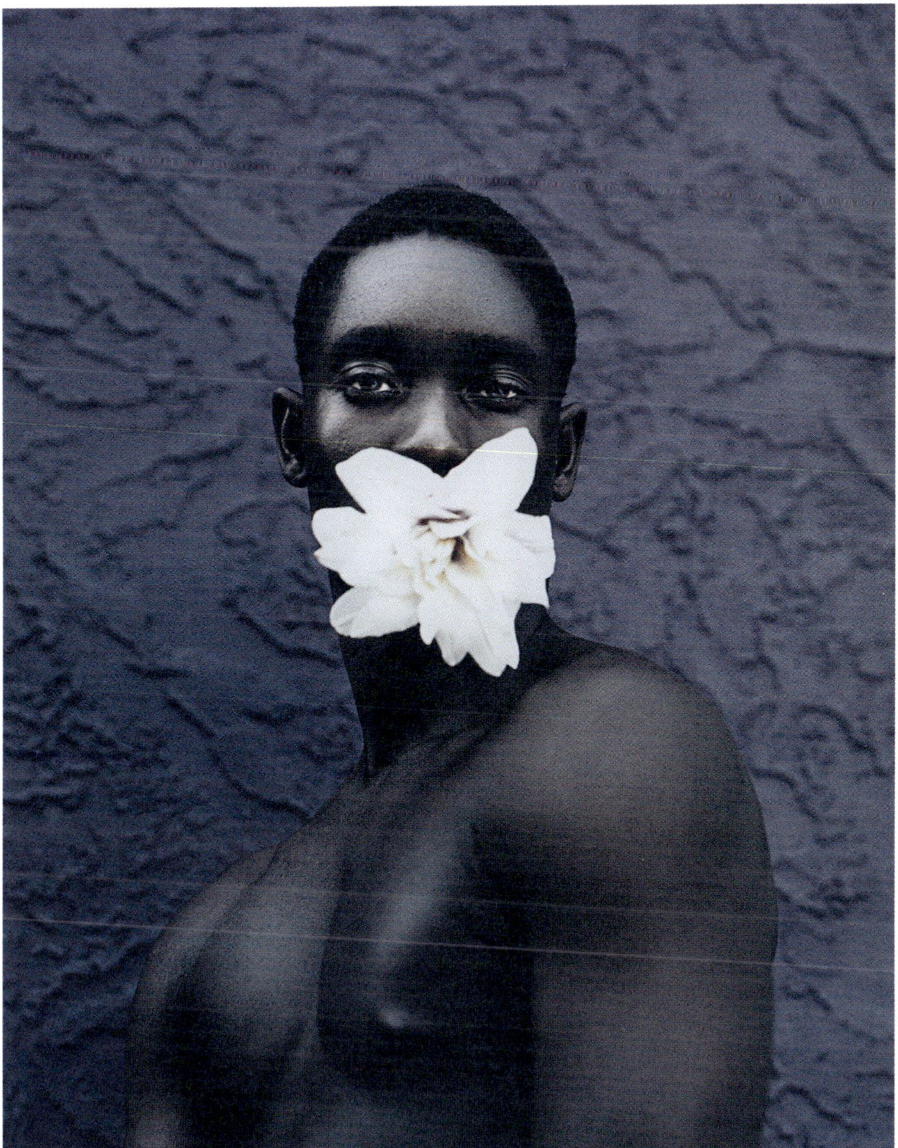

As Hard as a Rock

by Bartłomiej Jurecki

Witów, Poland

Wladyslaw Stopka Faktor lives in a house he built and has a small farm in Tatra County, a region where highlanders' faces are marked by struggle and pride. Highlanders are tough, but their hearts are big. Wladyslaw has worked as a carpenter and can also sew. 'God has given me manual skills and poverty has taught me everything.'

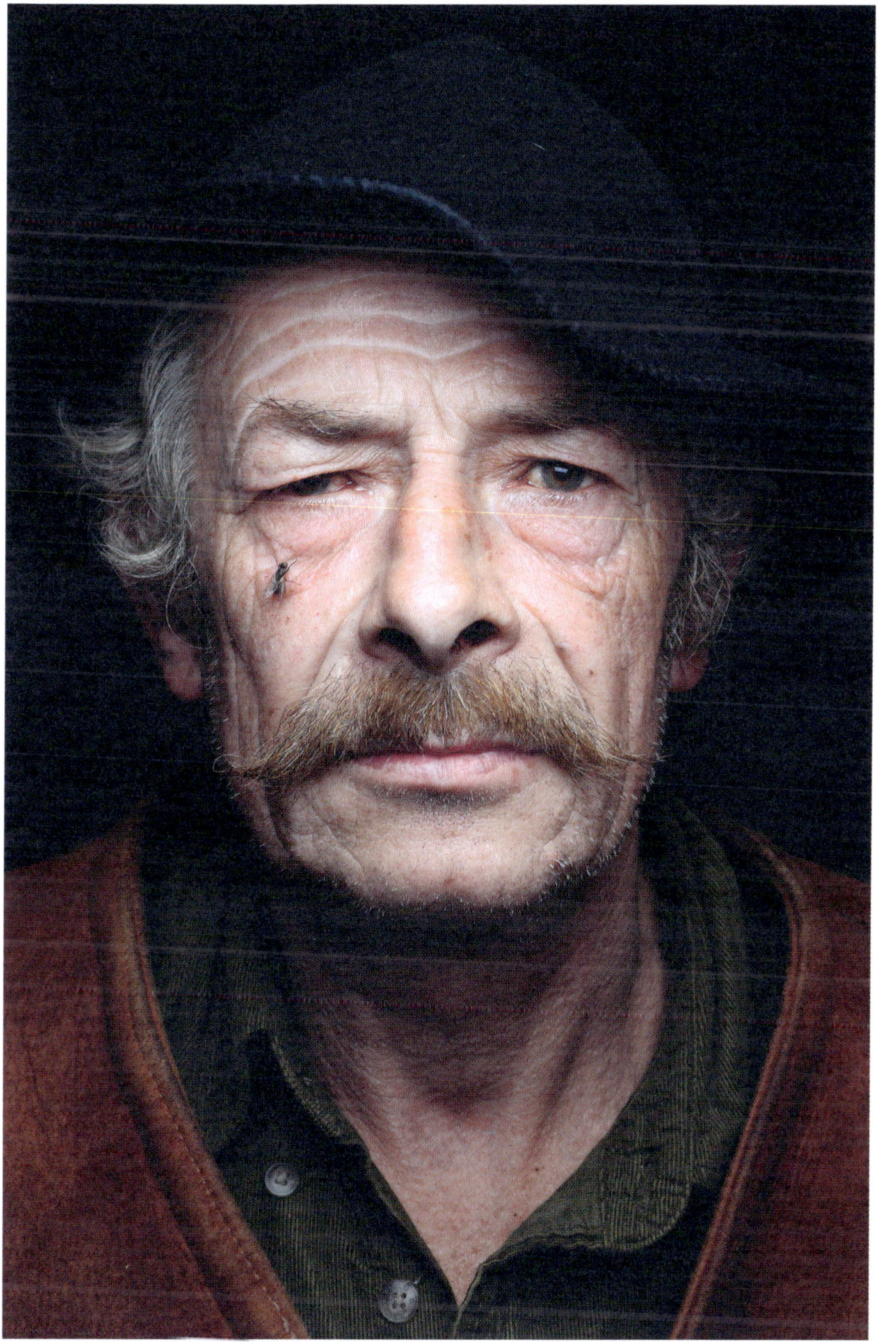

Worker, Coal Factory

by Roman Shalenkin

Mezhdurechensk, Russia

This is 28-year-old Alyona who works in a coal factory. When I spoke to her she said that everyone always asks why she works in such a dark, damp, dirty place. 'It is necessary to have a vocation and this is mine,' she said. 'I do not imagine anything else.'

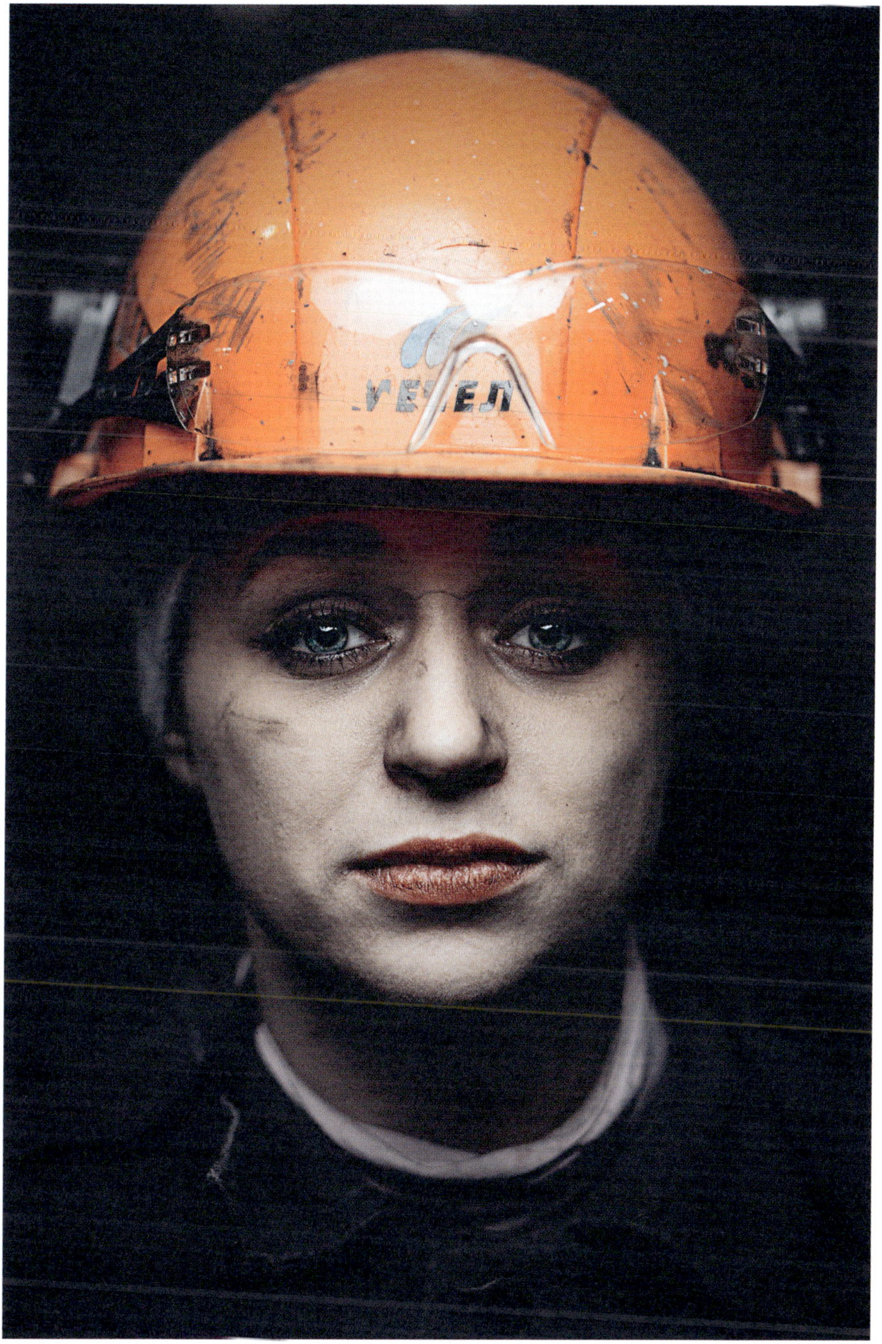

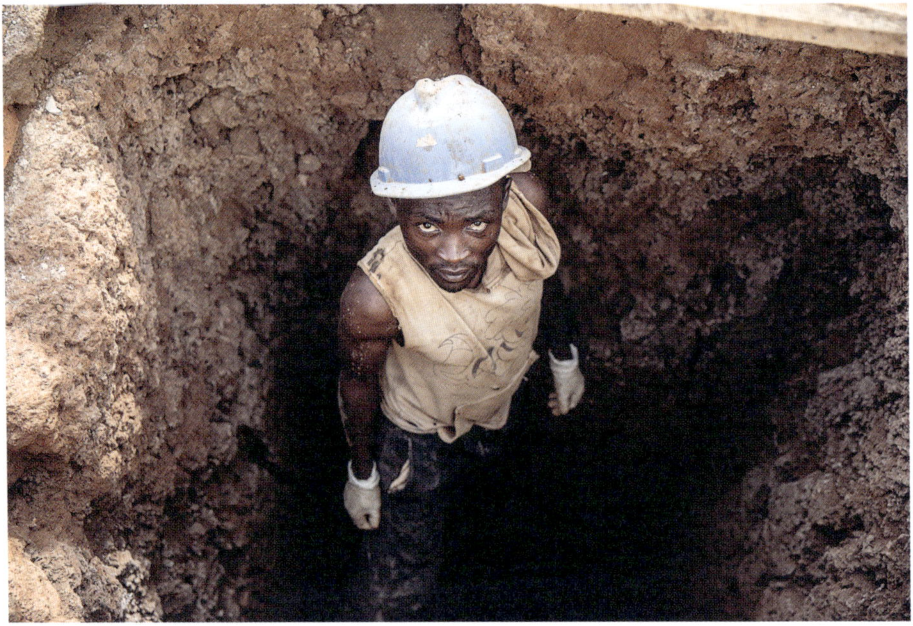

An Excavator Emerges from an 80-100ft Shaft

by Ty Faruki

Kigali, Rwanda

A volunteer searches for victims of the Rwandan genocide at an excavation site. In April 2018, four mass graves concealing the remains of tens of thousands of people were discovered.

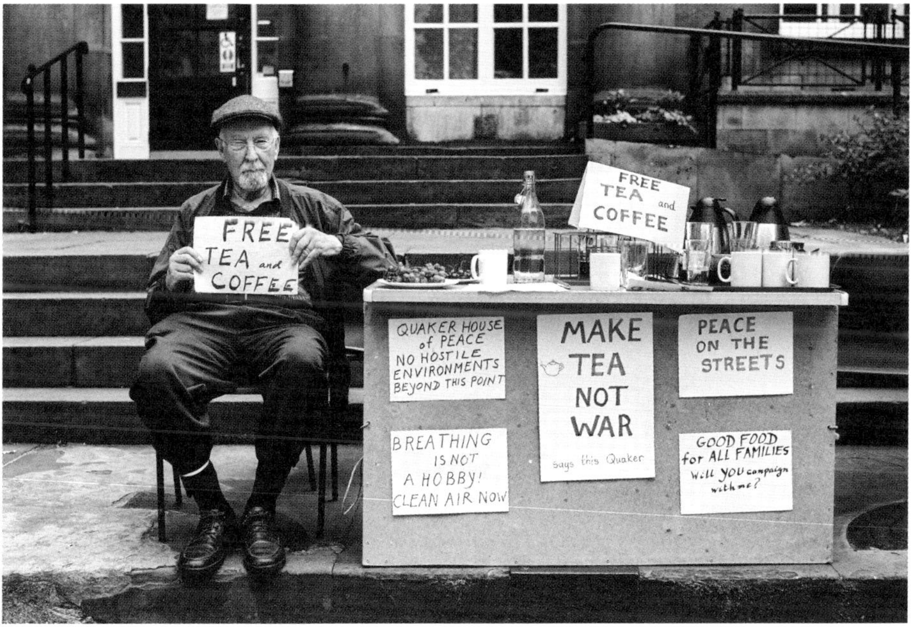

The Quaker

by Phil Melia

Manchester, UK

I saw this gentleman outside the Friends' Meeting House in Manchester, where the city's quaker community meet regularly. His beliefs of truth, integrity, simplicity, equality, peace and sustainability were not only represented in his public display but also in his persona.

Woman in Blue Cap

by Alice Zoo

London, UK

Ray swims daily at the Ladies' Pond in Hampstead Heath, even in winter when water temperatures reach as low as -1°C. When it's really cold, she wears rubber gloves secured with elastic bands.

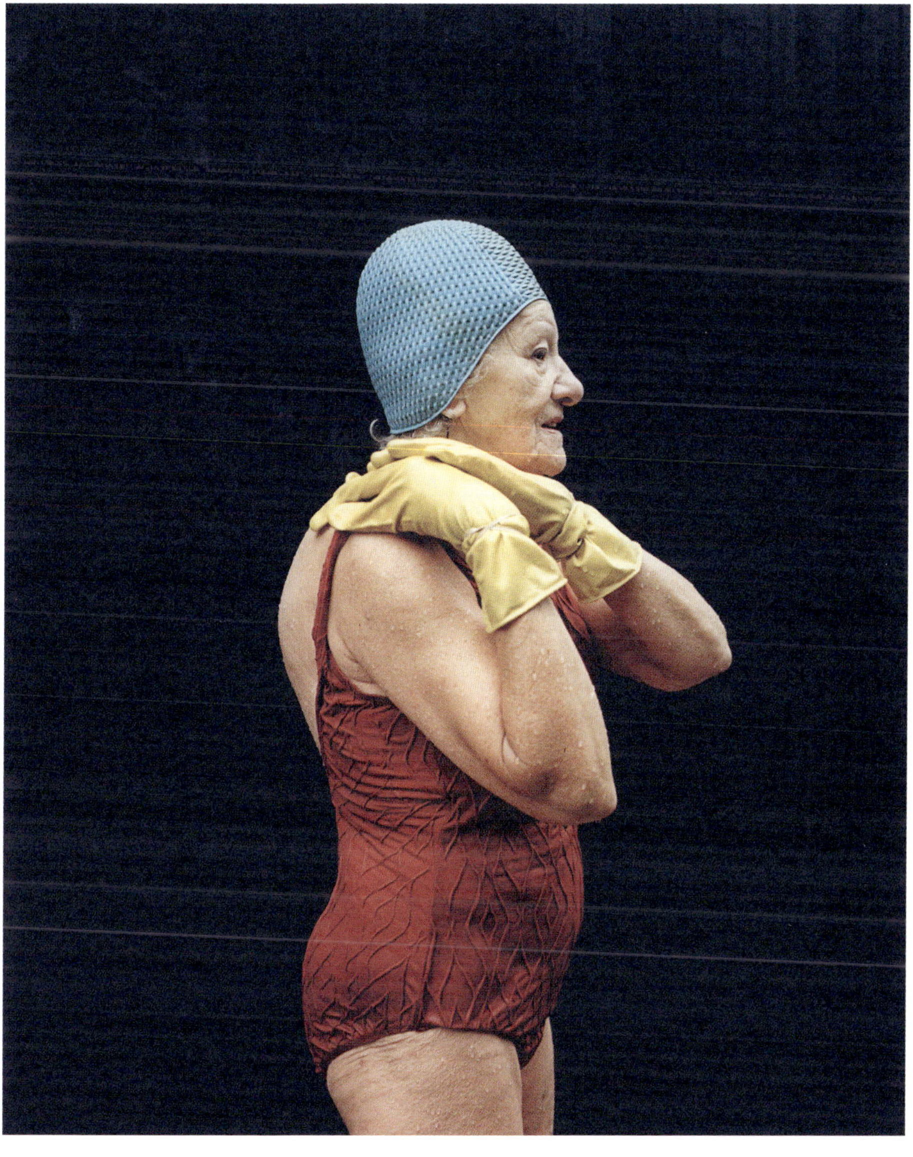

Stern Unicorn

by Sarah Weal

Lewes, UK

I took this photograph of 10-year-old Ella backstage at a production of *The Lion, The Witch and The Wardrobe*. She had a fantastic gaze.

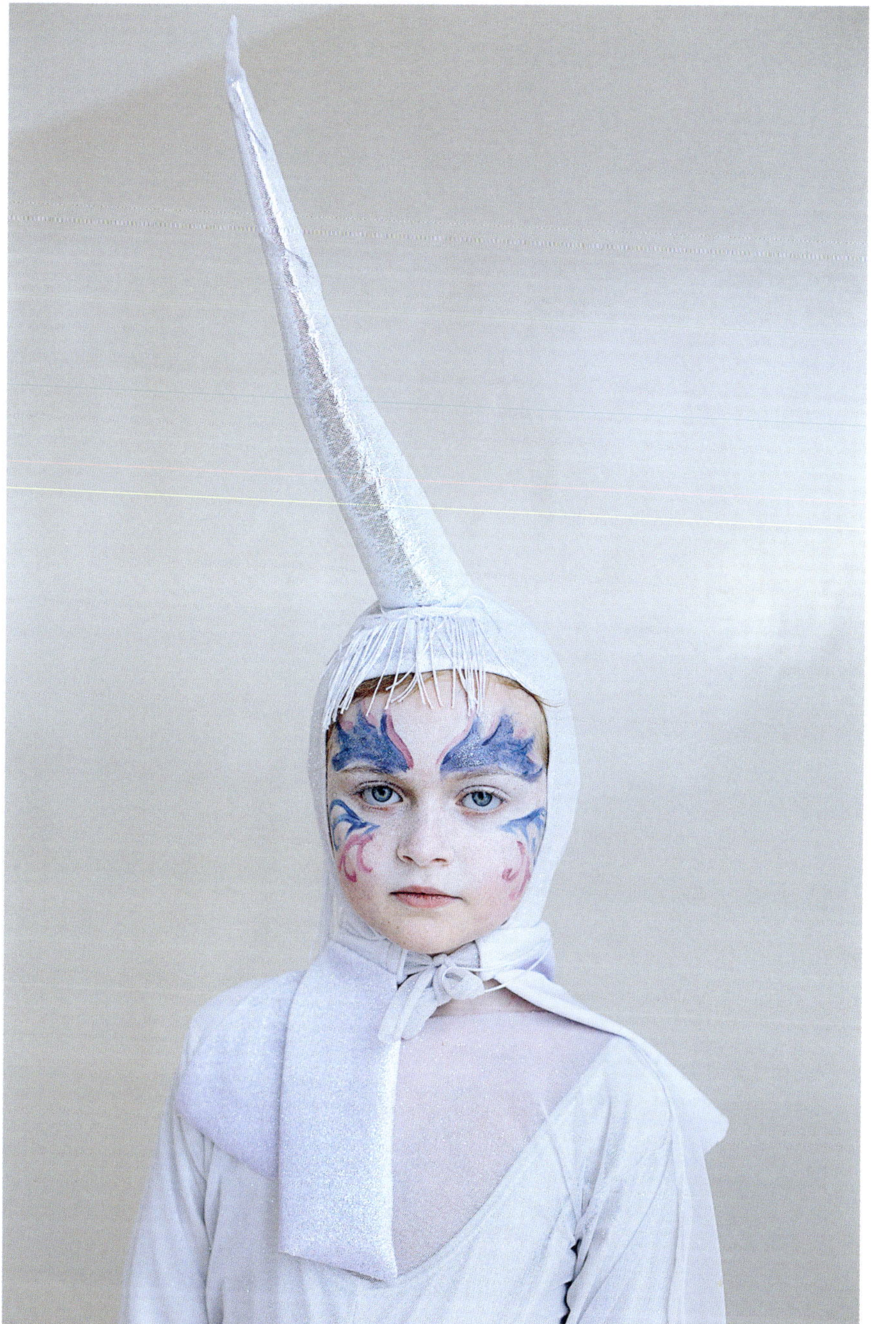

Luis Patterson Arboine,
Cuban National Fencing Team

by Katinka Herbert

Havana, Cuba

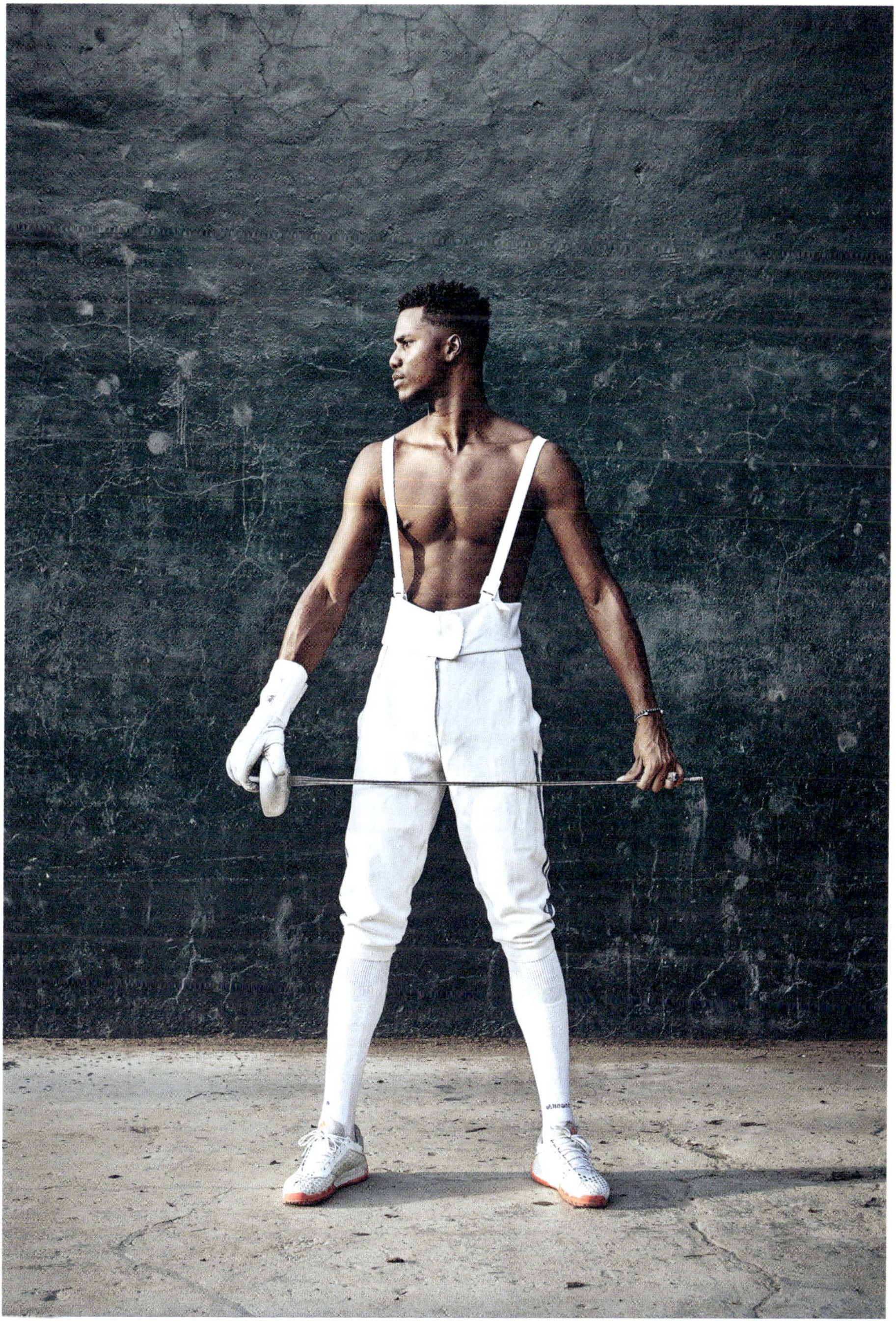

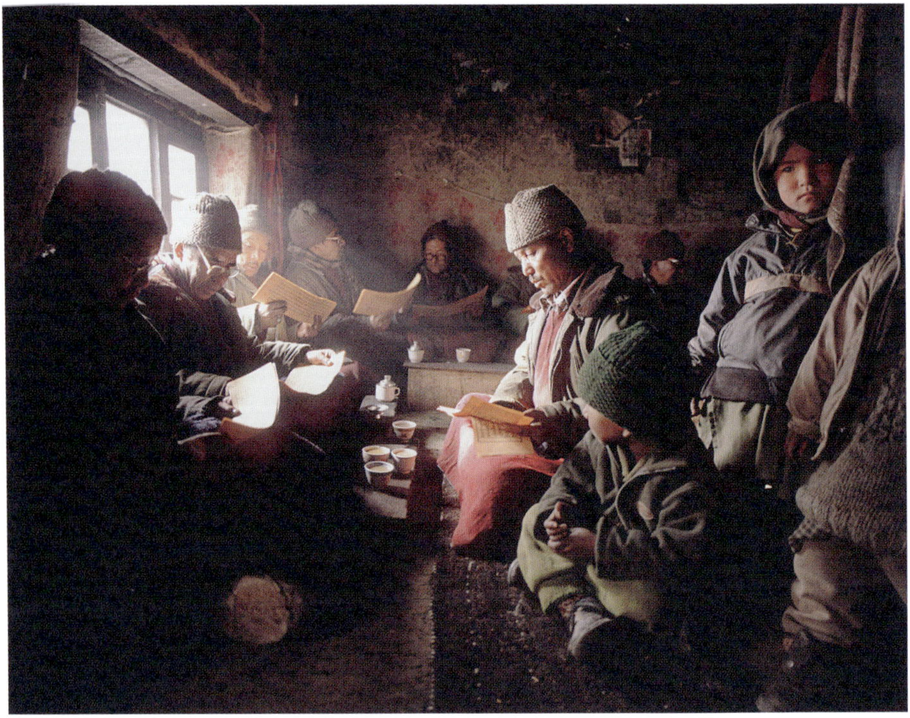

Puja Ceremony
by Martin Hartley
Padham, India

Men in a remote village in the Indian Himalayas gather together for a prayer reading during a Puja ceremony.

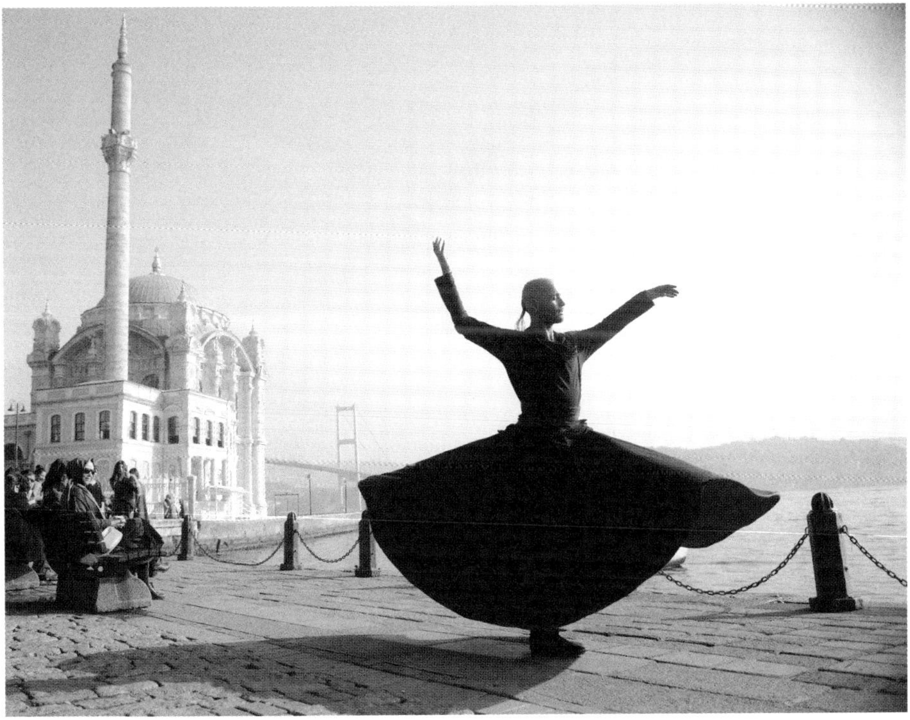

Dervish Whisper

by Dilan Bozyel

Istanbul, Turkey

My friend Alper Akçay, a whirling dervish, performs a Samâ dance [a sacred ritual among Sufis who are also known as 'mystic Muslims'].

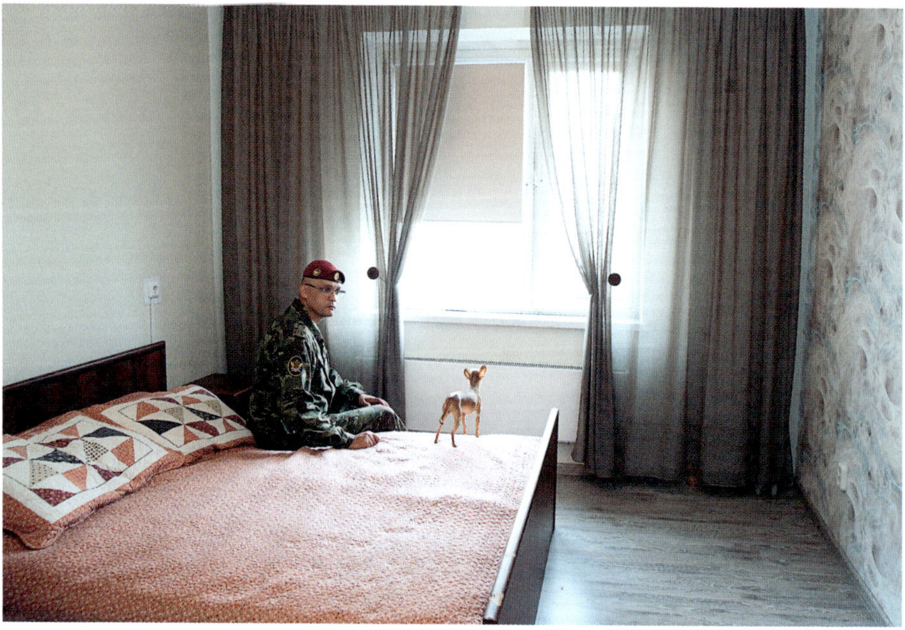

Russian Colonel

by Isabela Pacini

Moscow, Russia

Boris Nikolaev is a colonel in the Russian Armed Forces. I photographed him in his home in Moscow where he lives with his wife and daughter.

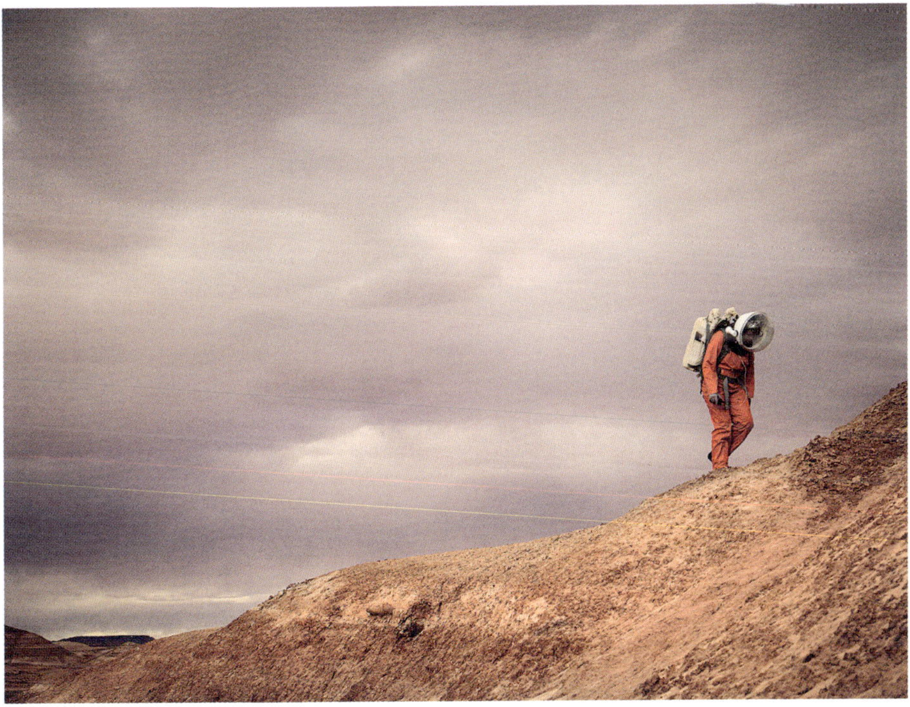

Untitled

by Olly Burn

Hanksville, Utah, USA

This is Commander Cassandra Klos at the Mars Desert Research Station, which is owned and operated by the Mars Society. Its primary function is to simulate life as it would be on Mars.

Shepherd Andrew Quinn

by Kevin Faingnaert

Kilkee, Ireland

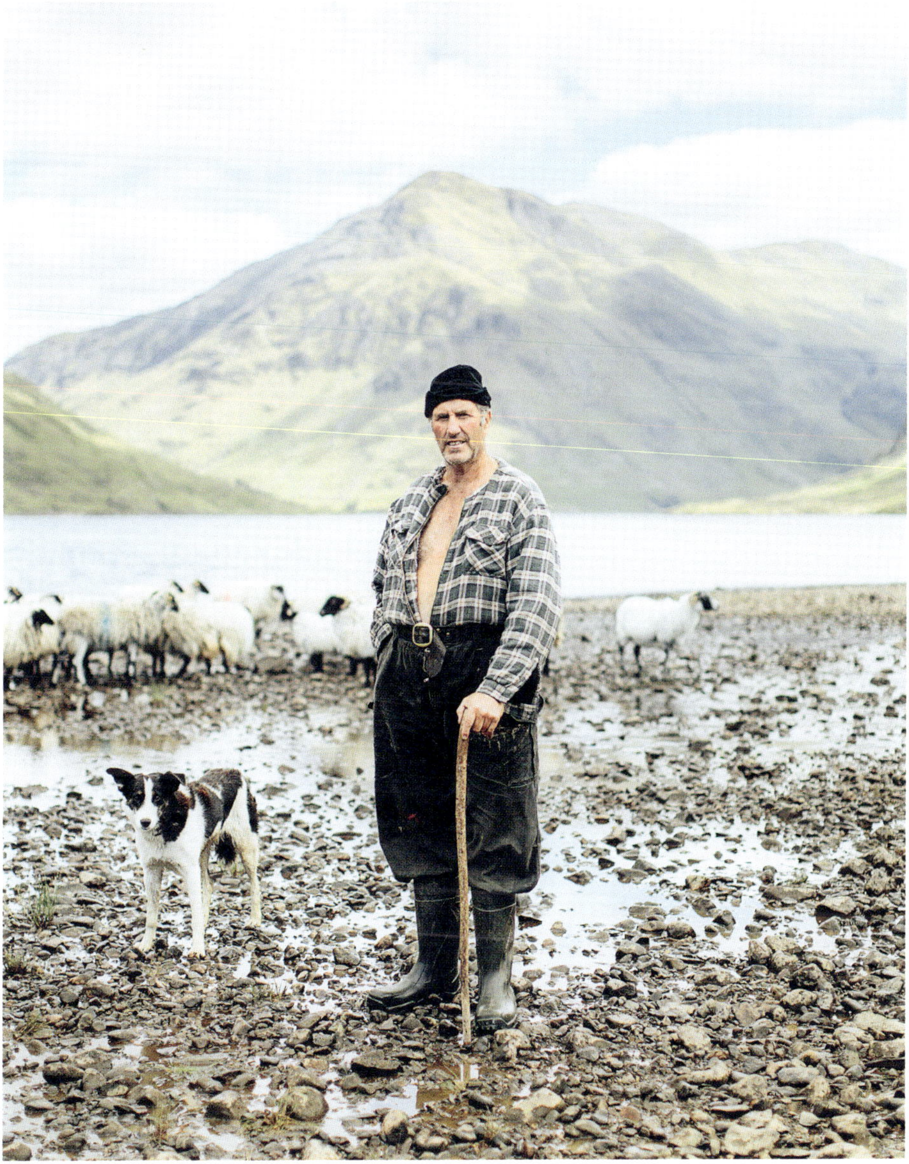

Faso on the Horse

by Iorgis Matyassy

Ouagadougou, Burkina Faso

Faso is a horseman and master of equestrian vaulting. I was impressed by how easily he got the horse to lie down, as though the animal was a pet dog.

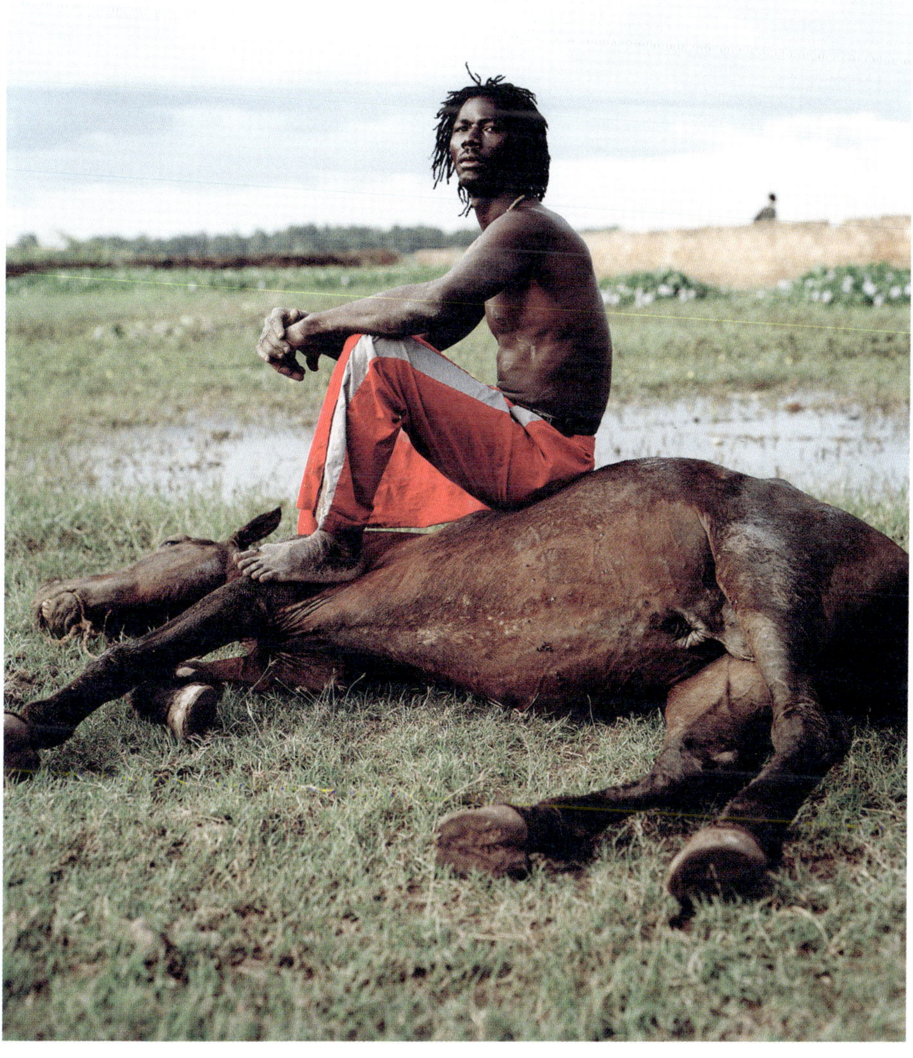

Maisie and Amy

by Javier Cortés

London, UK

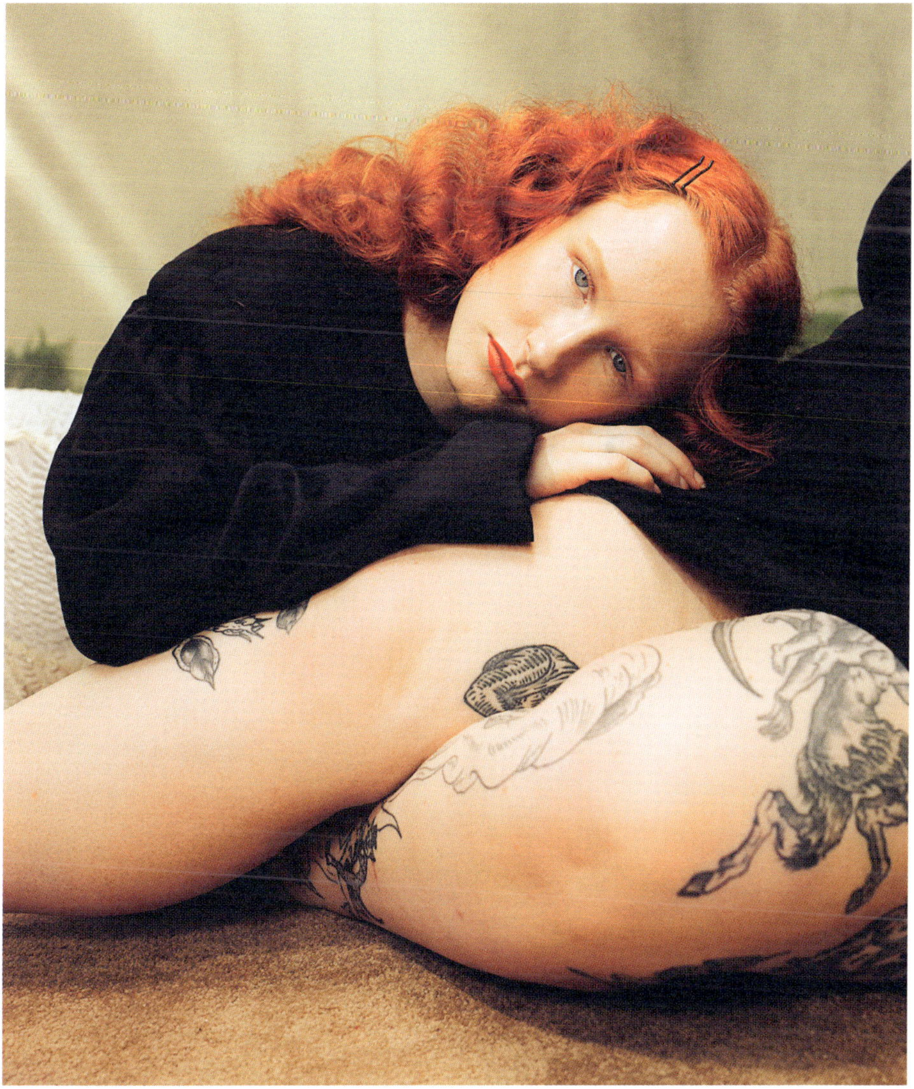

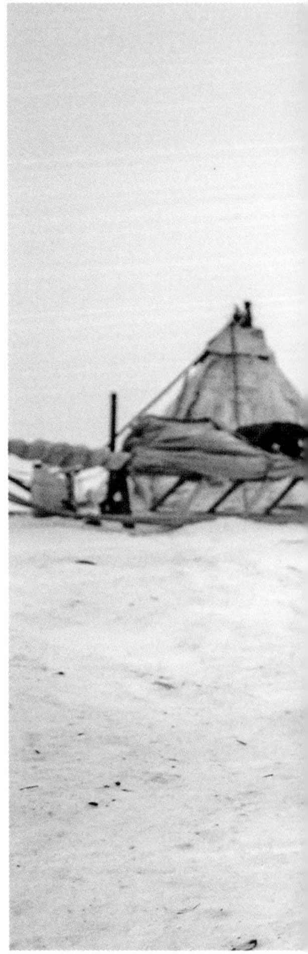

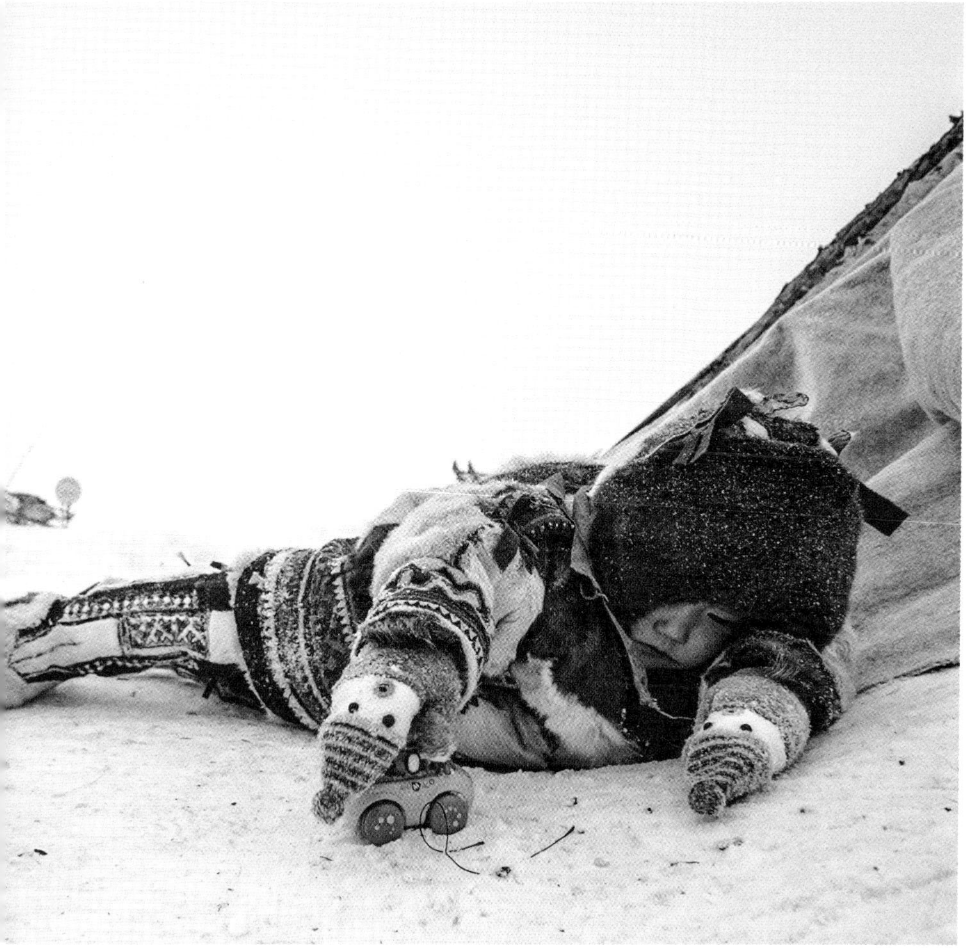

Driving on Ice
by Marco Marcone
Yamal, Siberia, Russia

A Nenets boy plays while his father and grandfather are out hunting. Nenets people are famous for herding reindeer but their way of life is under threat from the extraction of natural resources, pollution and climate change.

Daydreaming and Commuting

by Frankie Caradonna

London, UK

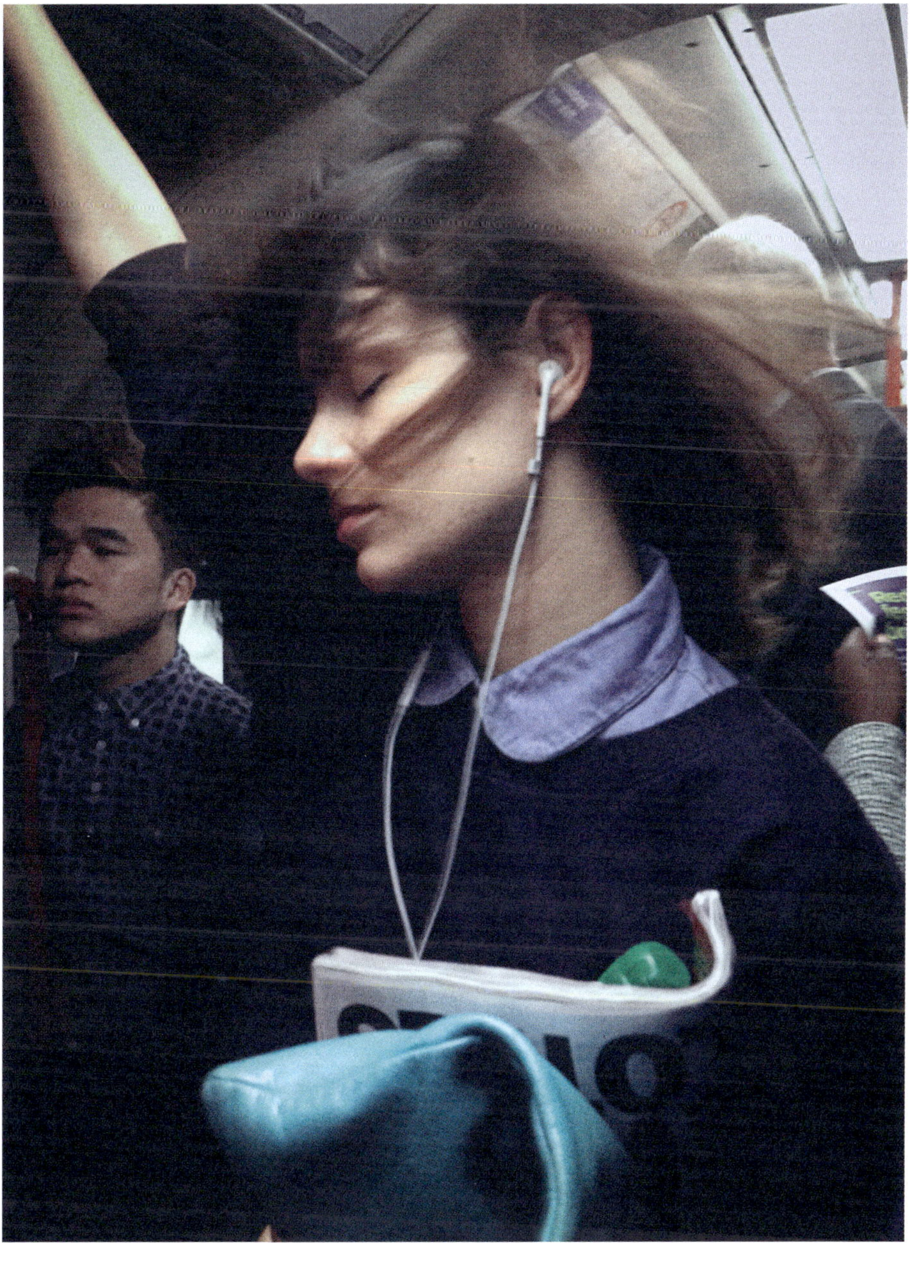

Circles of Light

by Joey Carrapichano

Red Hill, South Africa

This is Given Mlalazi who is originally from Bulawayo in Zimbabwe. He is the nephew of a friend of mine and lives in Red Hill, a shanty town close to the Cape Peninsula. The shacks and small dwellings of Red Hill are inhabited by a diverse population of African people, but levels of violent crime are high. People live very basic lives in an environment where anything can happen.

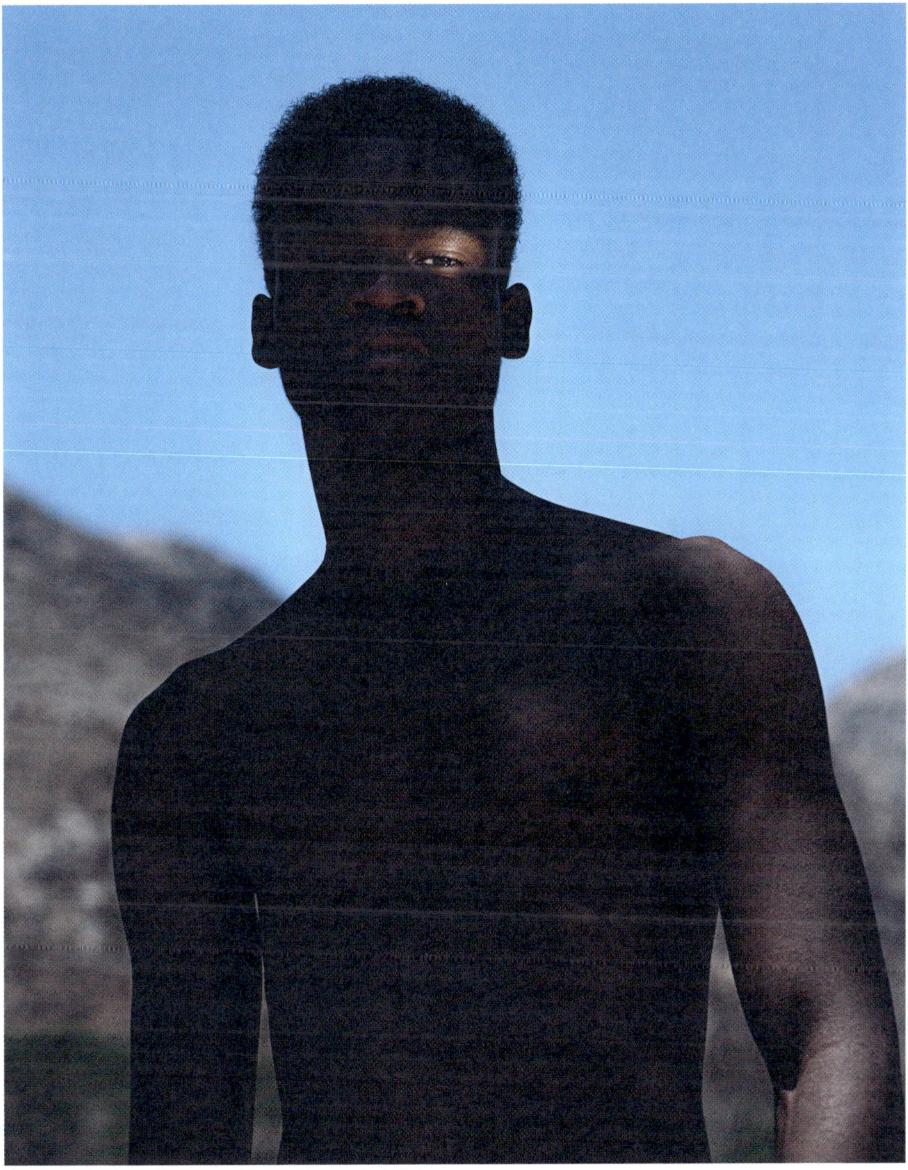

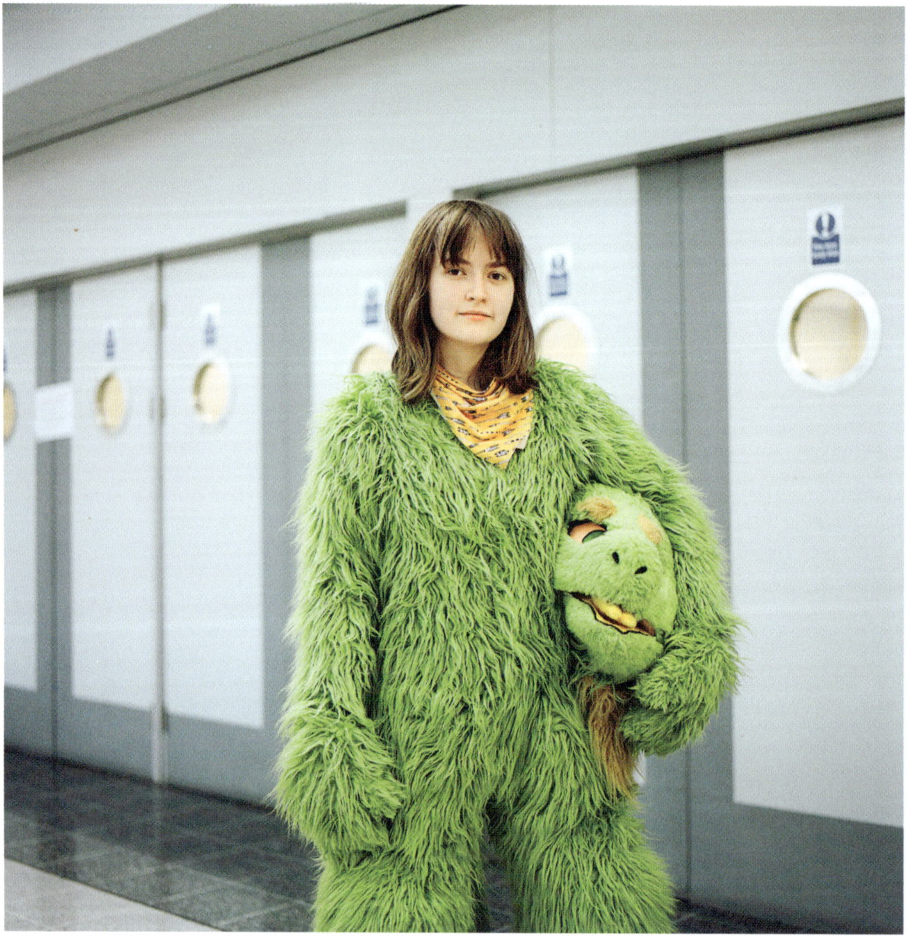

Silver Dressed as 'Lazlo'
by Ellie Smith
Birmingham, UK

Silver's costume was so different to anything else I had seen at Birmingham Comic Con. There was something endearing about the way she was walking along carrying her character's head under her arm.

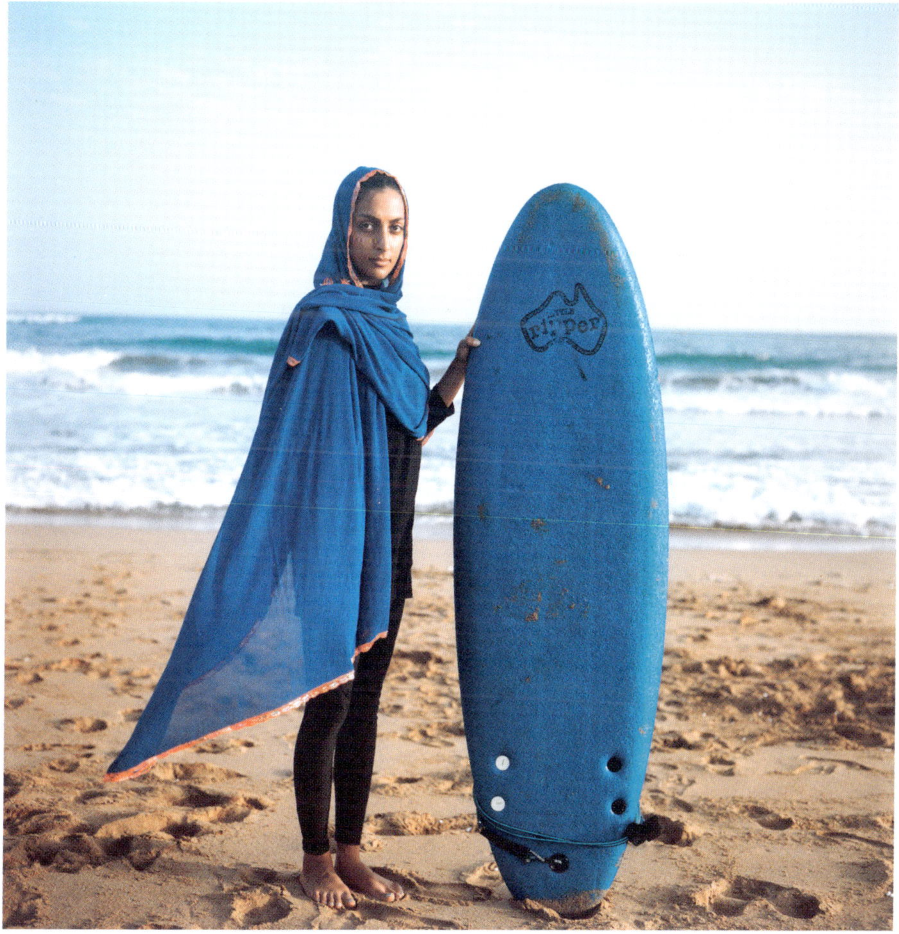

Surfing Iran
by Giulia Frigieri
Ramin, Iran

Since 2013, Shahla Yasini has been challenging stereotypes of Middle Eastern women by pioneering the surfing scene in southeast Iran. She represents a new Iranian youth who are proud, courageous and ready to fight for their freedom.

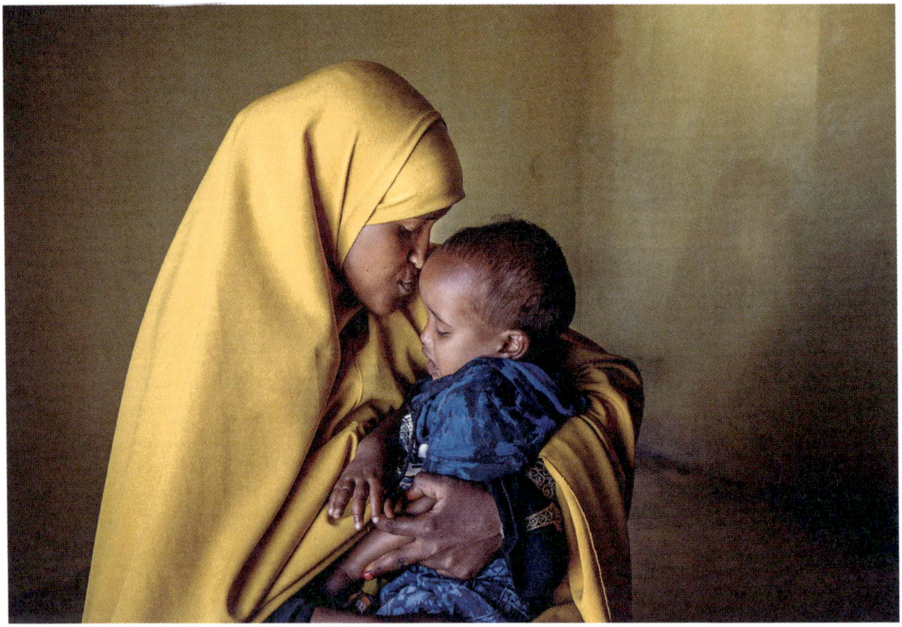

Fardouse and Ahmed

by Georgina Goodwin

Armale, Somalia

Fardouse Ibrahim Aden, 22, shares a quiet moment with her youngest child, one-year-old Ahmed. At the health centre she has access to nutrition supplements for her children who are suffering from malnutrition as a result of a two-year drought in the Sanaag region.

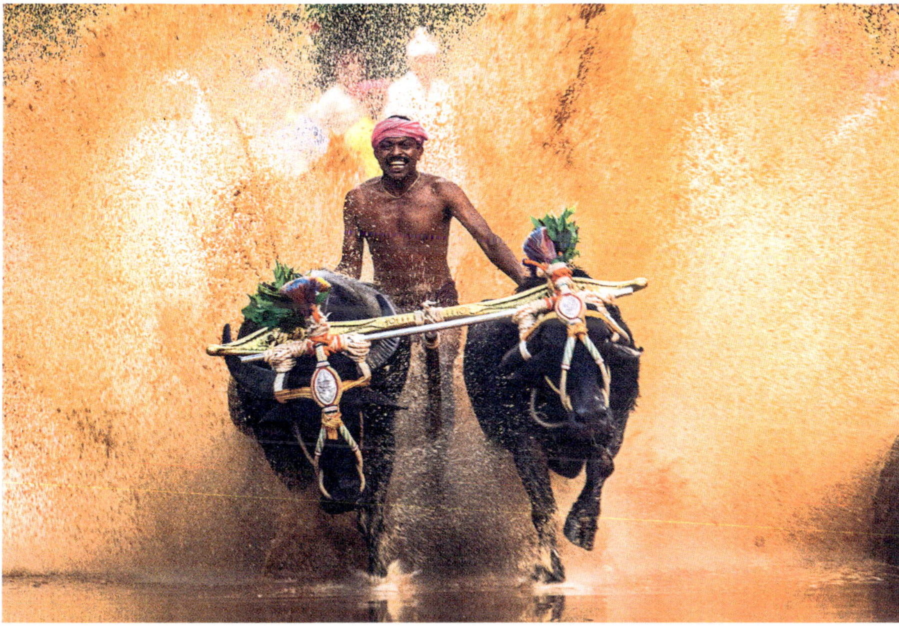

Drag Racing
by Kunal Gupta
Karnataka, India

Kambala is an annual festival centered around the traditional buffalo race, a popular and unique sport among Karnataka's farming community. Teams from across Karnataka and Tamil Nadu race pairs of buffalo down muddy paddy fields.

Samy Chabani

by David Cantor

London, UK

Samy was raised in western France but towards adulthood he found it challenging to reconcile the conservatism of his home region with his own flamboyant nature. Samy moved to London where he found the freedom to be himself.

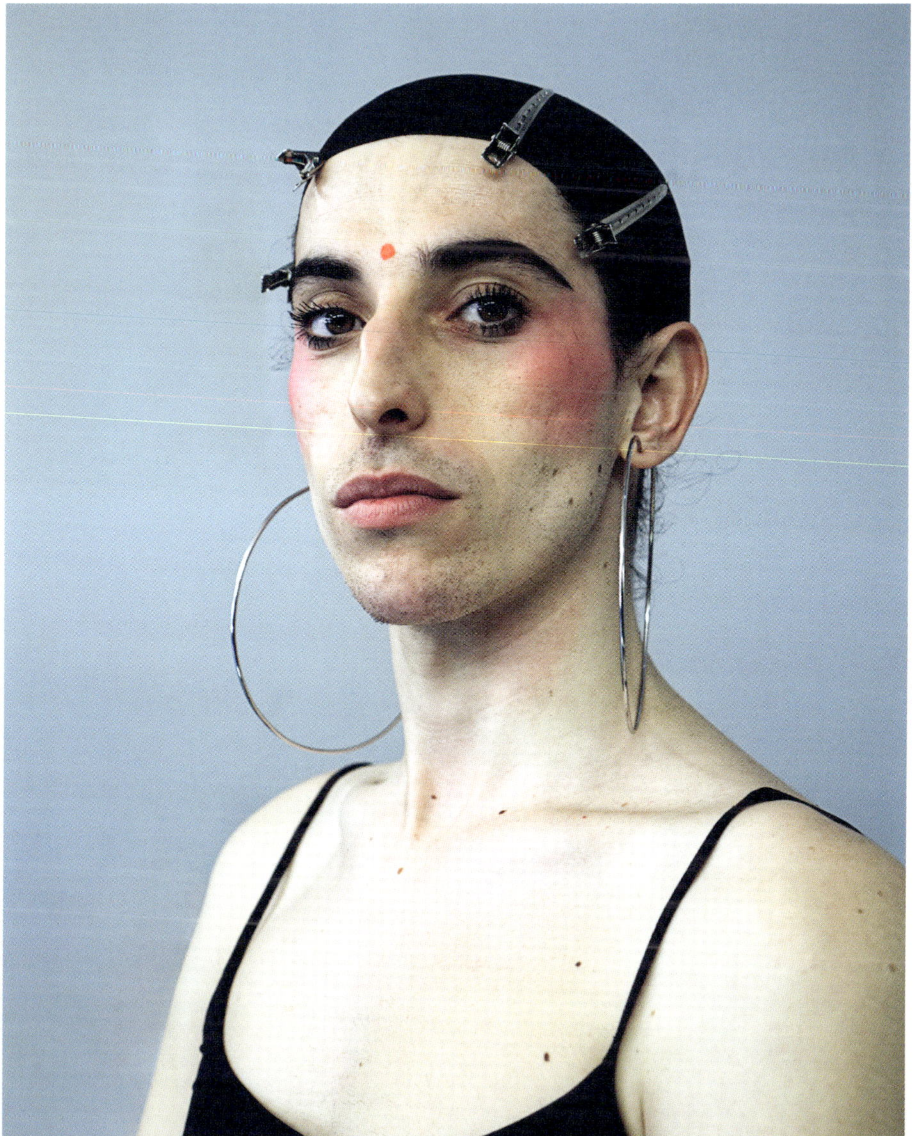

Boulaye and Hamza

by Sam Armstrong

Paris, France

I was walking down a quiet street in Paris when I came across a basketball court sandwiched between two large buildings. It was bursting with colours and I heard echoes of balls bouncing and kids' laughter. I returned to the court every day for months, got to know the people and slowly started taking some pictures.

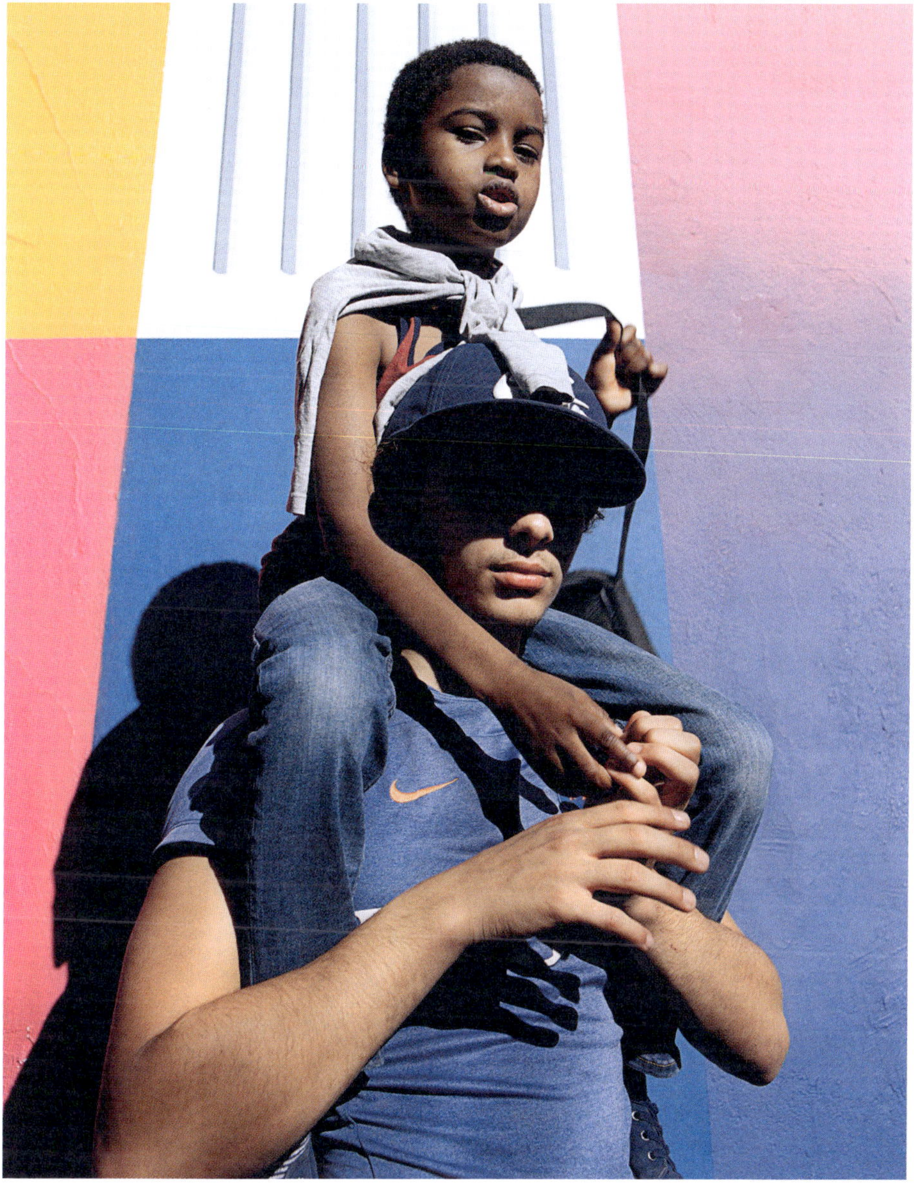

Brianna

by Stephanie Diani

New York City, New York, USA

Brianna came to my studio for a portrait session. I was going to change the light on her but as she stood and waited she turned just enough so that her face was mostly shadowed but her eyes still glowed.

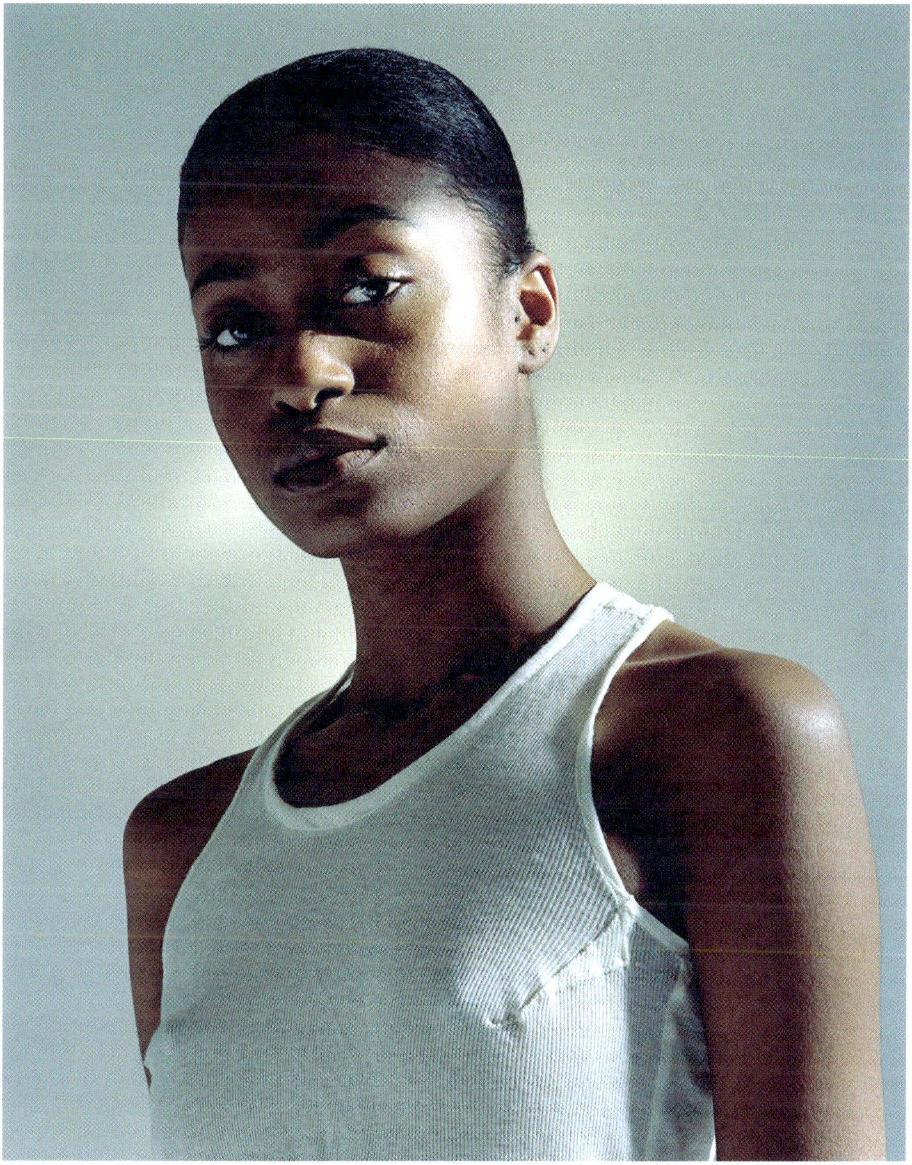

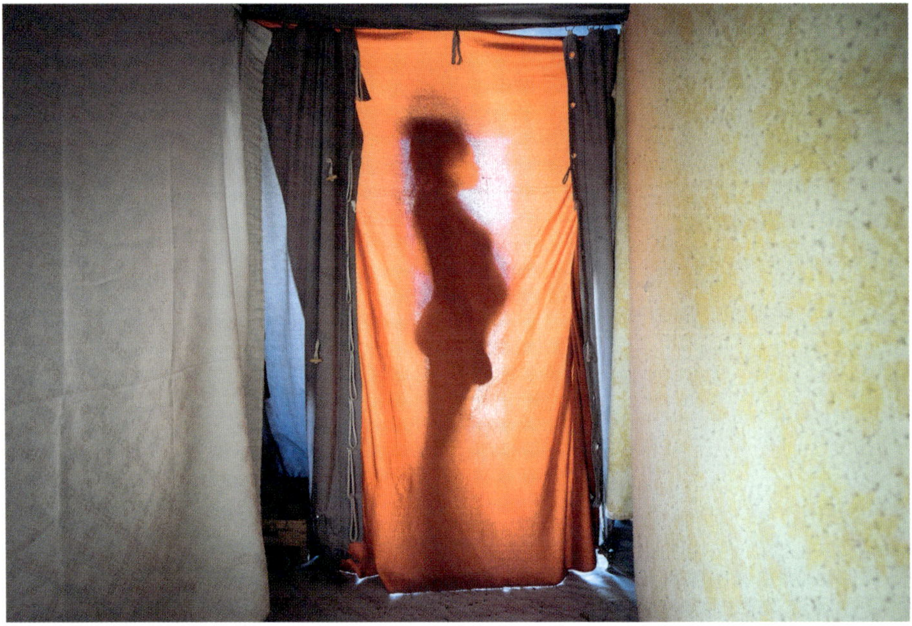

Life Goes On

by Marco Panzetti

Settimo Torinese, Italy

Fatima, originally from Mali, arrived in Italy after crossing the Mediterranean Sea during the migrant crisis. Fatima was with her husband, and she was pregnant. When I met her, she was waiting for her asylum request to be processed. I took this photograph at the entrance of her tent in the reception camp for asylum seekers where she was hosted.

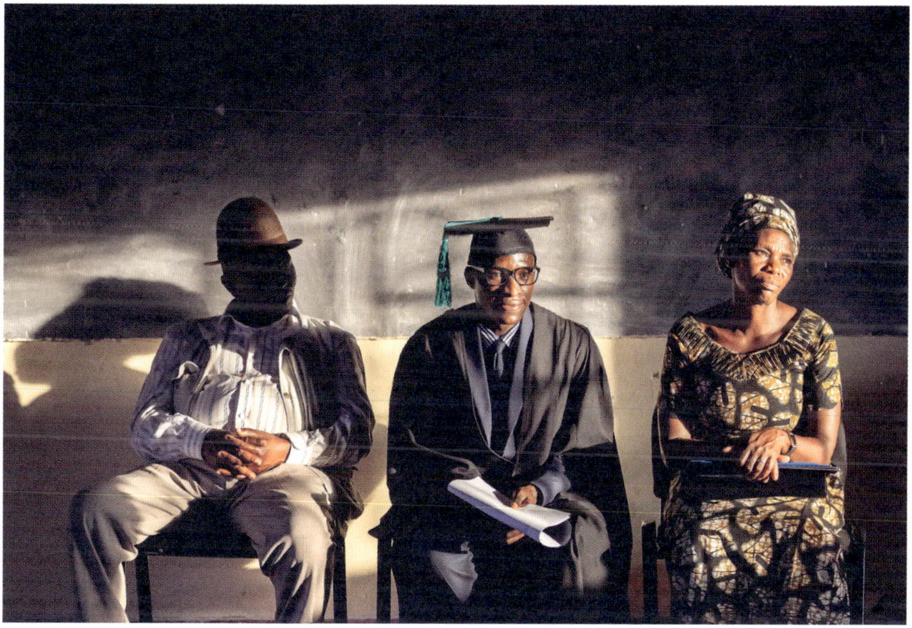

Niyonshuti Daniel
by Patricia Gutiérrez
Kayonza, Rwanda

Niyonshuti was five years old when he became an orphan and found himself living in the streets. At the age of 10 he was taken in by the Streets Ahead Children's Centre Association and had the chance to go to school. At 26, Niyonshuti graduated from the College of Medicine and Health Sciences at the University of Rwanda.

Madgo and Lokkhmi

by Karan Kumar Sachdev

Odisha, India

Madgo and Lokkhmi belong to the Dongria Kondh tribe. They are friends and live in the same village in the Niyamgiri Hills where they grew up together.

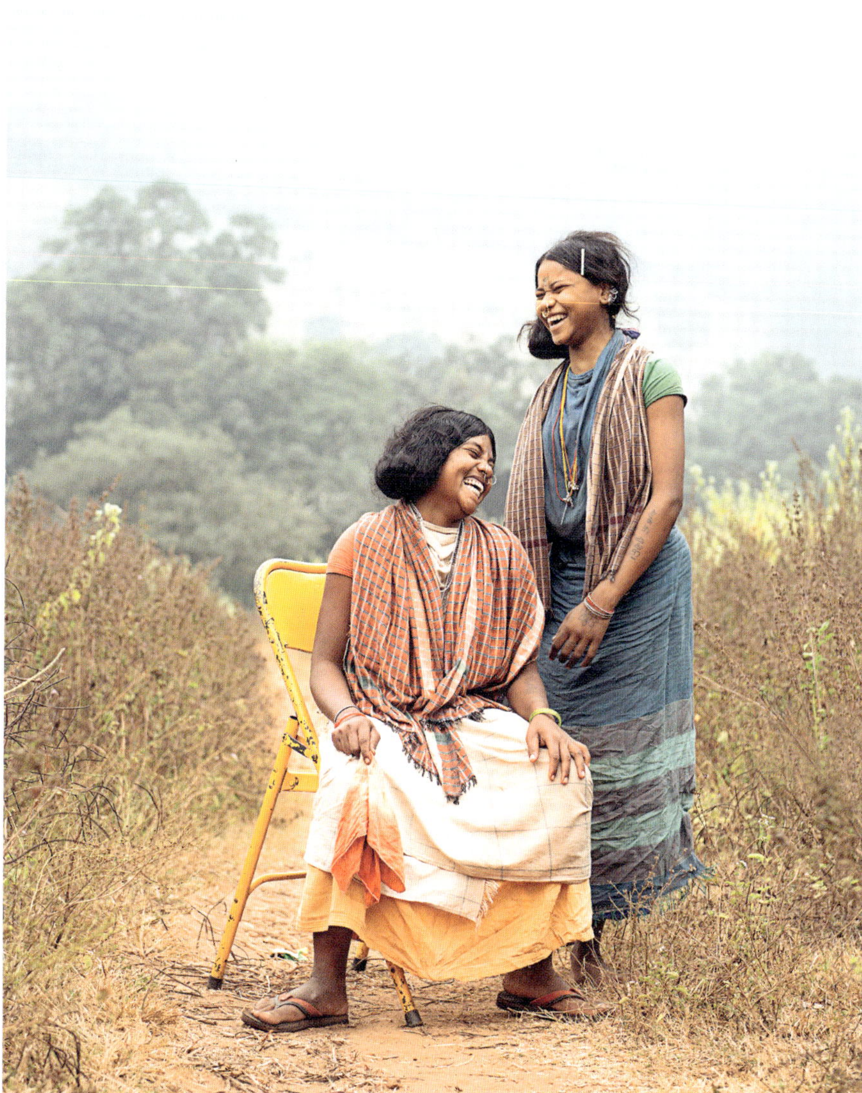

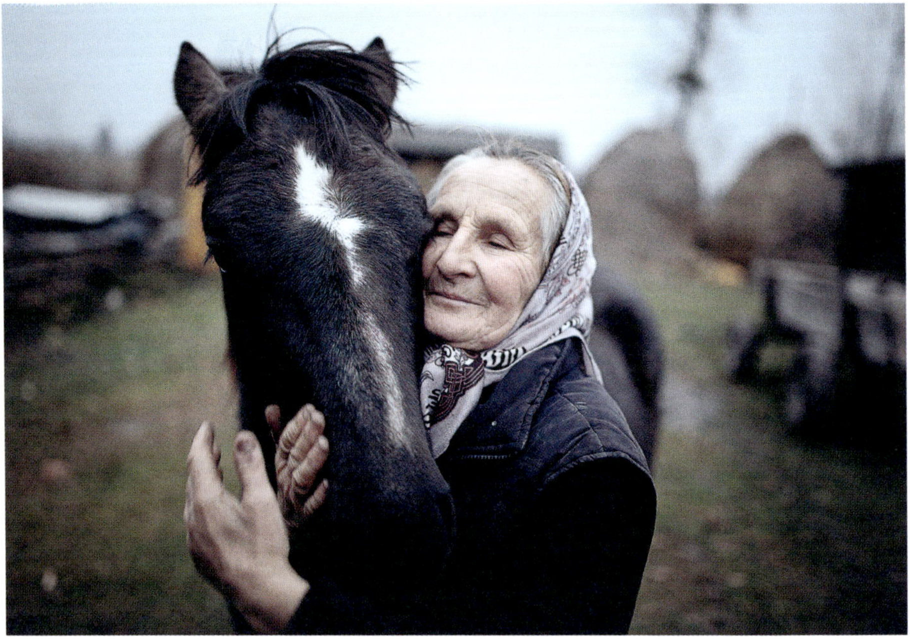

Tetiana
by Mateusz Baj
Melnyki, Ukraine

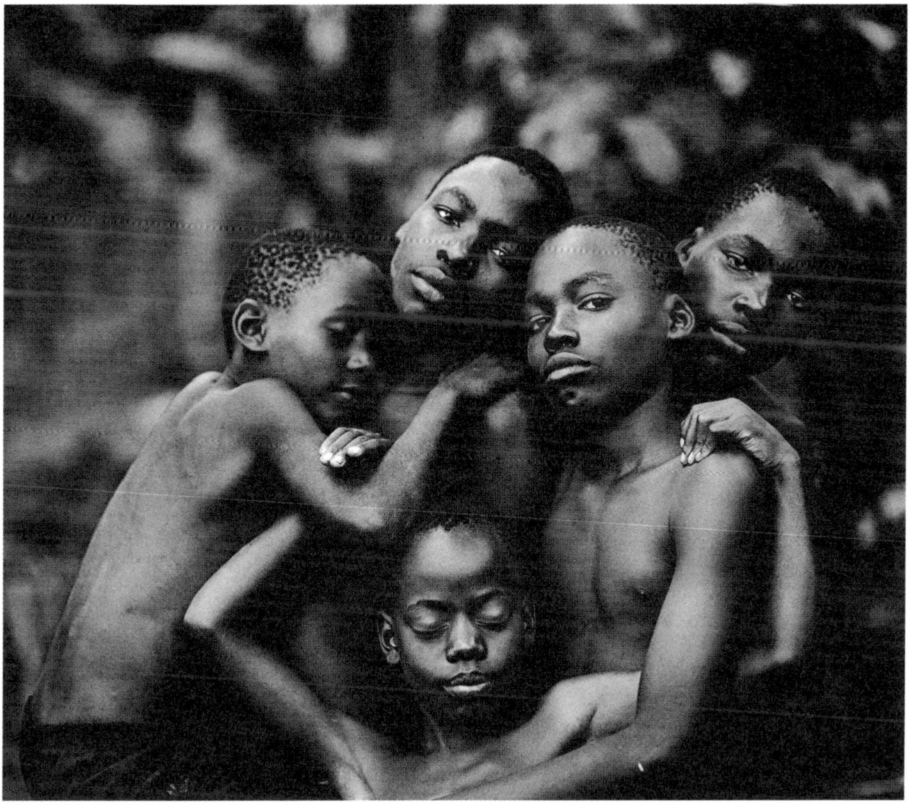

Band of Brothers
by Linelle Deunk
Mukono District, Uganda

The Kiss

by Karsten Thormaehlen

Los Angeles, California, USA

Ninety-nine-year-old Betty has been married to 101-year-old Morrie for almost eight decades. They have travelled the world together.

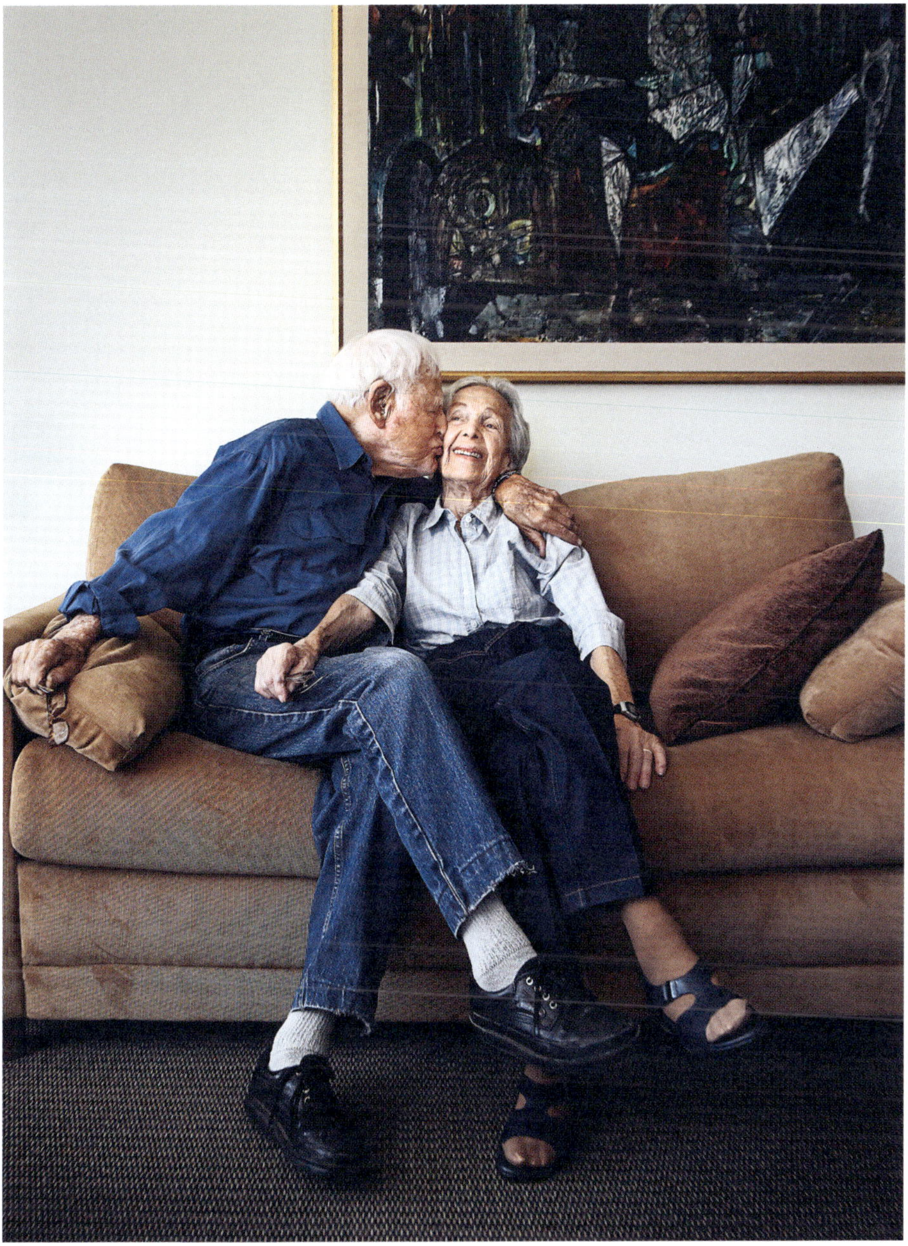

Machine Gun Motherhood

by Neil Thomas

Omo Valley, Ethiopia

This woman belongs to the Mursi tribe. Mostly it is the men who are armed, but she told me her husband was away and so she had to take over his role as protector of the family and their livestock.

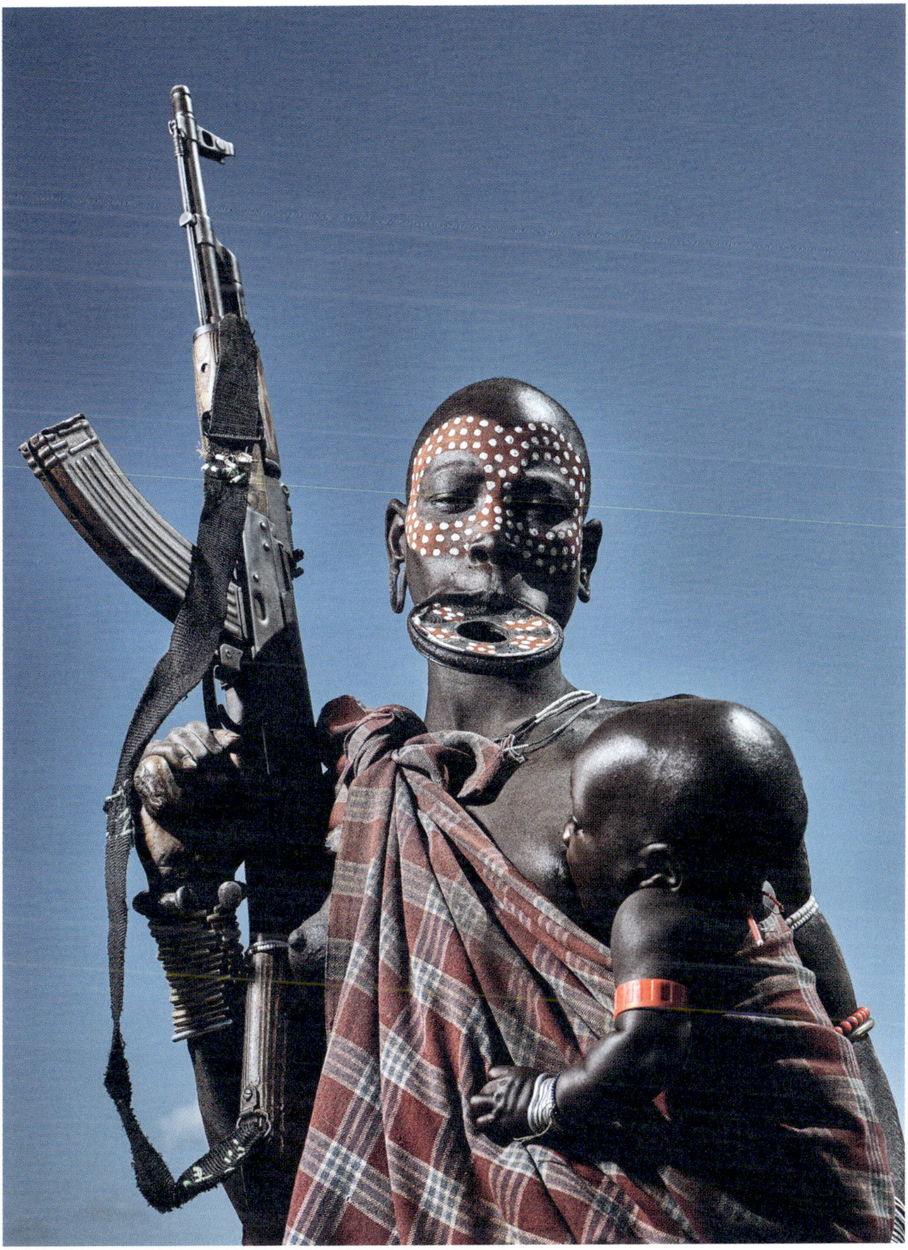

Red Light Sanctuary

by Darren Smith

Amsterdam, Netherlands

Cherry Poppins is a Dutch drag queen and performer. She is known as a funky, energetic, creative, fierce, fabulous soul-mama.

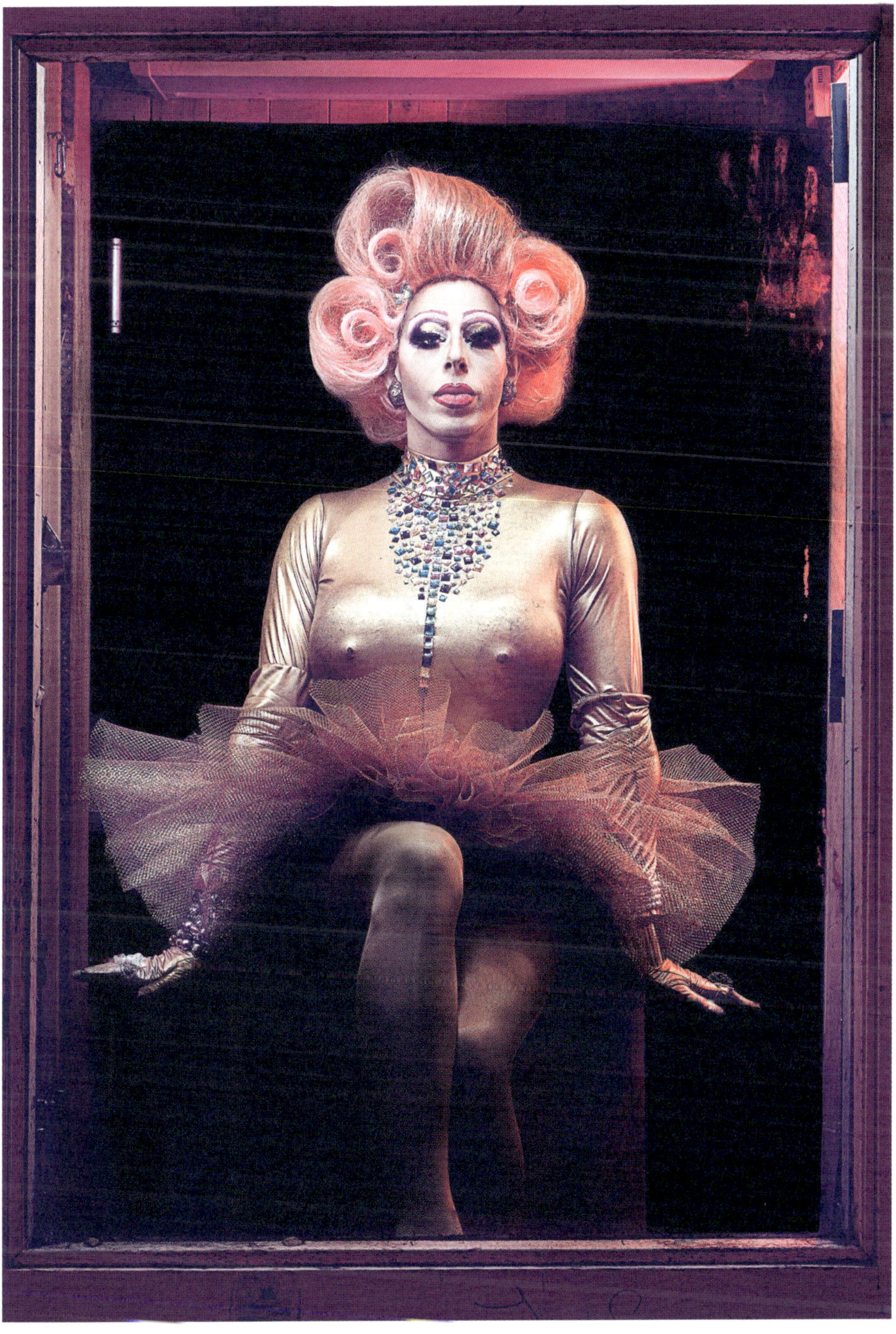

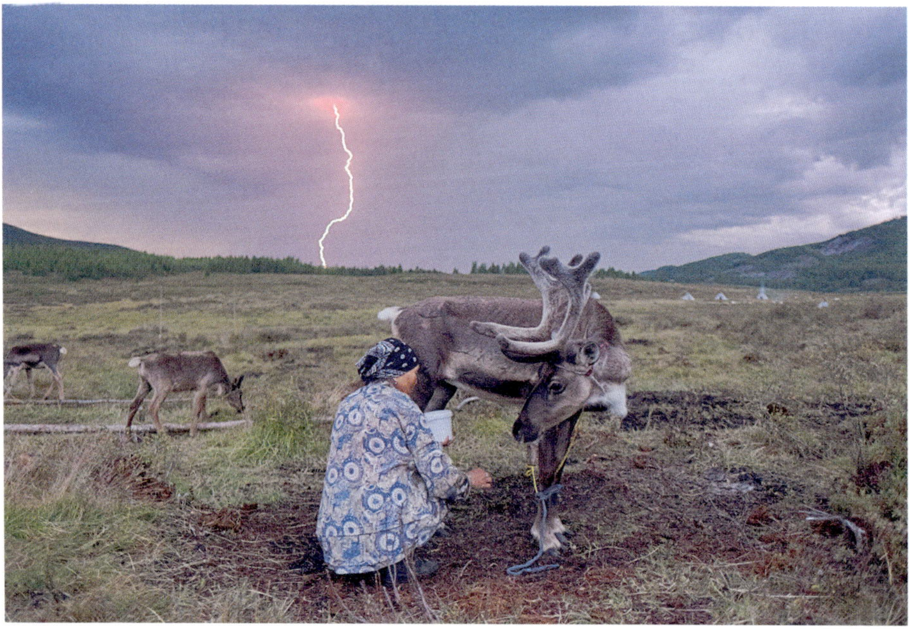

Harmony

by Luca Bracali

Khövsgöl Aimag, Mongolia

The Tsaatan people herd reindeer, but theirs is a precarious way of life. In late summer, the rainy season arrives and with it lightning, which ignites forests and kills reindeer. In these conditions milking the reindeer is dangerous and women often cover their hair with cloth to protect against static electricity.

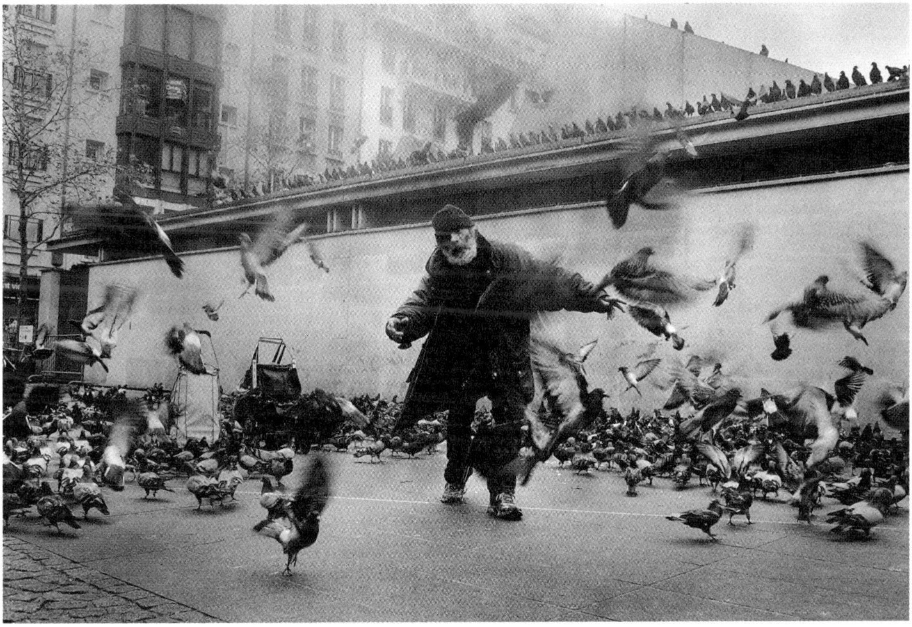

Giuseppe in Paris
by Magnus Cederlund
Paris, France

He came every day to feed the pigeons and really loved it, so he danced with them.

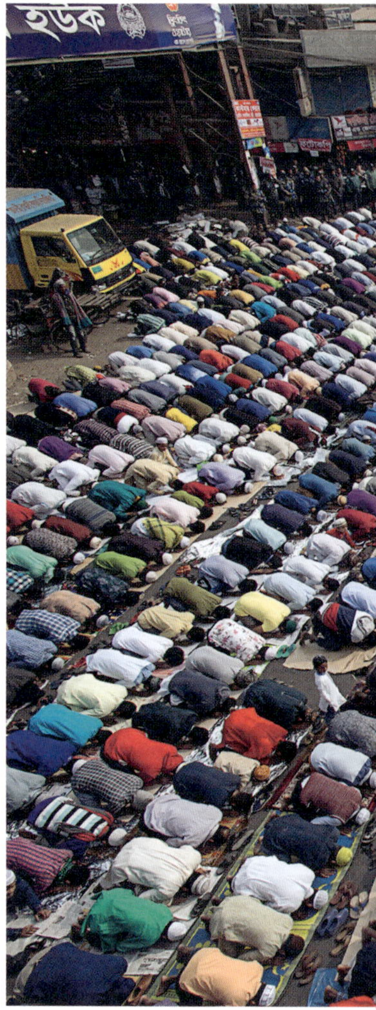
হউক

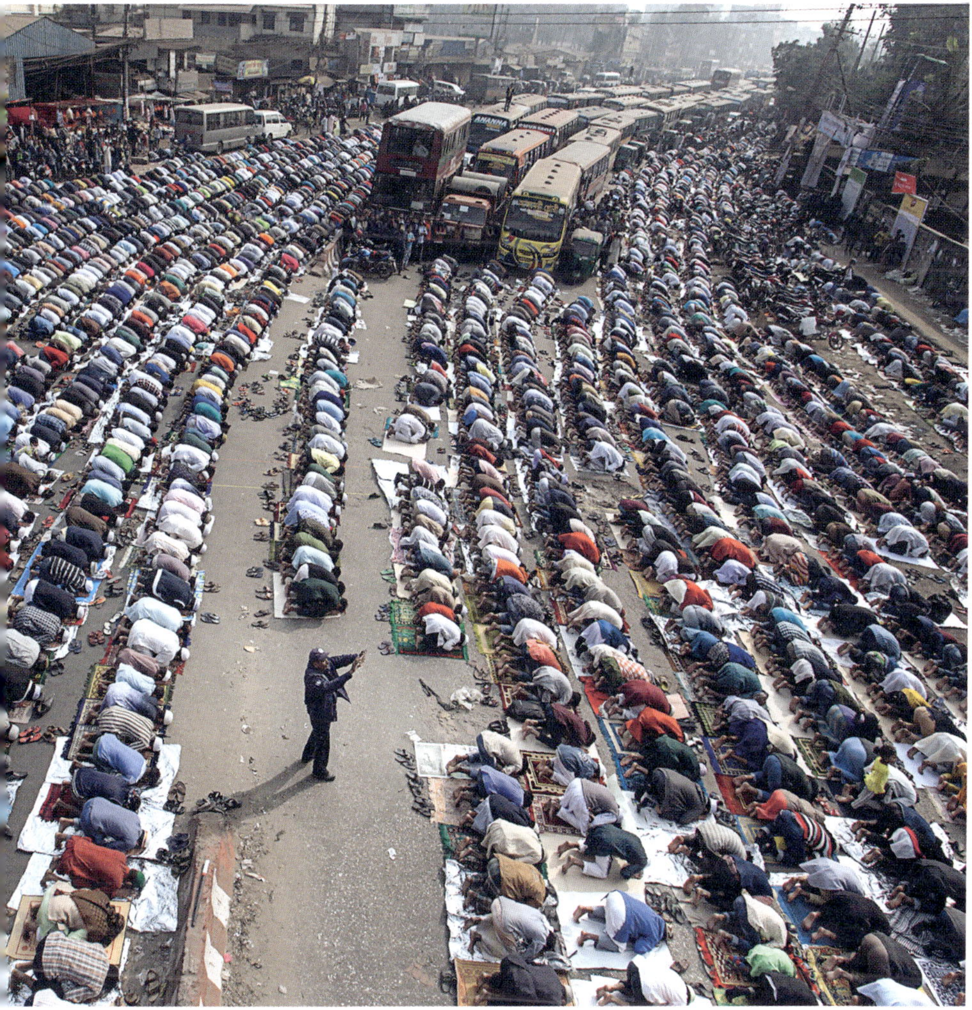

Ijtima Praying

by Kaan Yuan Chiam

Dhaka, Bangladesh

A congregation of devout muslims turns towards Mecca to pray.

Kids of Hackney #5

by Jørn Tomter

London, UK

Children at Kingsmead Primary School in Hackney lie on the ground and look up. Perhaps they are doing something we have all done, which is to contemplate what is ahead and what is out there.

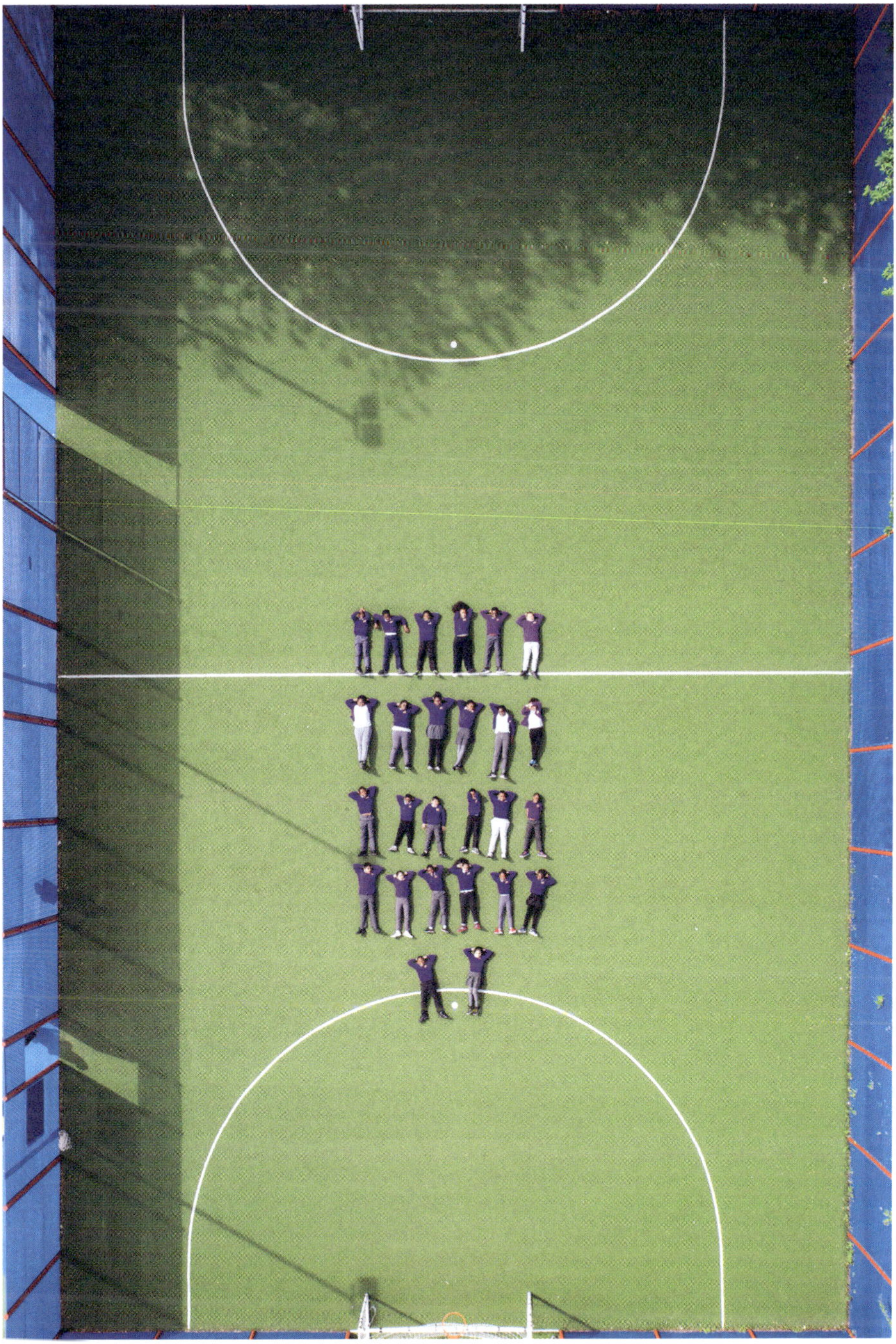

The Story Tree

by Pieter Henket

Mbomo District, Congo

We asked this group of kids if they could climb into the tree and within 20 seconds they had placed themselves in these spots. They have participated in storytelling workshops set up by Tales of Us, an organisation who communicates the urgency of protecting the world's most powerful and fragile ecosystems and the people who call them home. The kids' stories became the inspiration for a series of photographs called *Congo Tales*.

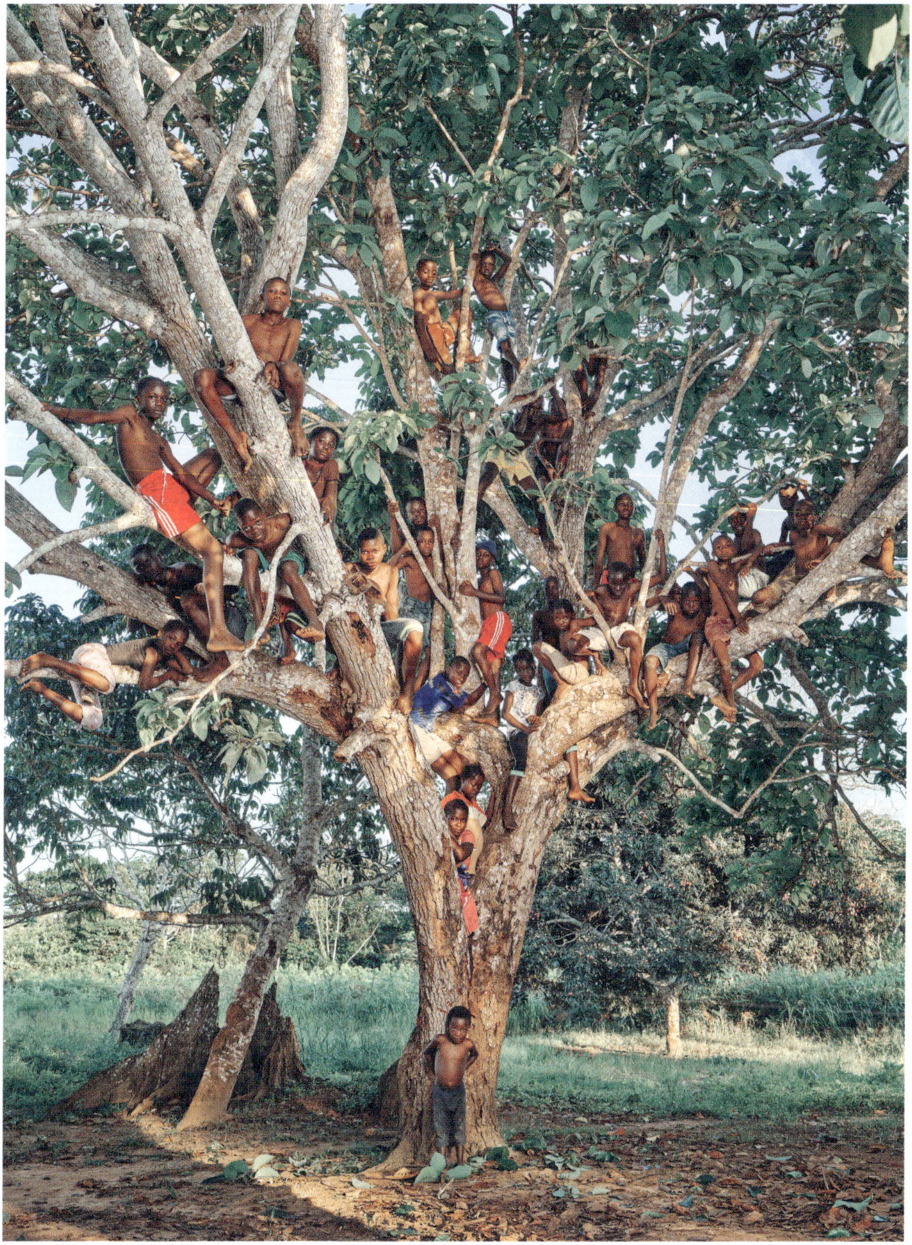

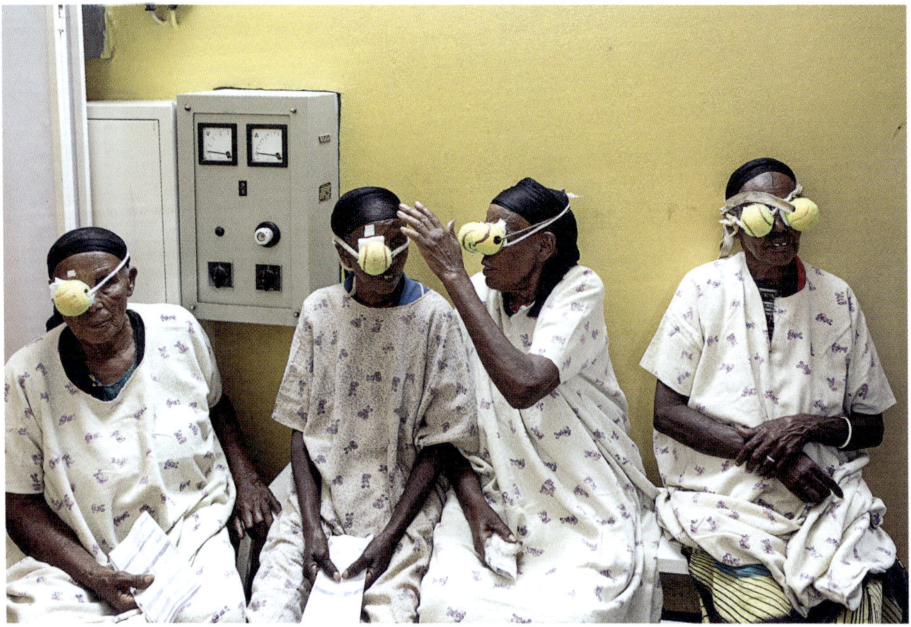

Blind Trust

by Jon Spangsvig

Bisidimo, Ethiopia

Four ladies who have just received local anaesthetic are minutes from getting potentially life-changing cataract surgery. Even though they don't know each other they find comfort in sitting close, touching and feeling.

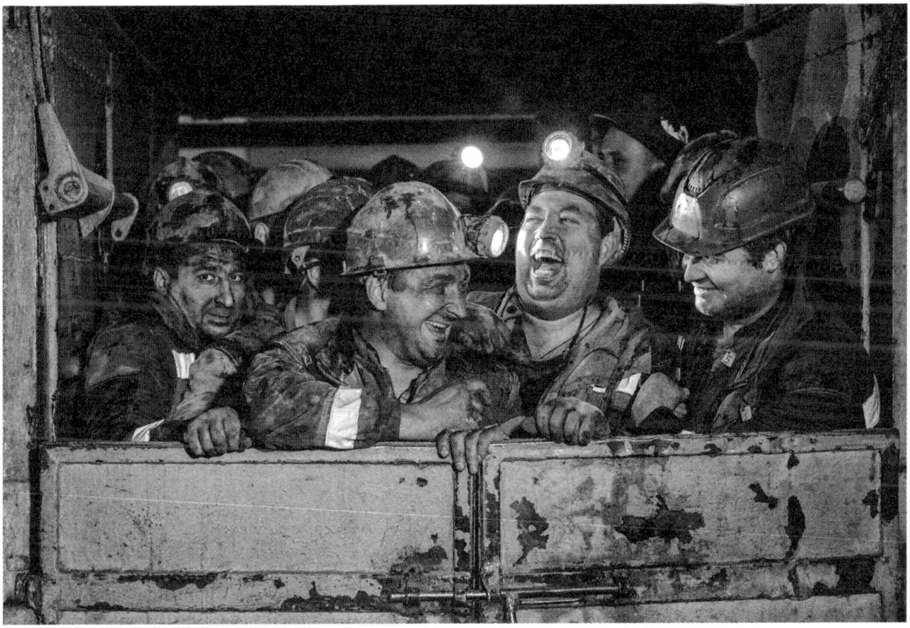

Coal People

by Maxim Marmur

Kuzbass, Siberia, Russia

Selina

by John Nassari

London, UK

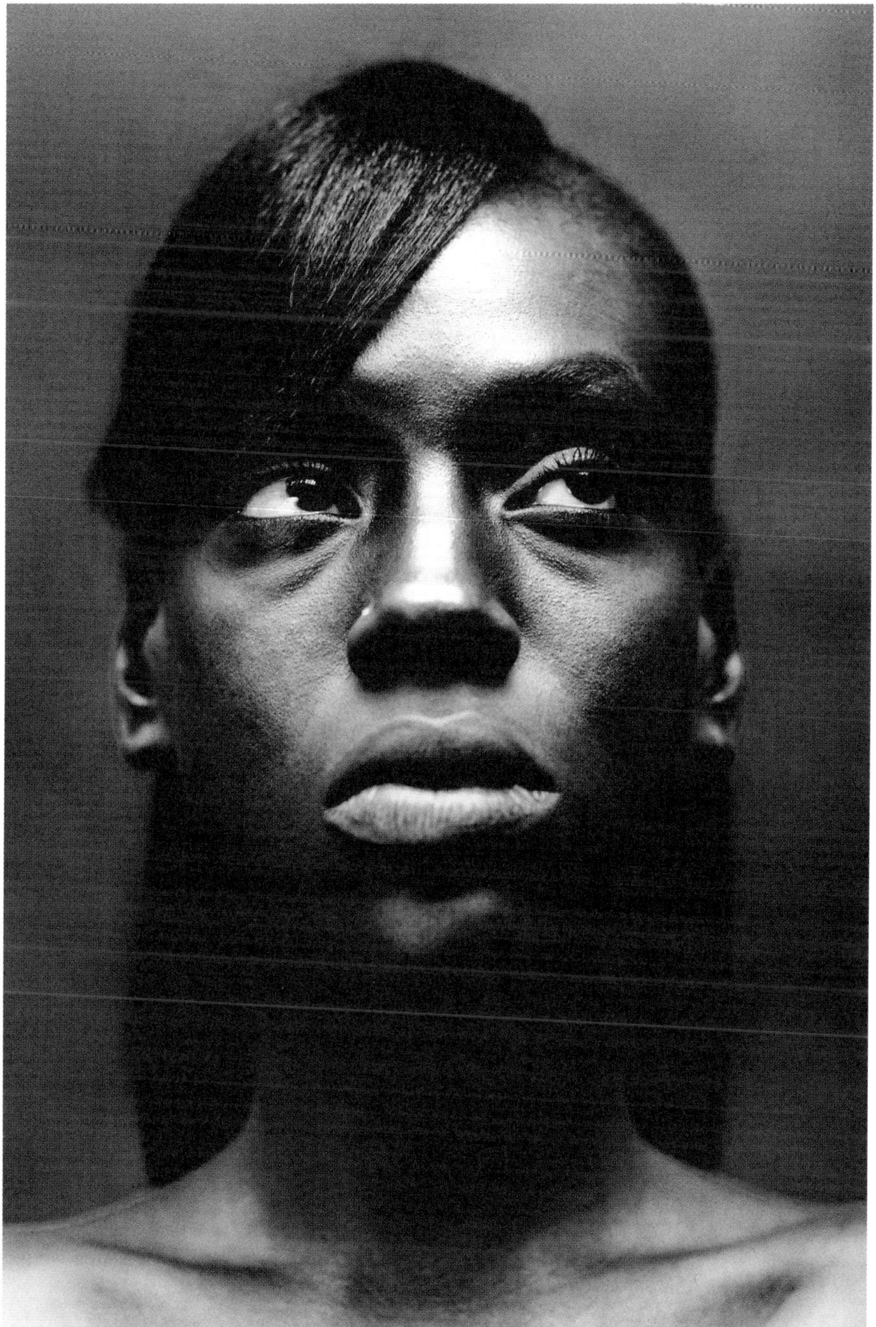

Nancy Harris
by Murat Ozkasim
Leeds, UK

'I was 28 when I had an accident on a trampoline and my leg was amputated above the knee 18 months later. It made me grieve for the active person I once was [as a former dancer and gymnast] but gradually I began to accept the new me and rediscovered my competitive spirit. I have achieved more as an amputee than I ever did before and absolutely love pushing myself. There are no limits anymore.' –Nancy Harris, model

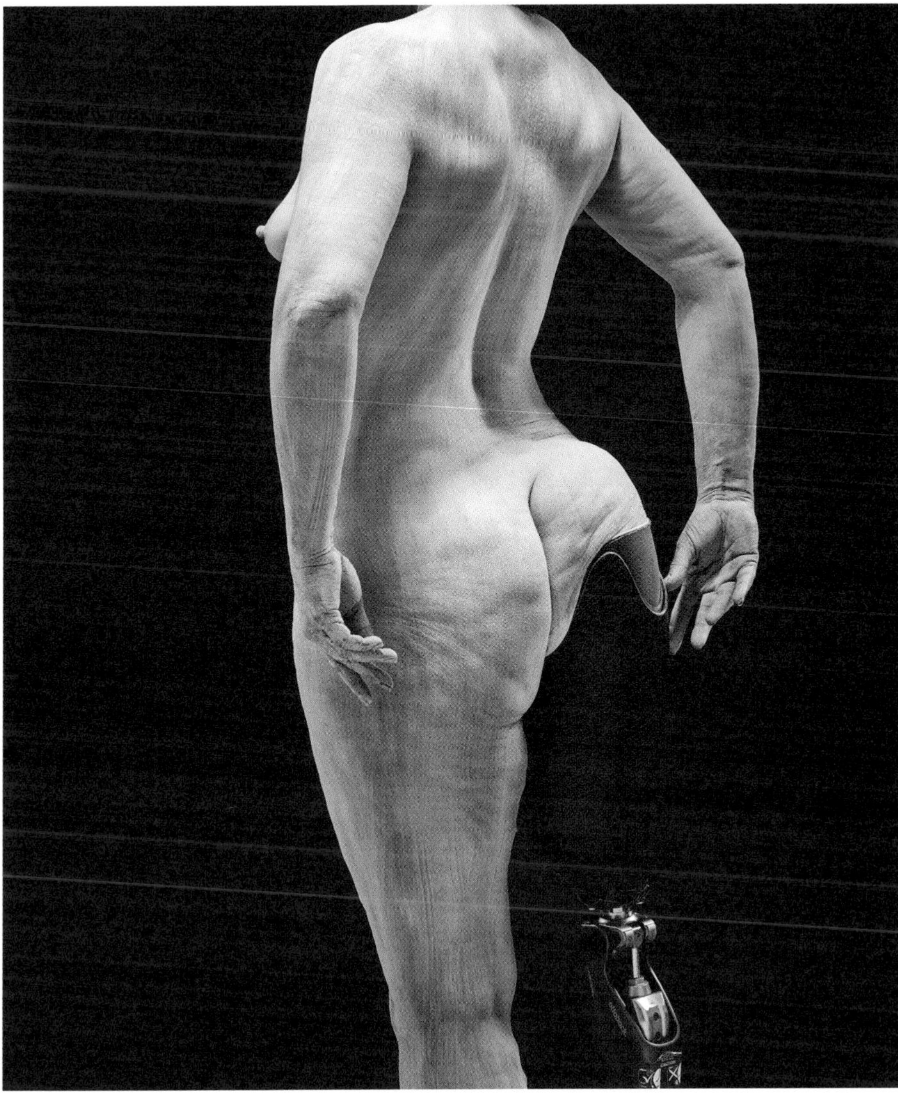

Kefulazia Juma

by Patrick Gries

Shinyanga, Tanzania

Because albinism affects the production of melanin – the pigment that colours skin, hair and eyes – many albinos have serious problems with their vision. Some, like Kefulazia, have a hard time opening their eyes at all when the light is strong. Kefulazia lives in a 'school' where some 120 children with albinism are confined.

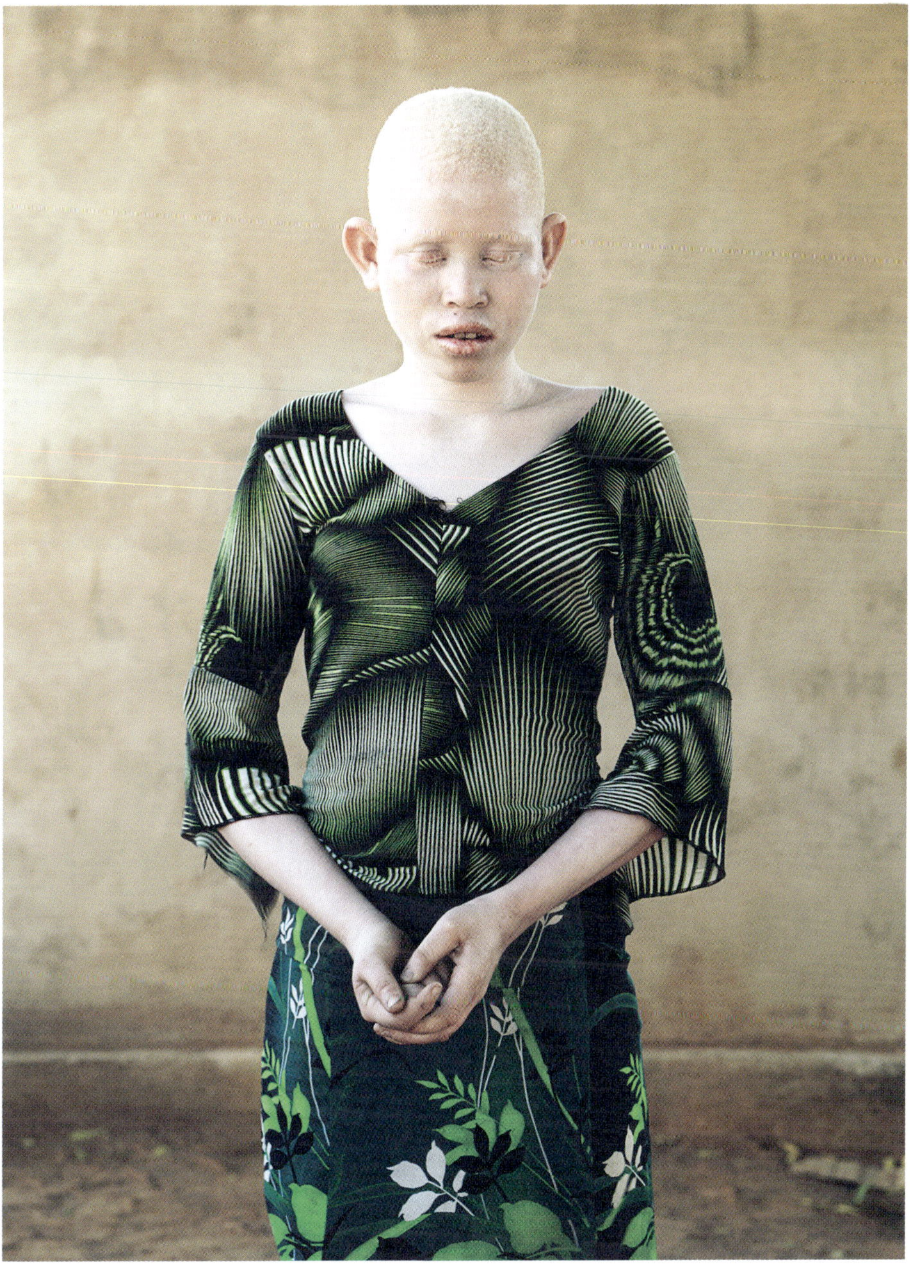

Pigment

by Andrea Zvadova

London, UK

Albinism, though beautiful and unique, is still misunderstood. Joanne is a young albino woman. She has an incredible persona, confidence and drive.

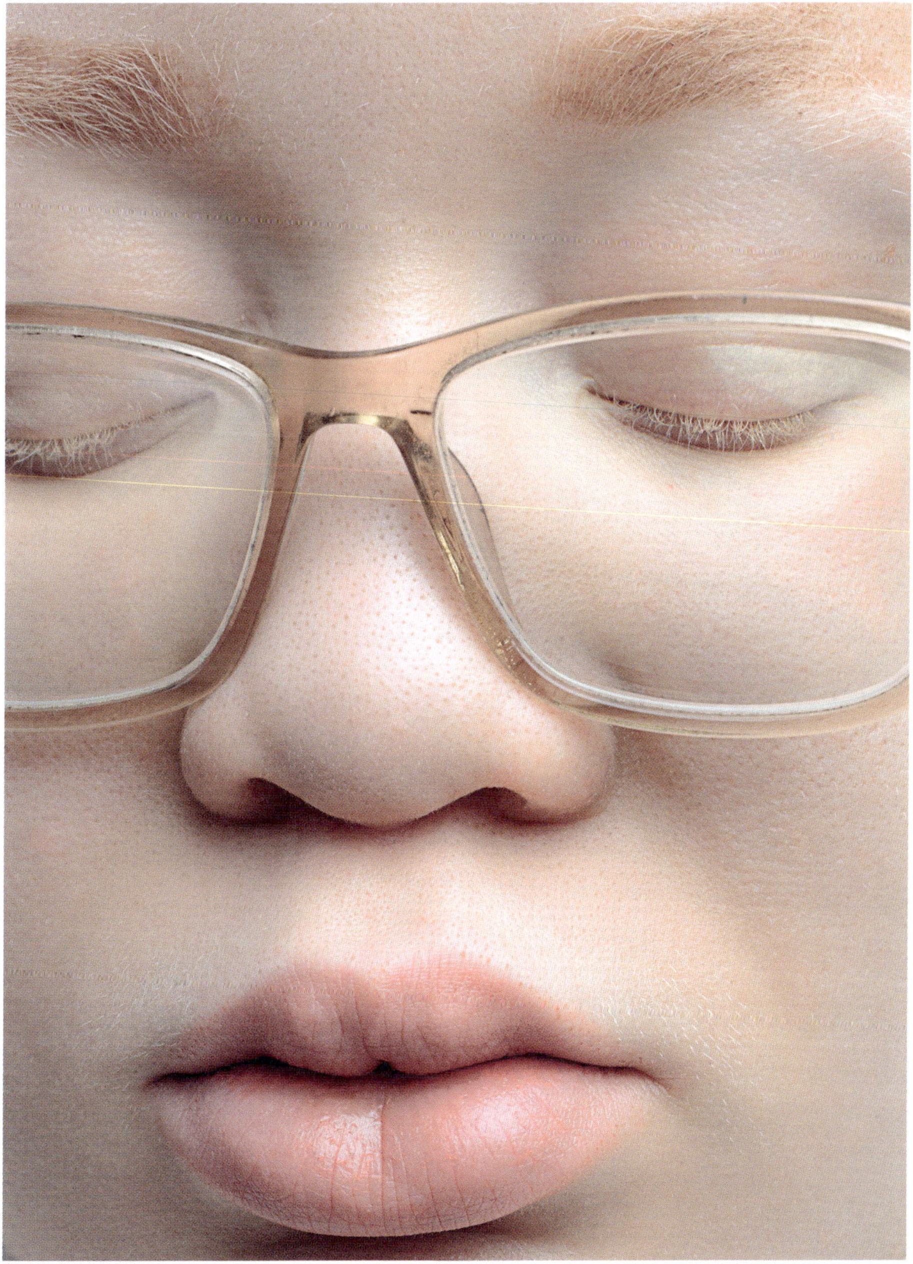

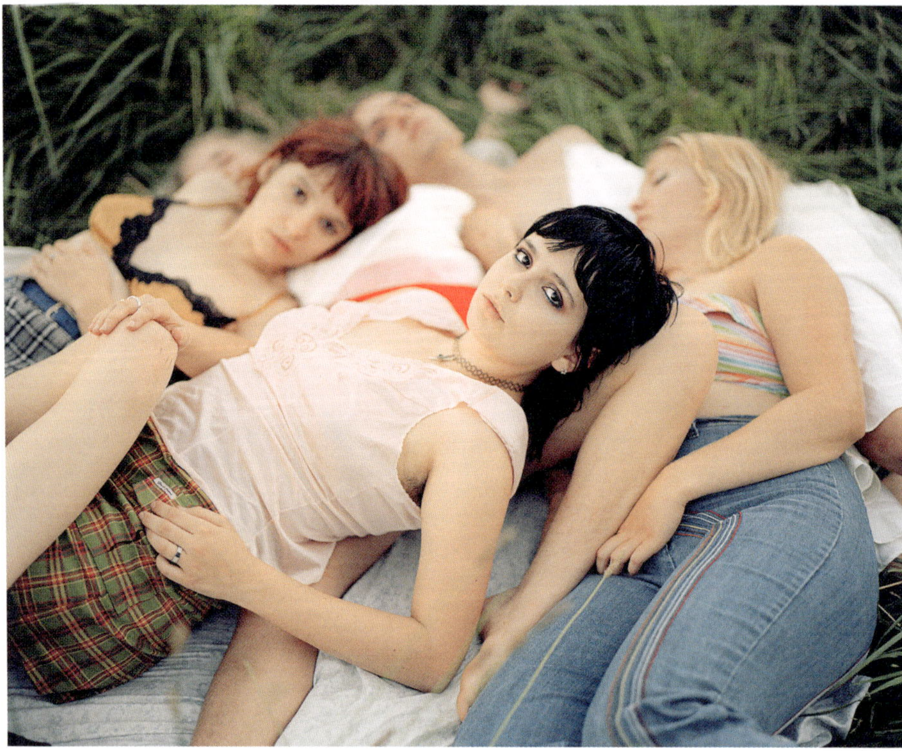

Rian with Friends
by Peyton Fulford
Athens, Georgia, USA

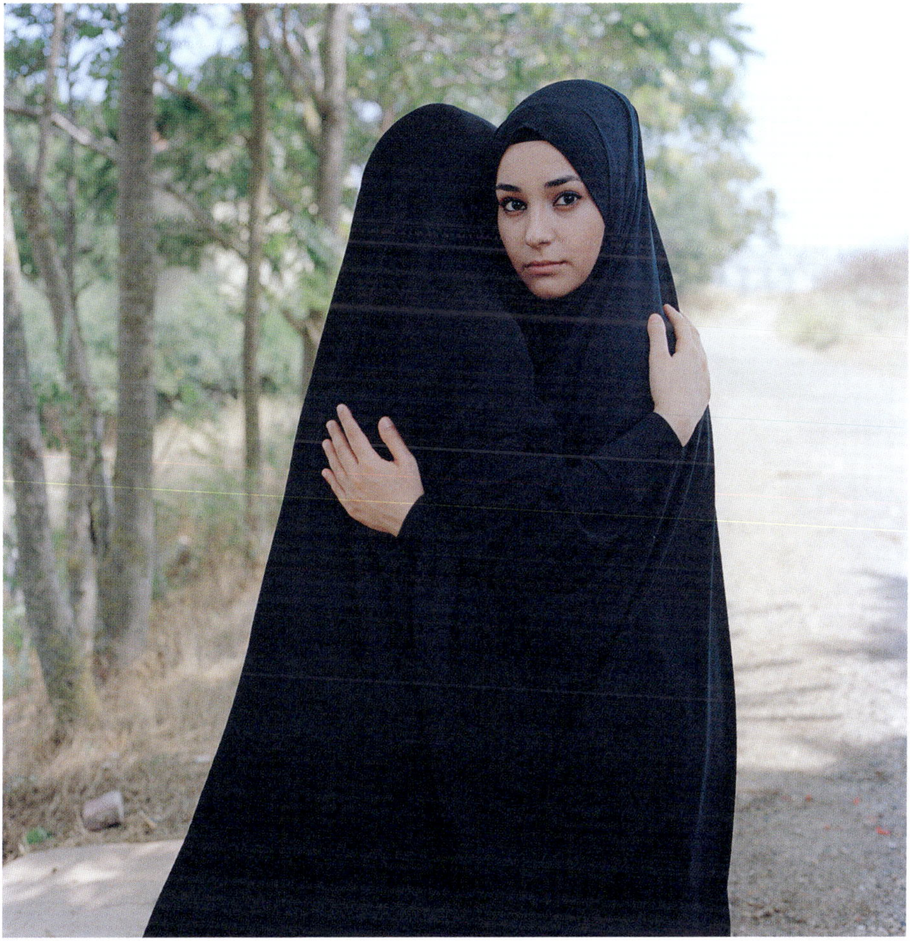

Embracing Soulmates
by Sabiha Çimen
Istanbul, Turkey

Nehir embraces her soulmate, Yaren, at a school event where they sing songs and eat watermelon. She whispers in her ear a secret that is between just them.

Girl with an iPhone

by Guoman Liao

Vancouver, British Columbia, Canada

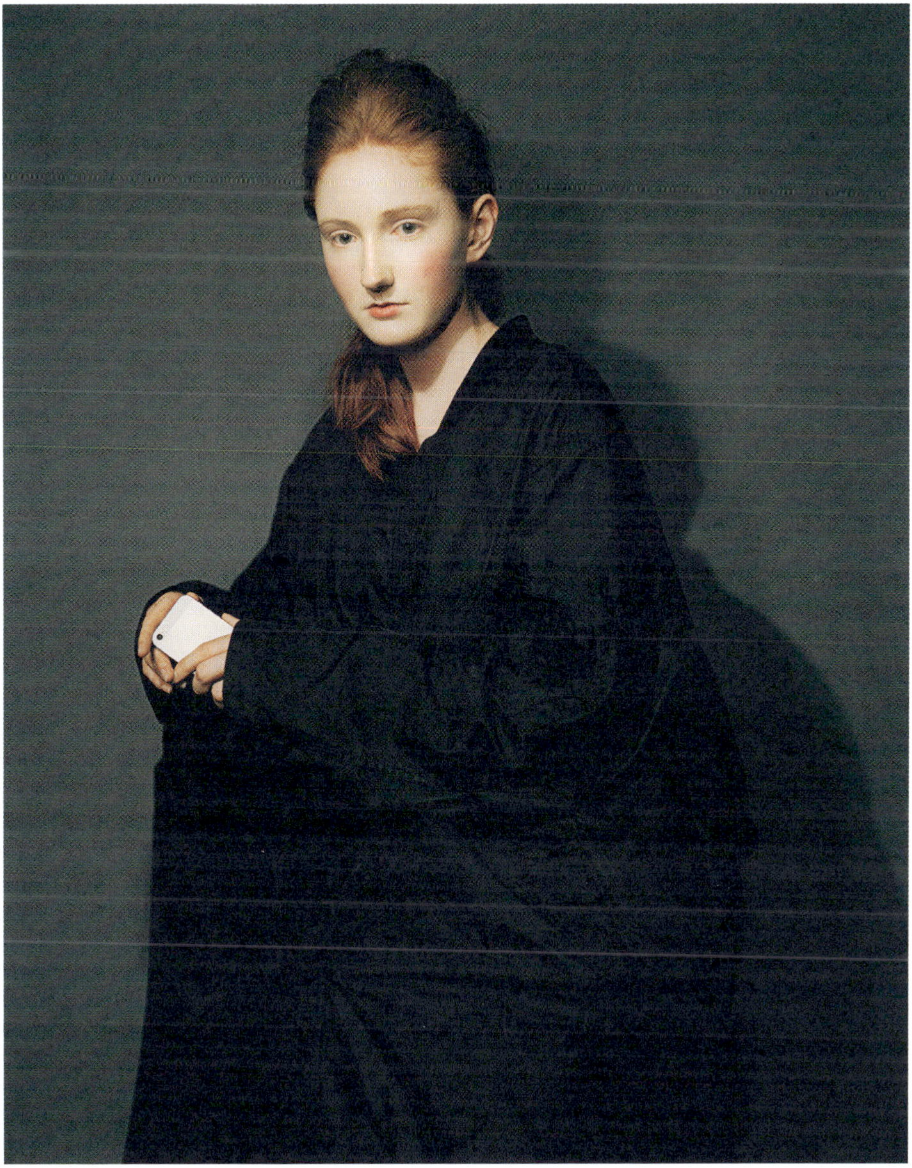

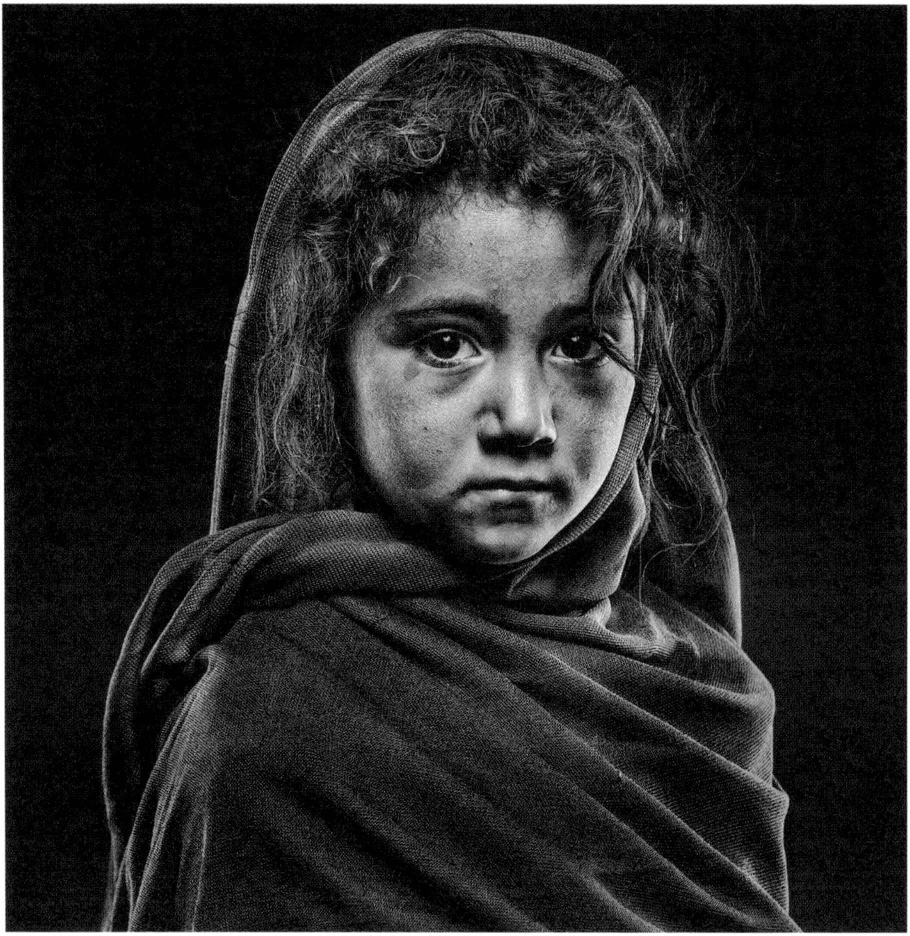

Sara

by Nour Eddine El Ghoumari

Rif Mountains, Morocco

Sara is five years old. She does not go to school like the other girls in the village. Sara will likely work as a shepherd and help around the house. When she is older, she will get married.

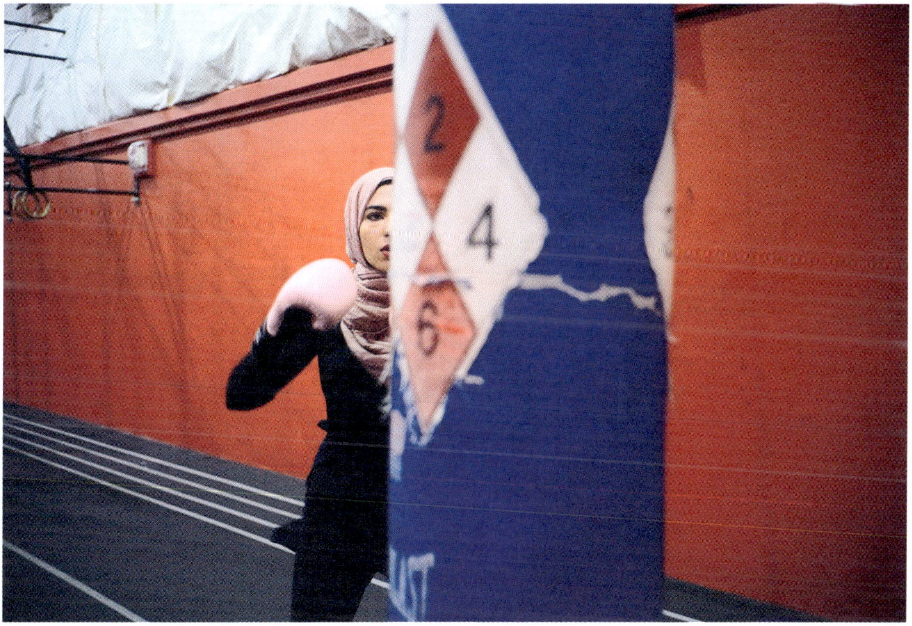

Mennah Kickboxing
by Anna Mia Davidson
Bothell, Washington, USA

'I'd like to be seen as a political scientist (I'm studying political science), a representative of my community, a muslim, a female, someone who is politically active, likes to kickbox and perform poetry. I am all of these things.'
– Mennah El-Gammal

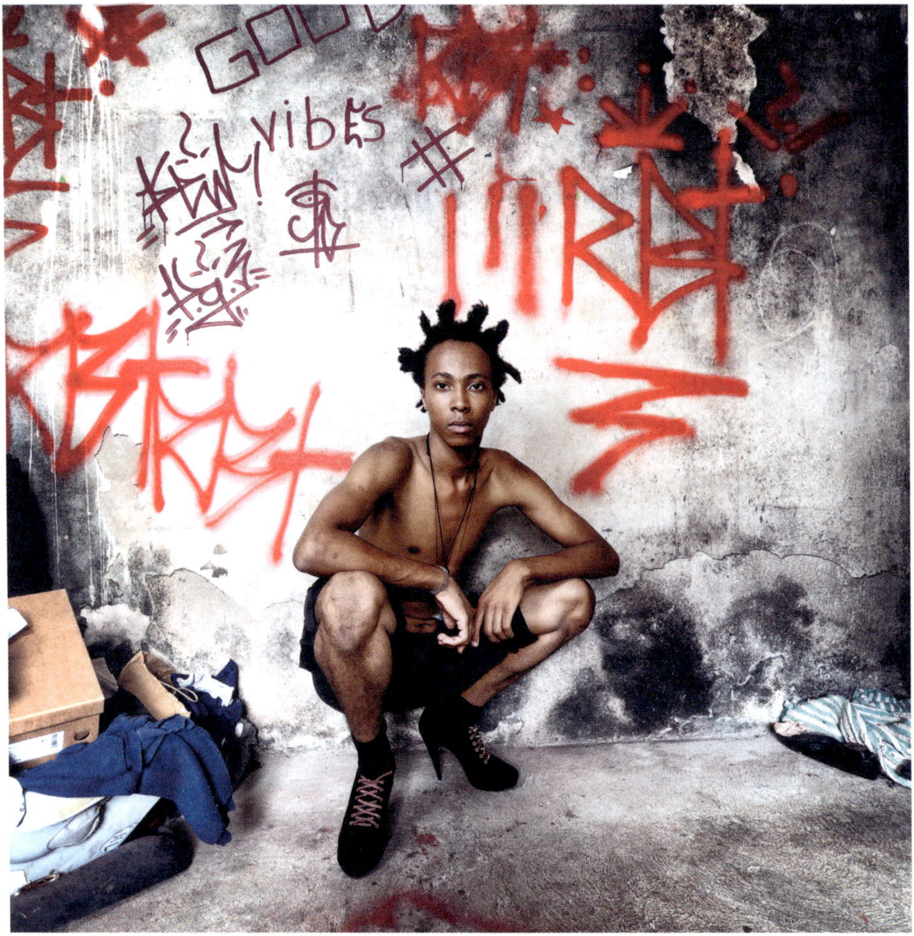

Portrait of Bruno Rabbit

by Edu Simões

São Paulo, Brazil

Every day, 59 young Afro-Brazilians are murdered in Brazil. The causes are complex but often involve criminal organisations, police corruption and poverty. Bruno is a ballet dancer who lives in one of São Paulo's many favelas.

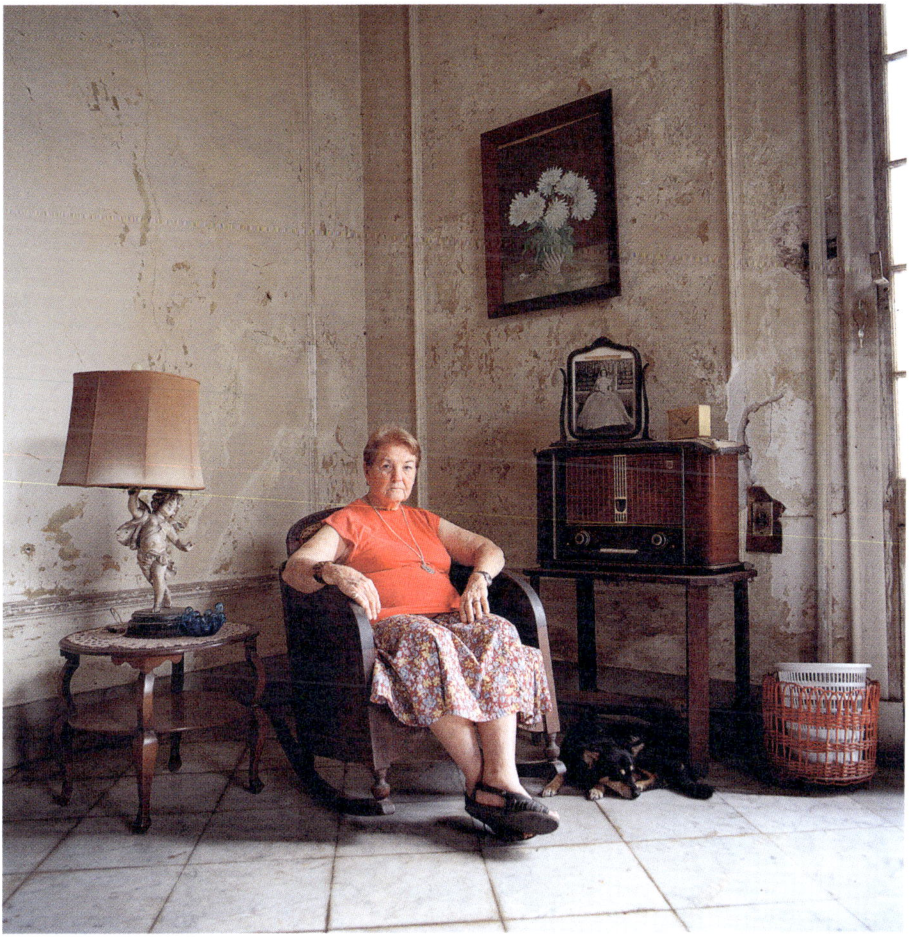

Josie Alonzo
by Carolina Sandretto
Havana, Cuba

'When I was a child I lived in this house with my parents and grandparents. All my family left Cuba after the revolution. Only my late husband and I stayed to take care of the house.' – Josie Alonzo

Zlata

by Michal Solarski

Odessa, Ukraine

I met Zlata on the waterfront in Odessa. She had come to the city with her mother to take part in a beauty contest. I thought her Ukrainian dress looked beautiful against the setting sun over the Black Sea. Traditionally, the floral headdresses are worn by young, unmarried women as a sign of their purity; they were once even thought to protect them from evil spirits.

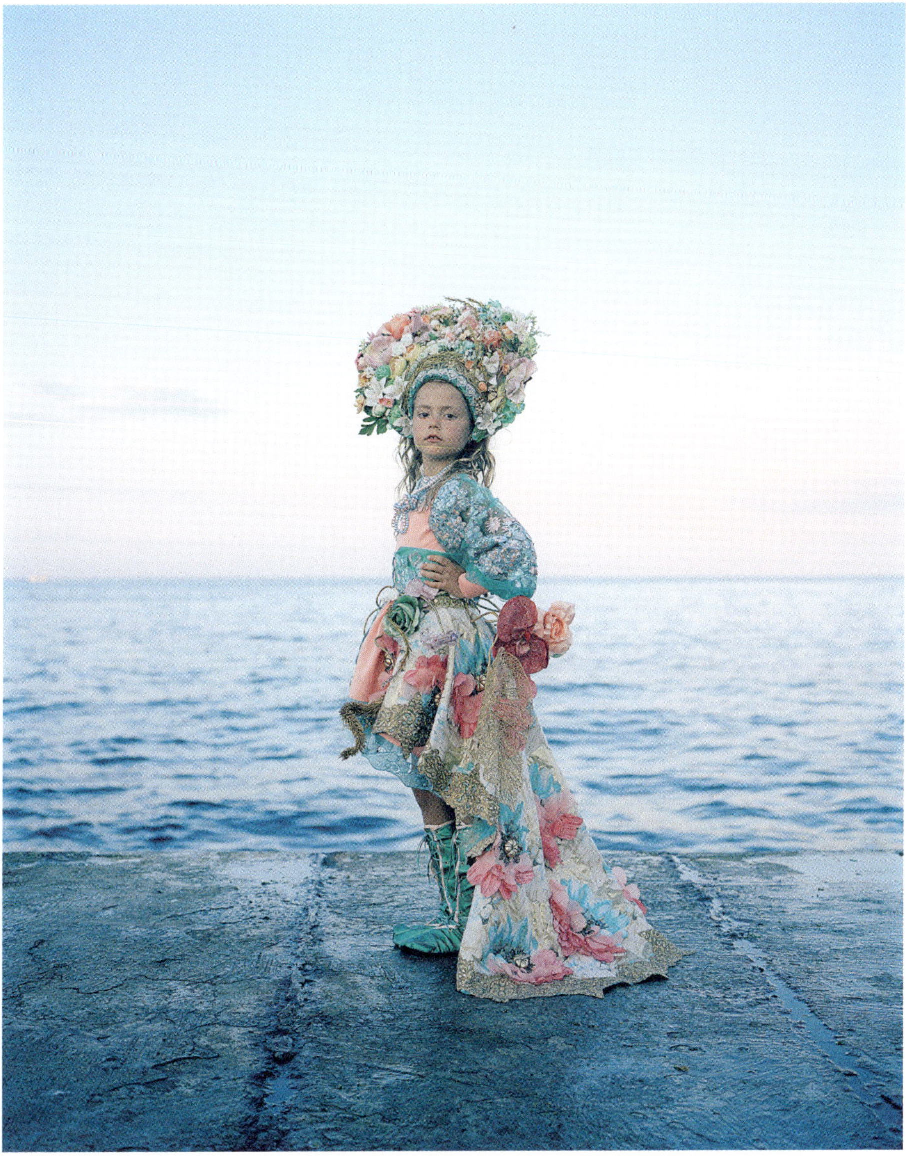

Kontakt XXXV

by Máté Bartha

Tiszafüred, Hungary

I took this photograph at a military-themed summer camp while a few boys were enacting a jungle mission through a swampy area.

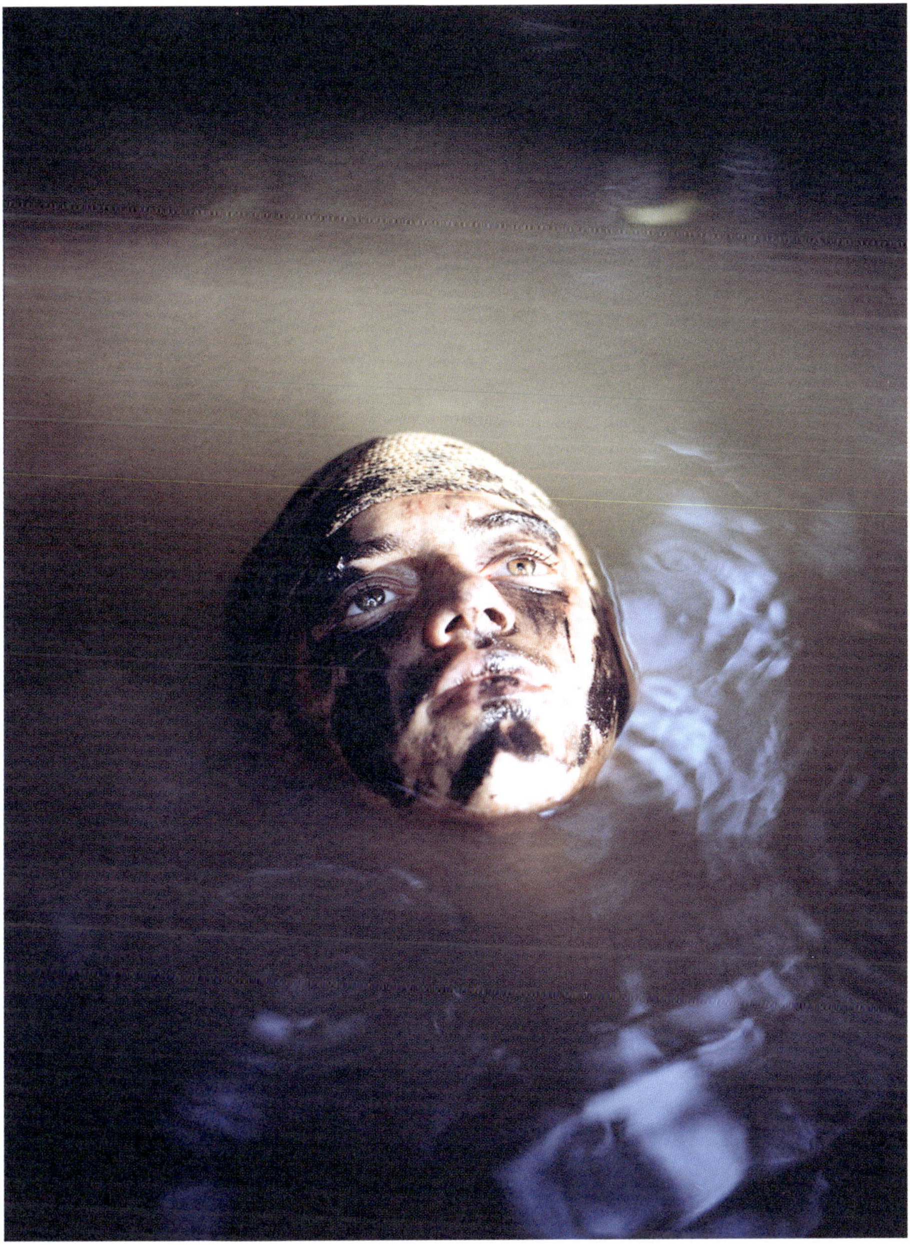

Remembering Life

by Luka Łukasiak

Warsaw, Poland

This is a portrait of Szymon Bojko when he was 97 years old. The last months of Szymon's life were difficult. He did not remember many things and wrote down his most important thoughts on small pieces of paper that were distributed everywhere. He was a very charismatic man, an artist, a dandy and a huge womaniser. I spent time with him during the last three years of his life, making portraits of him almost every day.

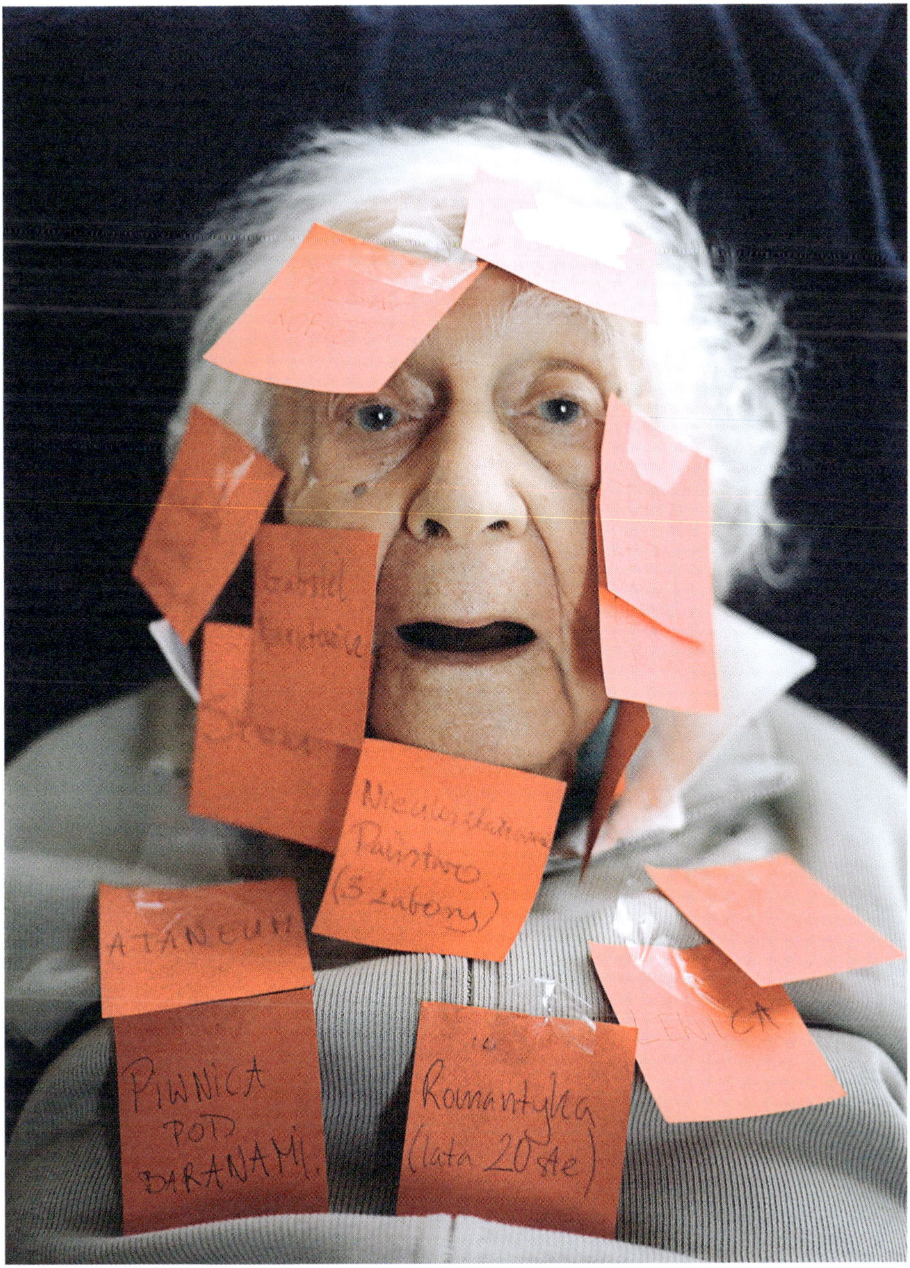
PIWNICA POD BARANAMI.
Romantyka (lata 20-te)

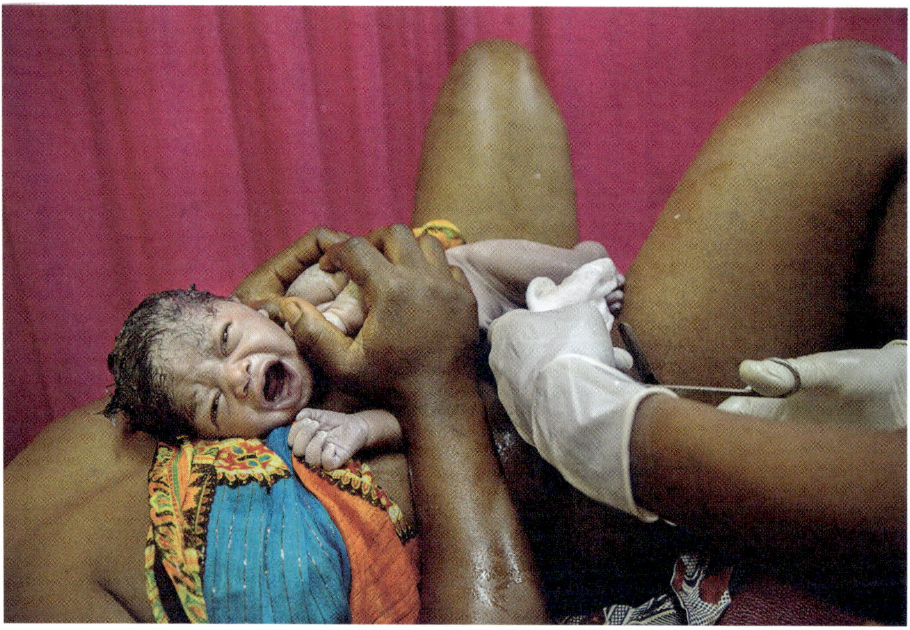

Born a Refugee: 30-seconds-old Marian

by Georgina Goodwin

Nyarugusu refugee camp, Tanzania

Newborn Marian is one of approximately 10 babies born every day in the maternity wards of Nyarugusu refugee camp's main hospital. Her mother, Tosha Sangan, arrived in the camp in 1989 after fleeing violence in her native Democratic Republic of Congo.

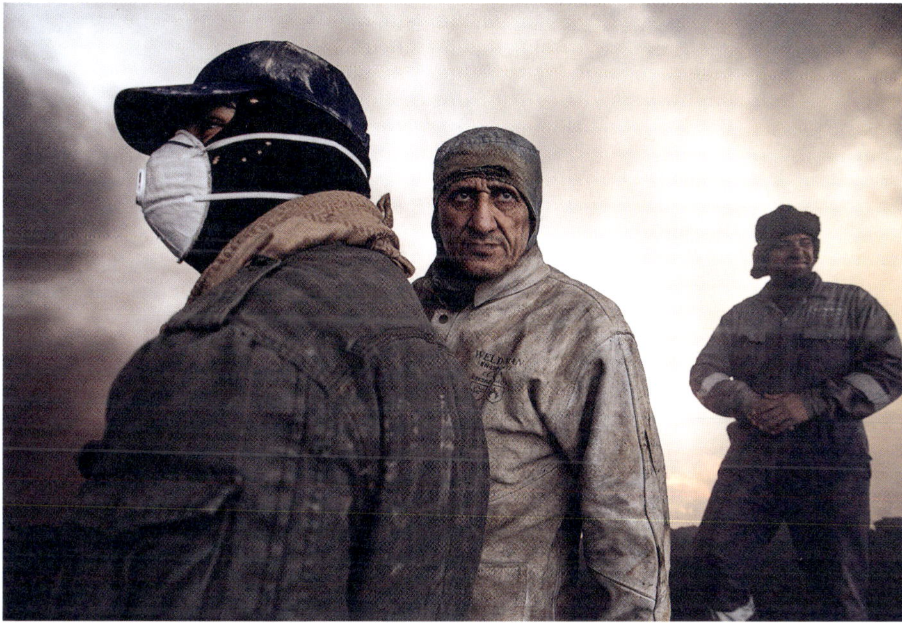

Workers Assess Oil Fires

by Ty Faruki

Al Qayyarah, Iraq

Workers pause for a moment while working to contain oil fires caused by ISIS who set fire to oil fields in Al Qayyarah, Iraq. This was the town's main source of income. The workers' main concern was contamination of the local water supply.

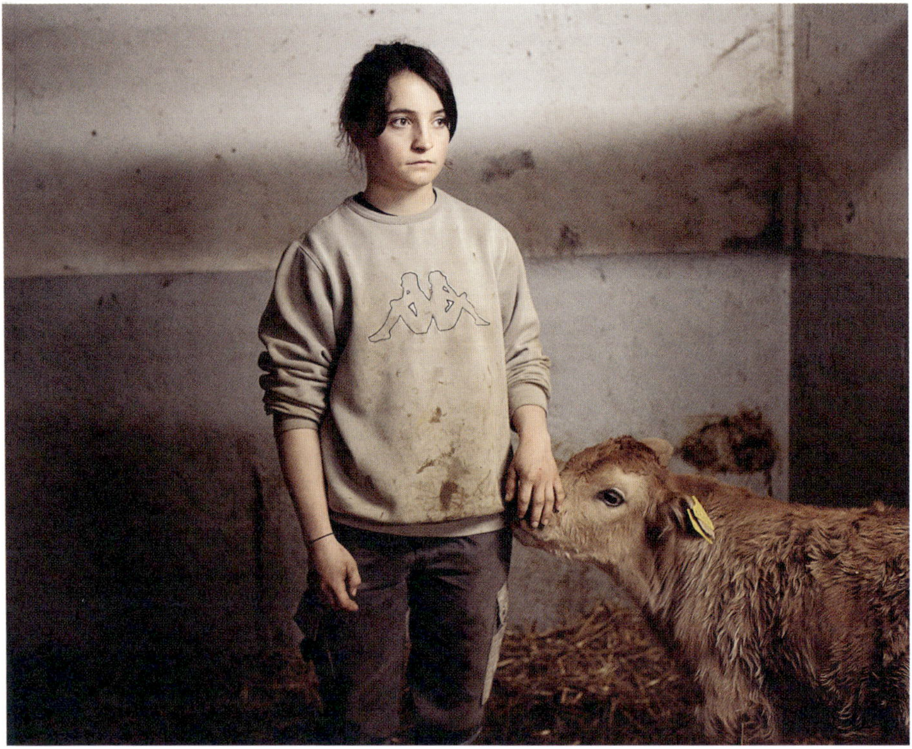

The Last Farmer of Largario

by Alfio Tommasini

Largario, Switzerland

At the age of 18, when this portrait was taken, Doris took the place of her mother in managing the family-run farm. She is now the only farmer in the village. Largario is experiencing a constant decline in population as young people move elsewhere to live and work.

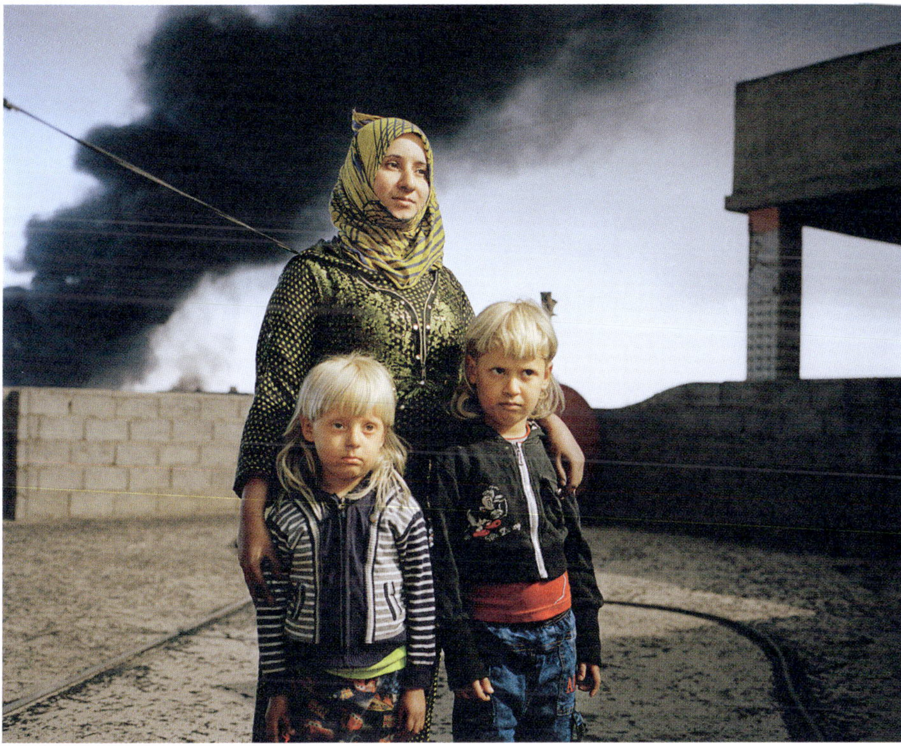

Burning Oil

by Abbie Trayler-Smith

Al Qayyarah, Iraq

Rana, 38, with her sons Ali and Mohammed stand on the rooftop of their house. ISIS set 19 of the town's oil wells on fire when they retreated a few months ago and the fires have been burning ever since. Smoke can be seen in the sky up to 60 kilometres away. The fires were eventually extinguished two months after this photograph was taken.

What Still Remains

by Katharina Dubno

Twardawa, Poland

I grew up in Twardawa, a place that once had a convivial, family-like atmosphere. Now, almost all the farms are gone and only the older generation and a few families remain, while younger people have moved abroad to try to make a better living. I went back after many years to meet and photograph the villagers who still live there and who had a strong connection to their homes and the animals that had been their loyal companions. This is Mr Cichoń with his favourite wild duck.

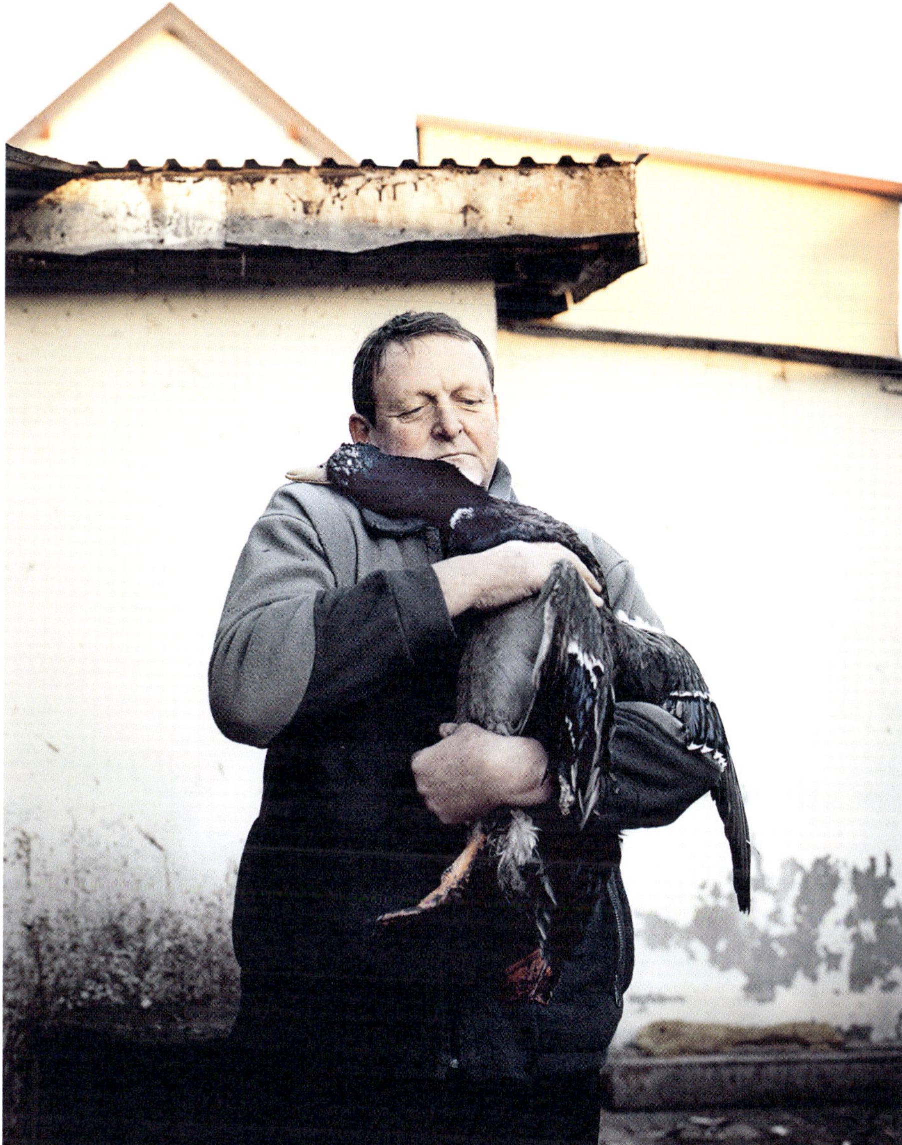

Love at Agbogbloshie

by Natasha Drewnicki

Accra, Ghana

Razak and Rukayå are workers at Agbogbloshie, the world's largest e-waste dump. It's where other countries discard their unwanted phones, computers and other electronic goods, and Ghanaians are forced to carve a precarious living through collecting and burning toxic scrap metal, like copper. It was hard to walk in as an outsider. Nobody wants the outside world to witness what goes on there.

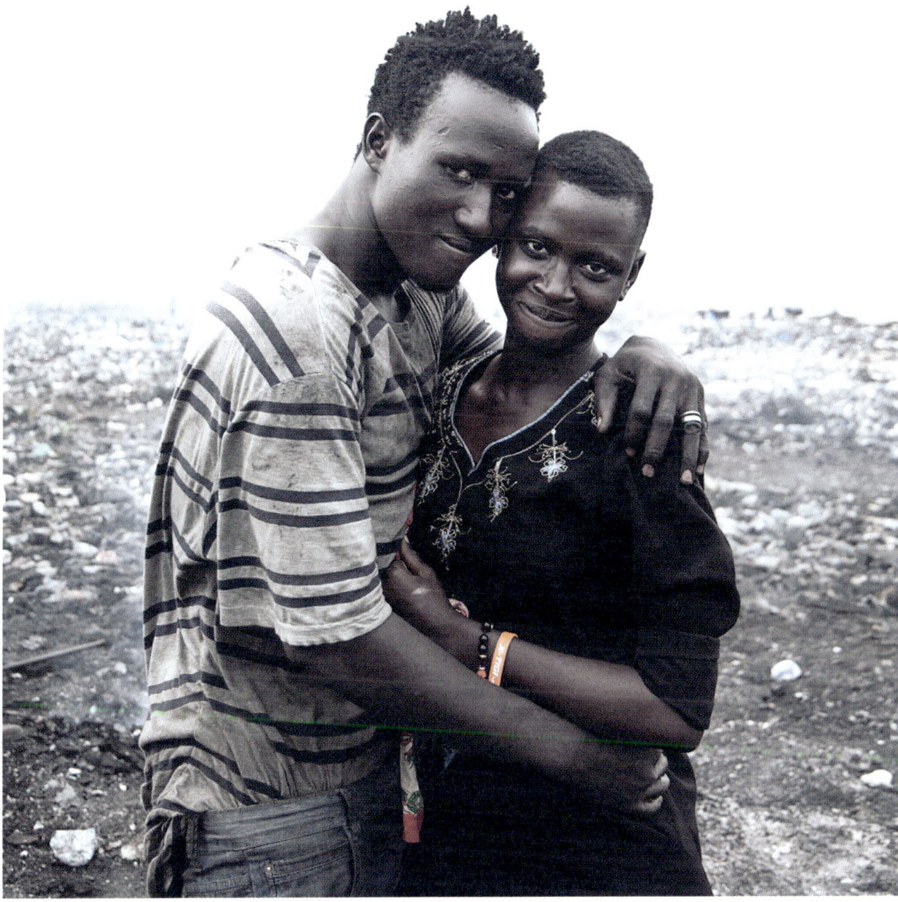

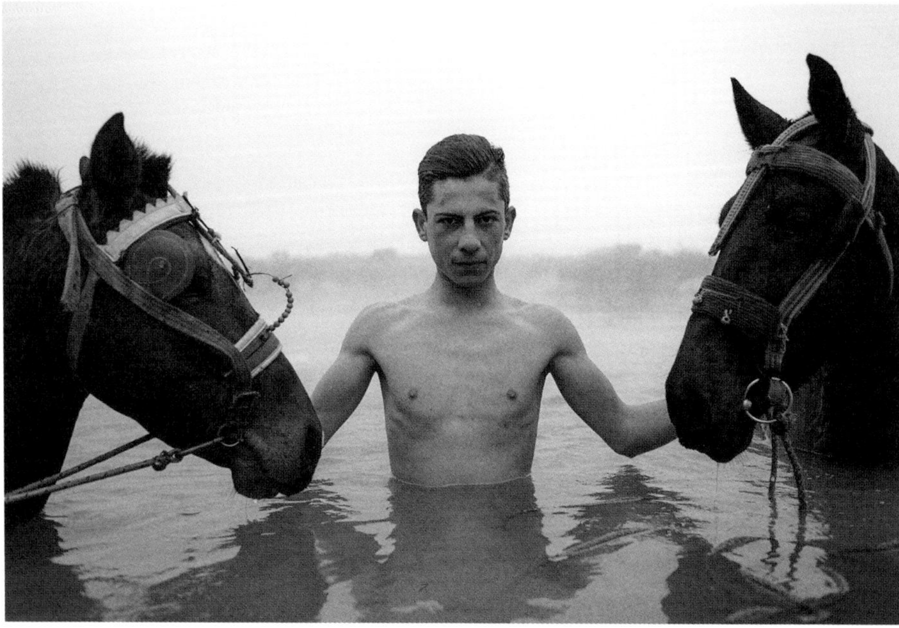

Hope Keeper
by Ferhat Celik
Tatvan, Turkey

Muhammed takes his family's horses to the lake on weekends to wash them. The area is very cold in the winter with temperatures as low as -20°C but the water comes from a hot spring so it's warm. He lives in a remote town where terror and poverty is high, and has to work while studying to support his family.

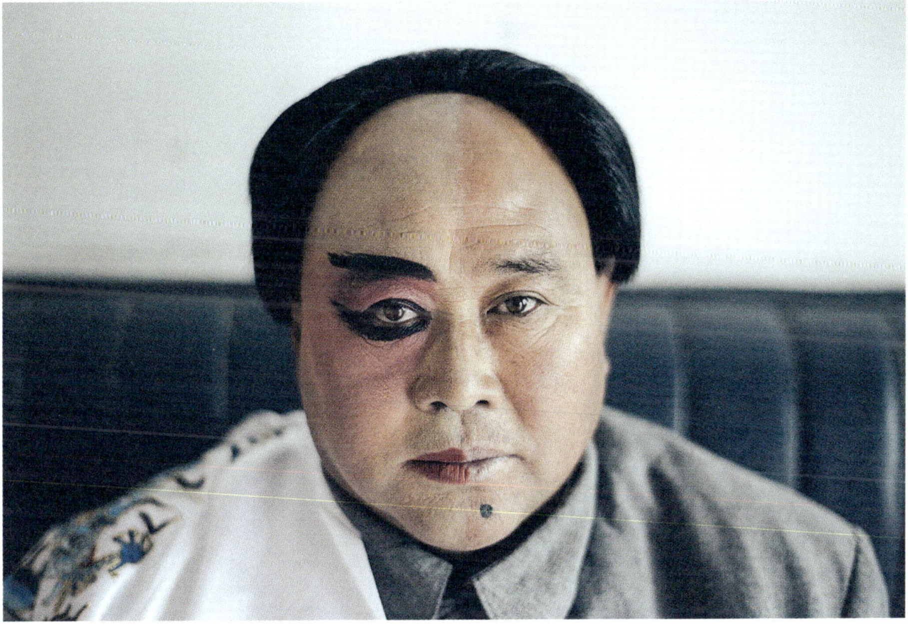

Under the Skin

by Ying Wang

Shijiazhuang, Hebei, China

Sanming Bai is a Mao Zedong impersonator, one of many in China. The makeup he is wearing on one side of his face points to Bai's experiences as a performer in opera and we also see him in role as Chairman Mao. Bai works as a farmer.

Vincent

by Gregor Kuntscher

Manga, Burkina Faso

Twelve-year-old Vincent Adouabou has been deaf since birth and does not speak out loud. He also has a skin condition called vitiligo. The majority of children with disabilities in Burkina Faso have never been to school, but Vincent is lucky and attends a school that champions inclusive education. He is learning sign language and wants to become a doctor.

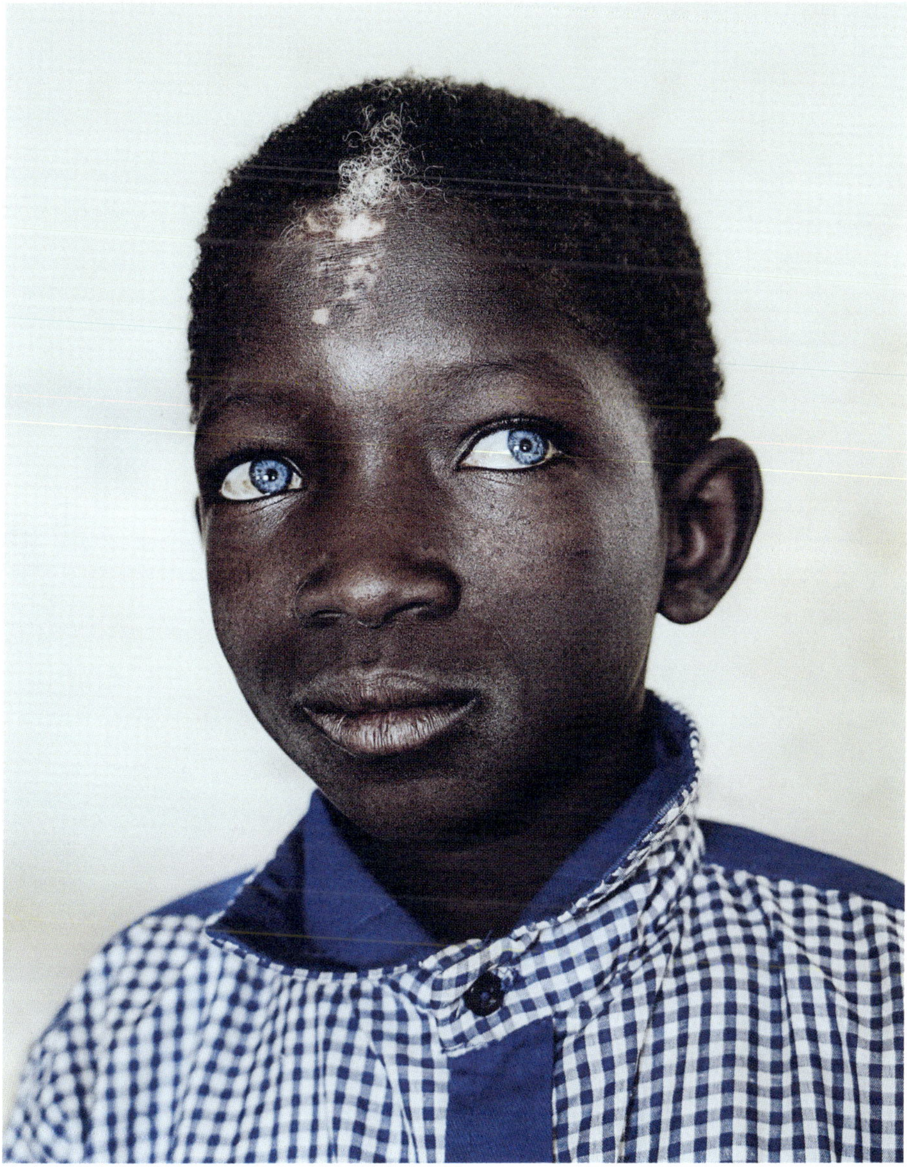

Soledad

by Néstor Díaz

Buenos Aires, Argentina

'I went through cancer at the same time as my sister, and my brother died from lymphoma. The difficult part is being able to turn adversity into something positive. I was able to achieve this thanks to my family and friends and I manage to be in the present more than ever.' – Soledad

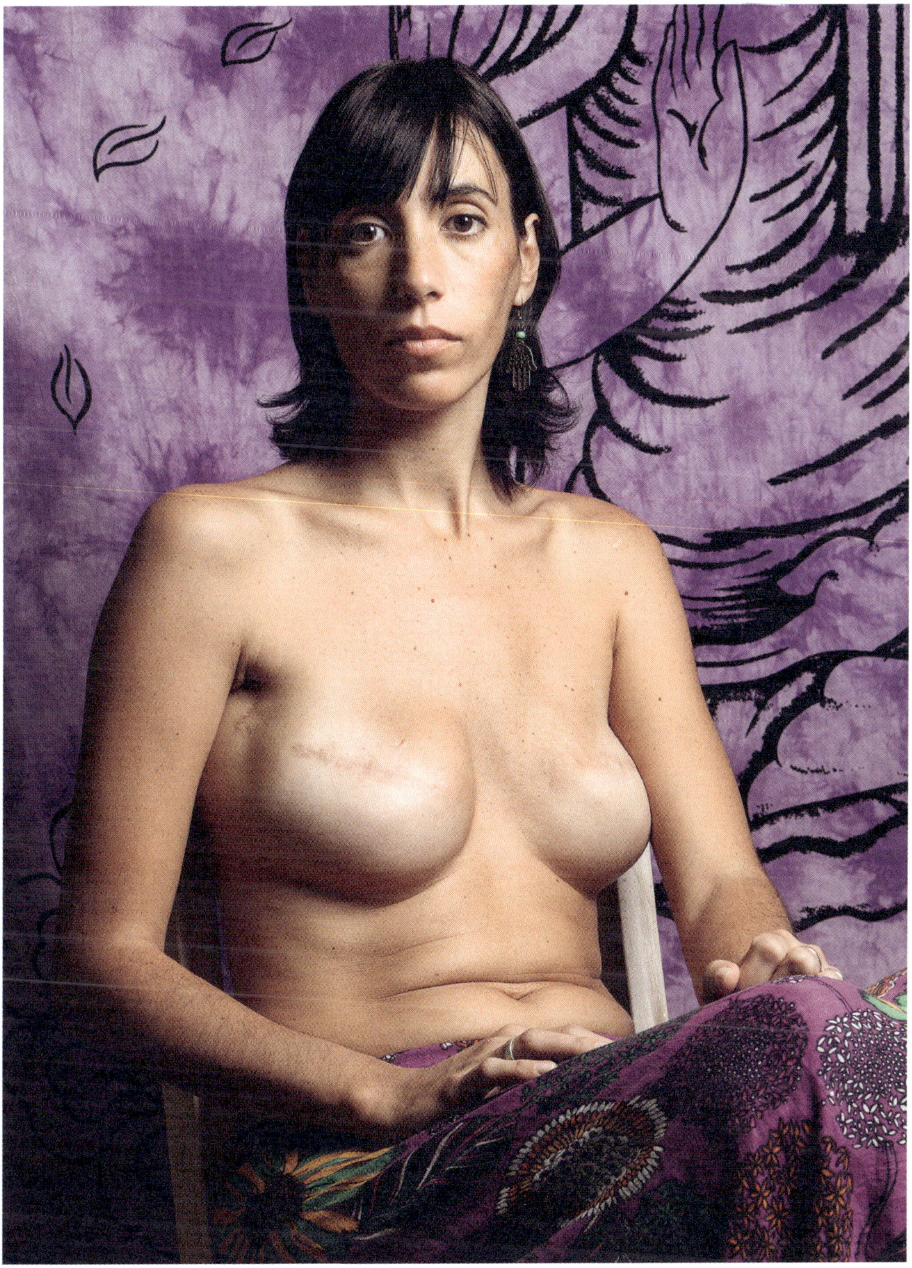

Untitled

by Dustin Thierry

Berlin, Germany

To this day, homosexuality is stigmatised and condemned within the Caribbean community. With this in mind, I made portraits of members of the black LGBTQ community in Berlin, Amsterdam, Milan and Paris who are part of an underground ballroom scene. The project is an ode to my late brother and all people of Afro-Caribbean descent who are denied the right to express their sexuality freely.

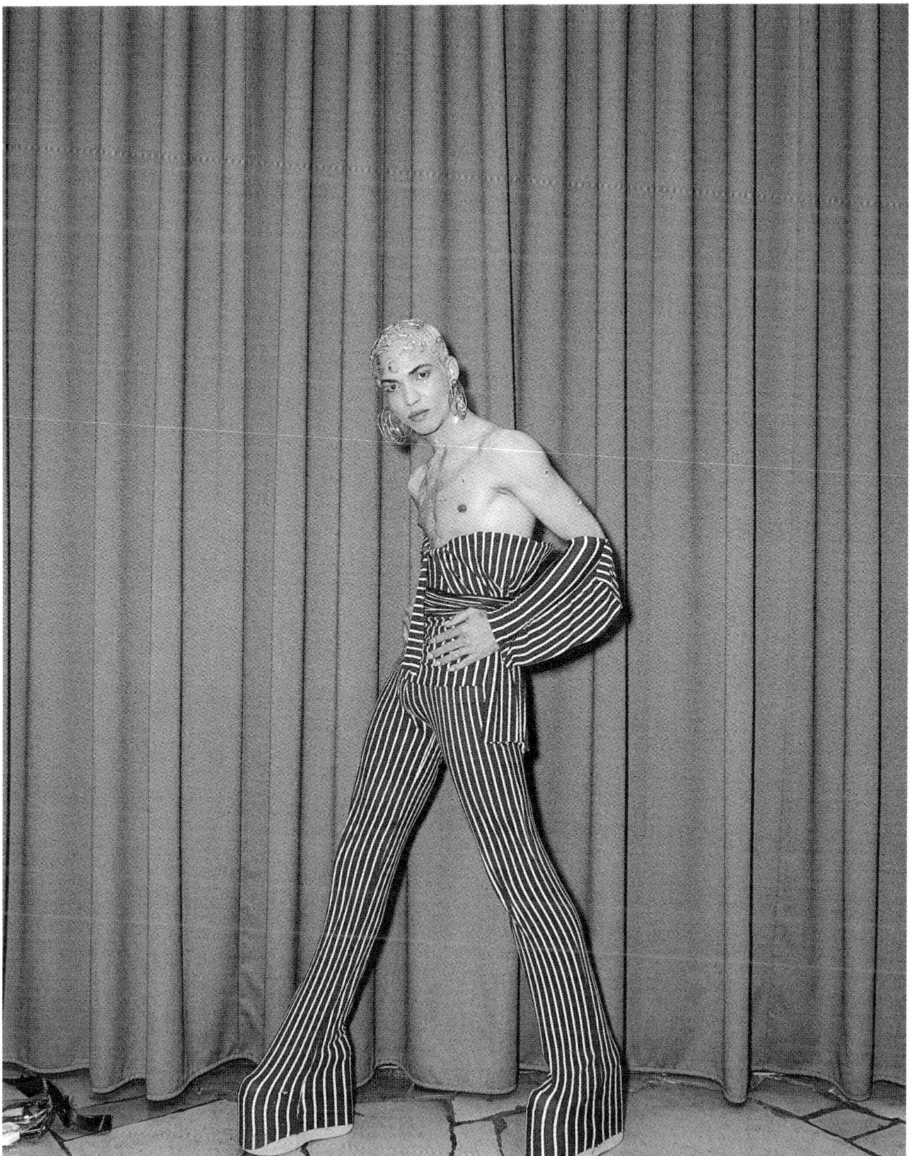

Emil

by Nana Varveropoulou

London, UK

I took this portrait of my son for a community art project, the aim of which is to produce a collective portrait of residents in a mixed-tenancy apartment block in Hackney. Emil loves Greek mythology and decided to turn his top into a headdress and pose as a character from one of his books.

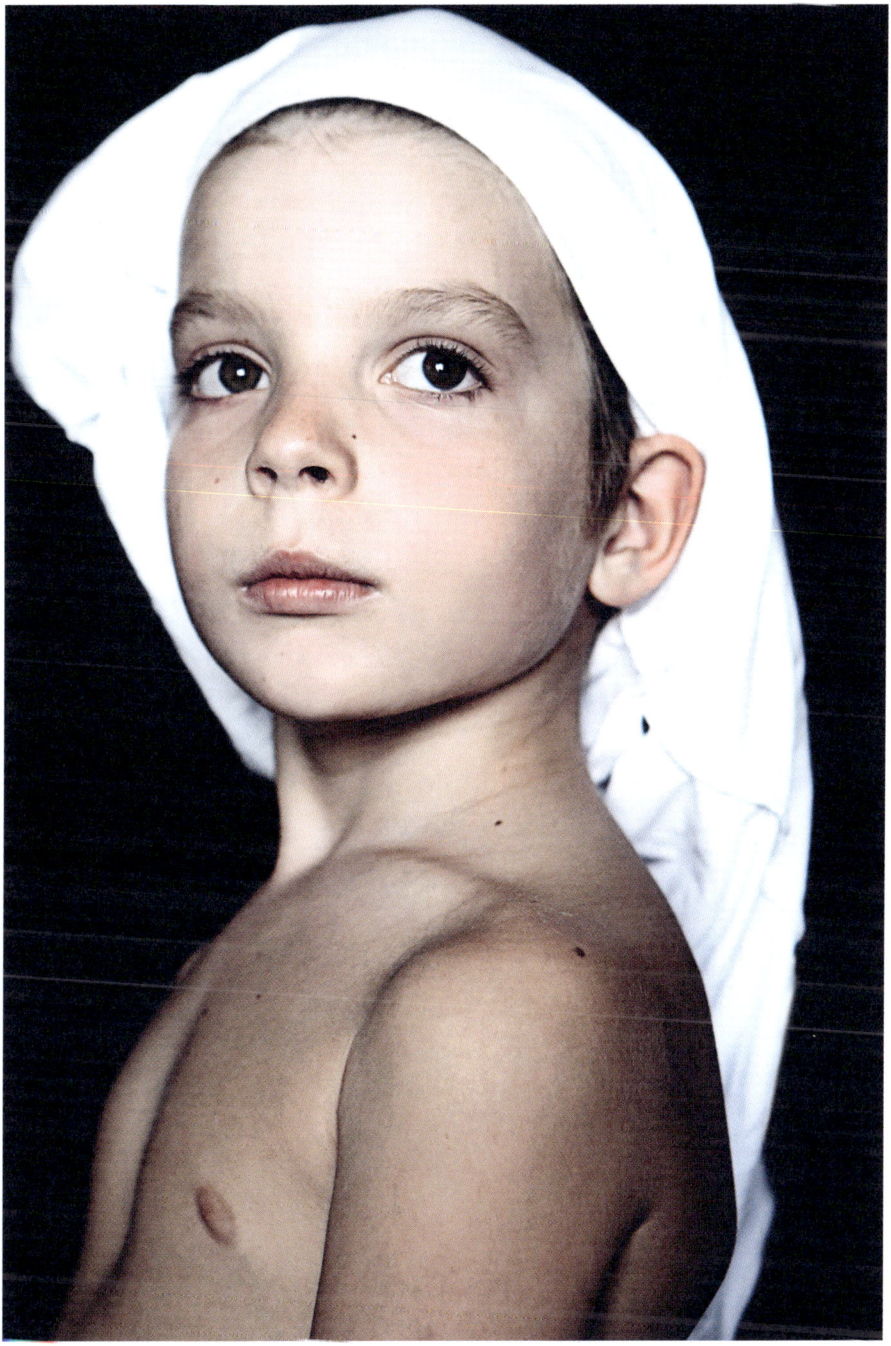

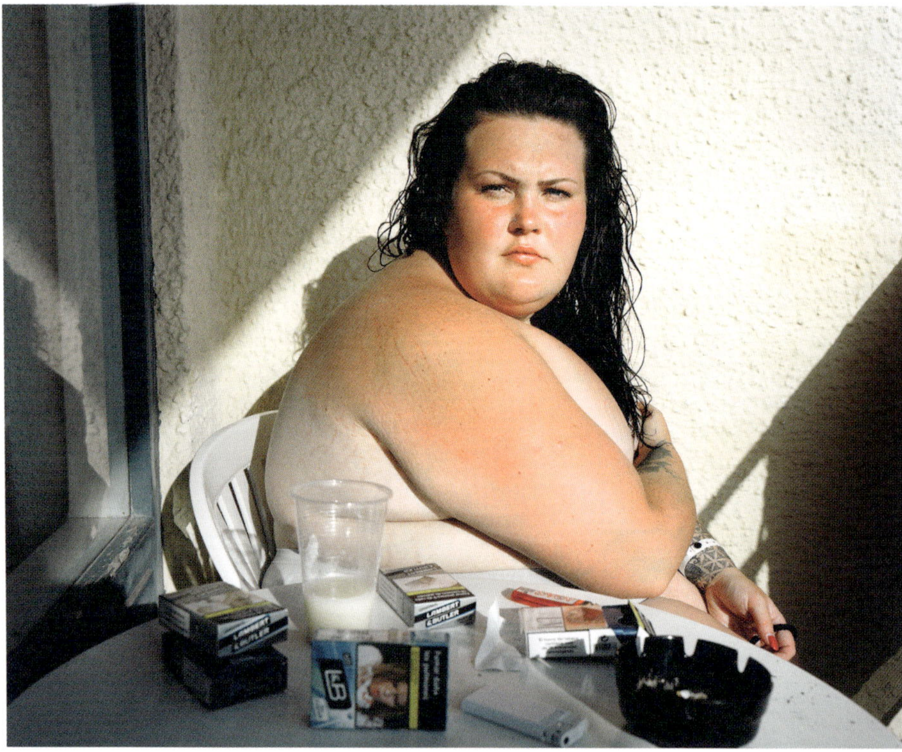

Shannon: Going Large on the Costa Del Sol

by Abbie Trayler-Smith

Fuengirola, Spain

I spent a week with Shannon and her best friend on a girls' holiday in Spain. I have spent eight years photographing Shannon in Sheffield for my project, *The Big O*, an intimate portrait of the young people behind the UK's obesity statistics.

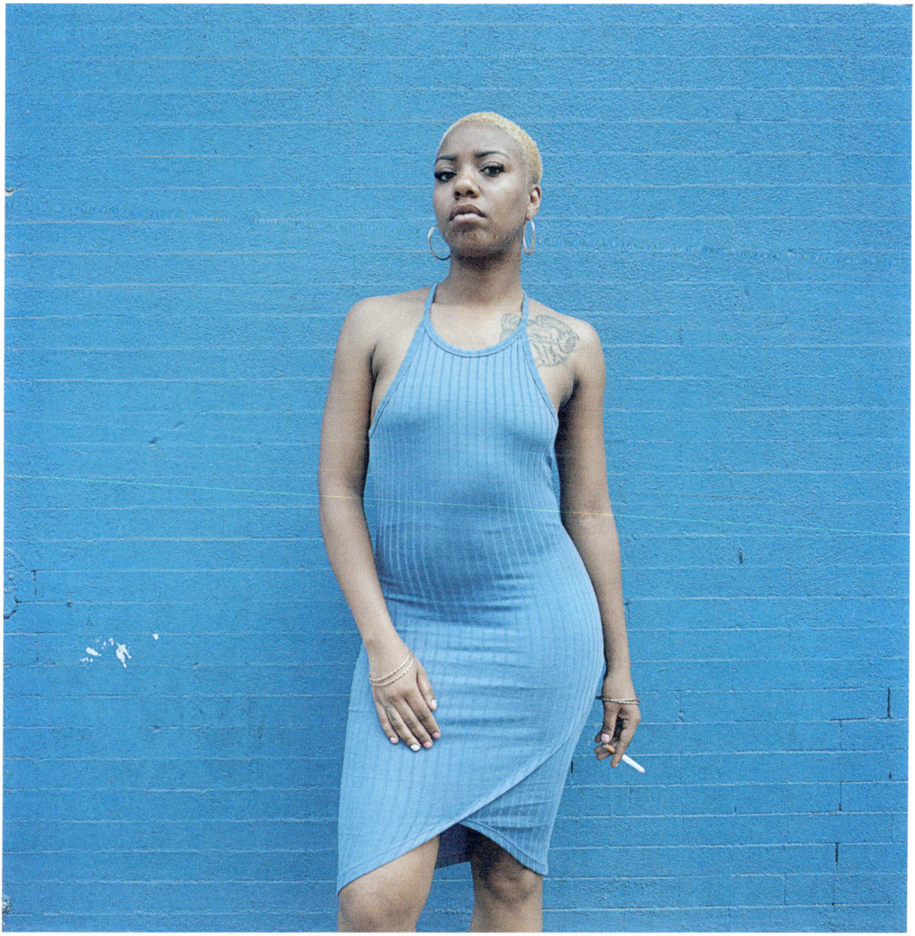

Woman in Blue

by Louise Amelie and Aljaž Fuis

New York City, New York, USA

Harlem native Latisha walked out of a grocery store in front of this wall. We only had five minutes before she had to leave and I later found out that she is a rapper.

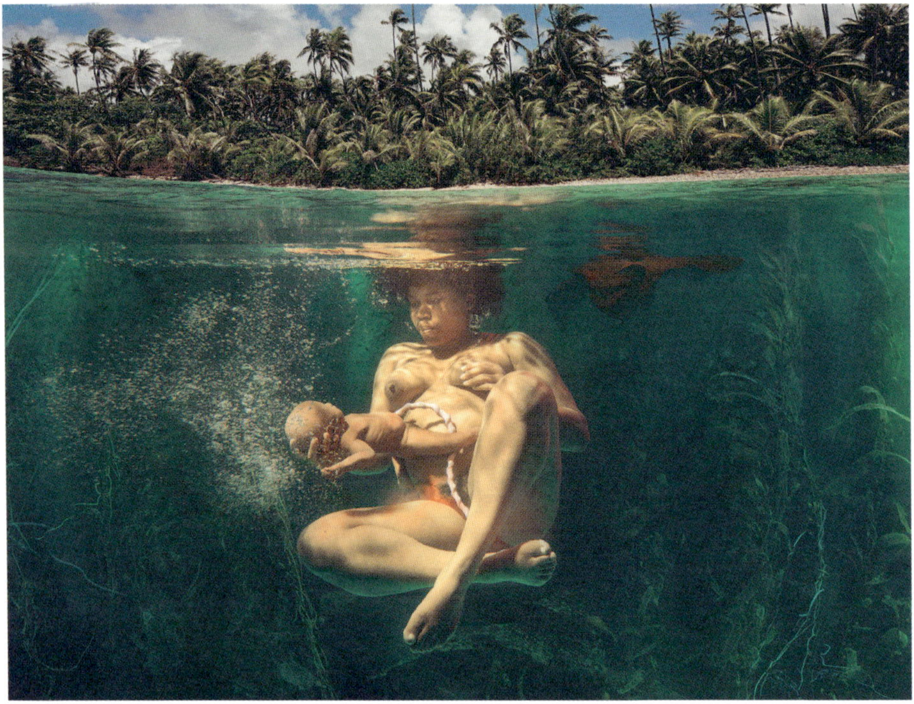

Aquadural
by Natalie Lennard
Uckfield, UK

Ijeoma Sady, a mother who experienced a breech free birth in water at home, poses in a swimming pool with a silicone baby to represent the ancient roots of waterbirth. Women were known to give birth in shallow sea water and rivers in ancient Crete, Japan, South America and New Zealand.

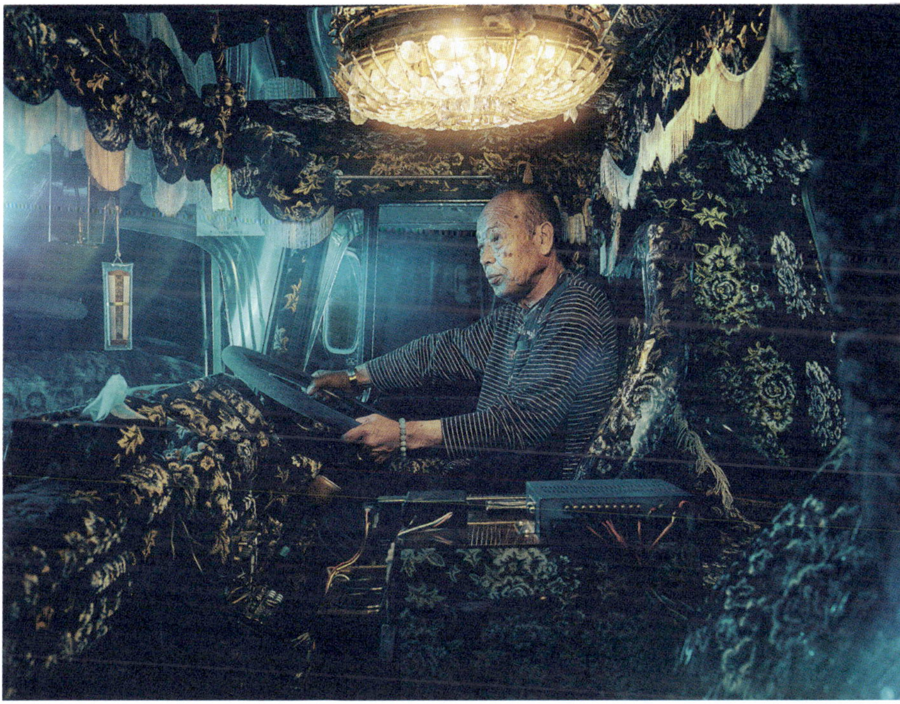

Junichi Tajima
by Todd Antony
Honjo, Japan

The Japanese subculture of dekotora, meaning 'decorated trucks', stems from the 1970s Torakku Yarō ('truck guys') films. Junichi Tajima is the head of Utamaro Kai, a dekotora association. He said that with the right truck a driver can make even dark times feel bright.

Runner-up

by Sam Wright

London, UK

Levi Cooper, an amateur teenage boxer, had suffered a tough bout with a bigger opponent, but he stood proud of what he had achieved. Going toe to toe at a young age takes determination, passion, dedication and self-belief. I like to think of this portrait as a metaphor for anyone who has been knocked down but got up and carried on.

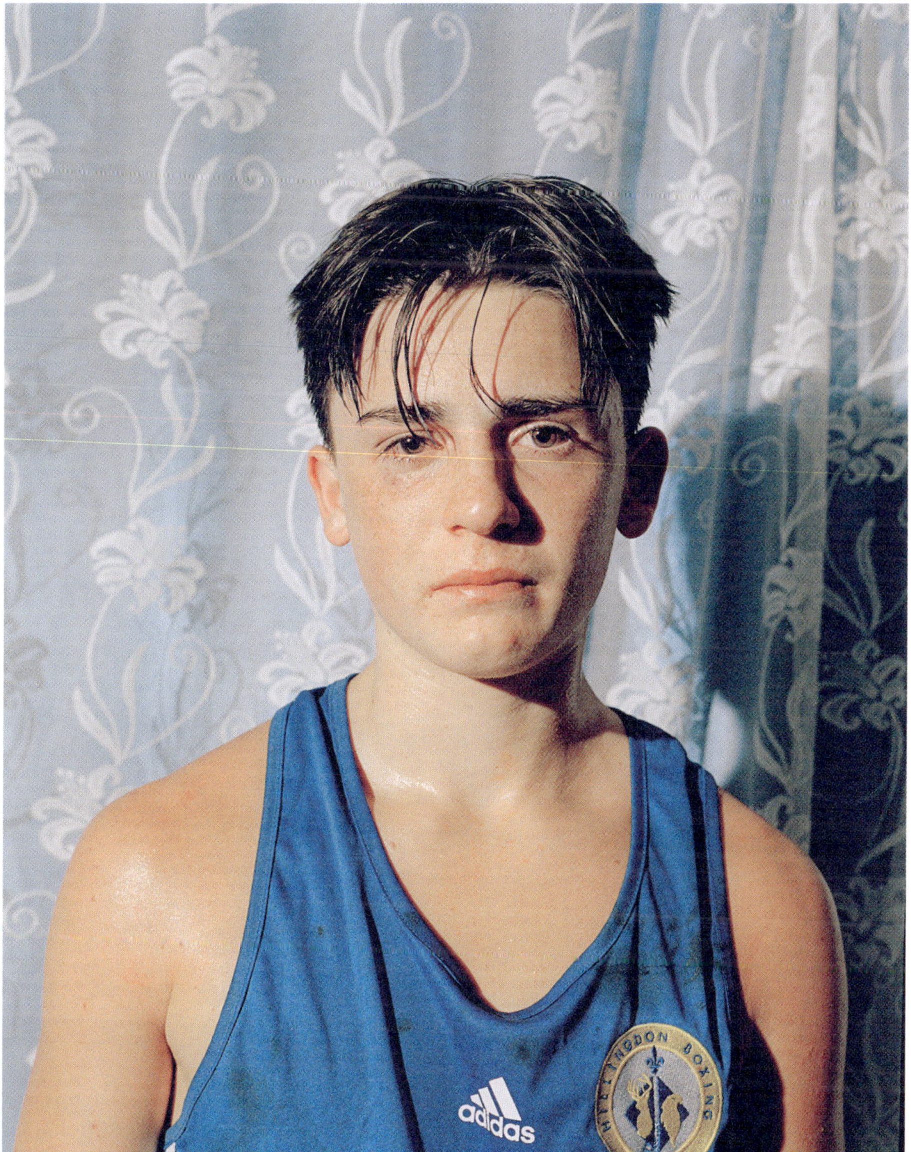
HILLINGDON BOXING
adidas

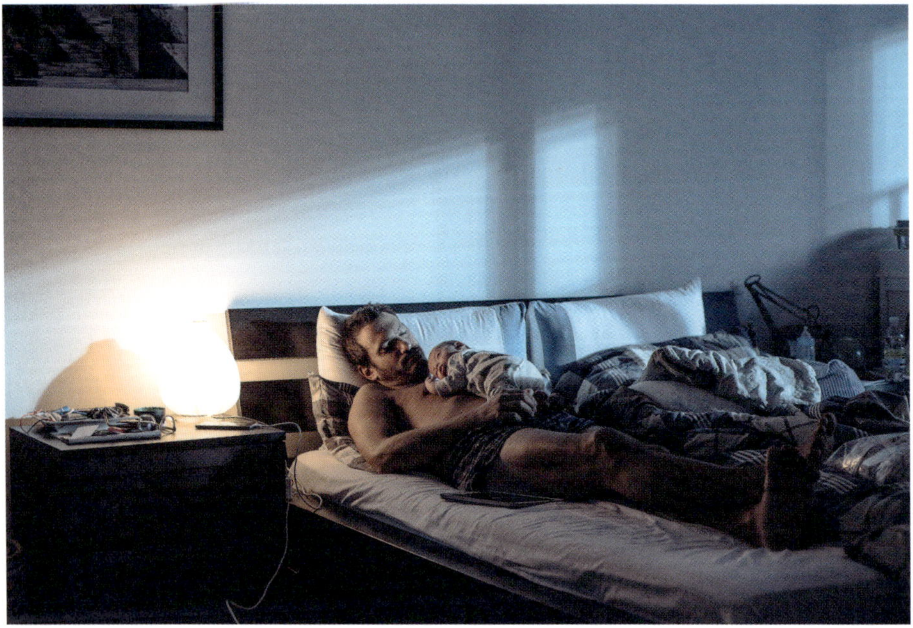

Next to Me

by Sandra Zarneshan

Dubai, United Arab Emirates

This is my husband Fabrizio and our six-week-old son, Filippo. I took this photograph because I was exhausted and didn't know what else to do. Having a baby shocked me in a way I never expected. I felt that neither my body nor my time belonged to me anymore. Taking the camera in my hands makes me feel like I am still the person I was before.

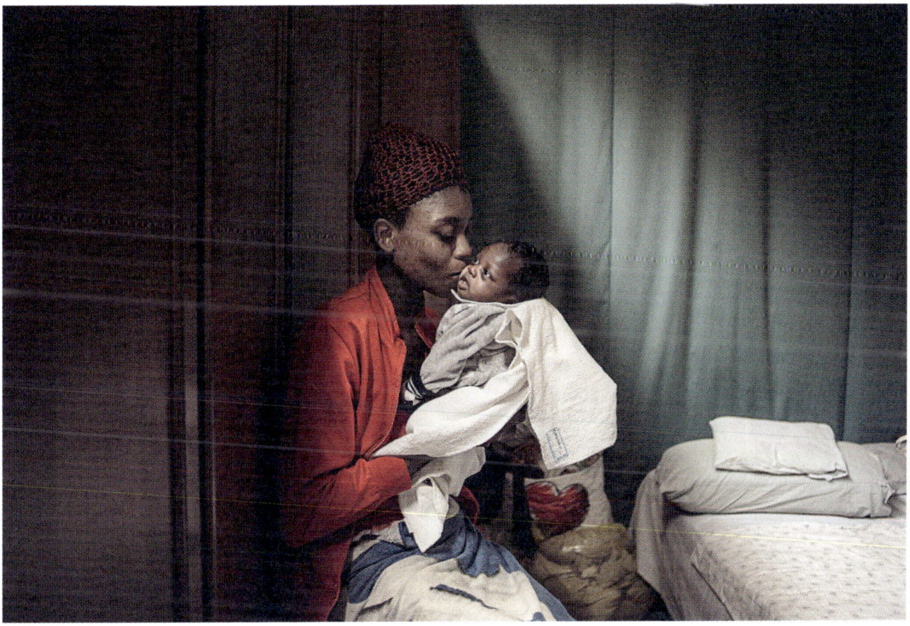

Motherly Love

by Federico Tisa

Turin, Italy

Angela, a young Nigerian woman, pictured with her newborn daughter, Gift.

Maeli and Luna

by David Dufeal

Paris, France

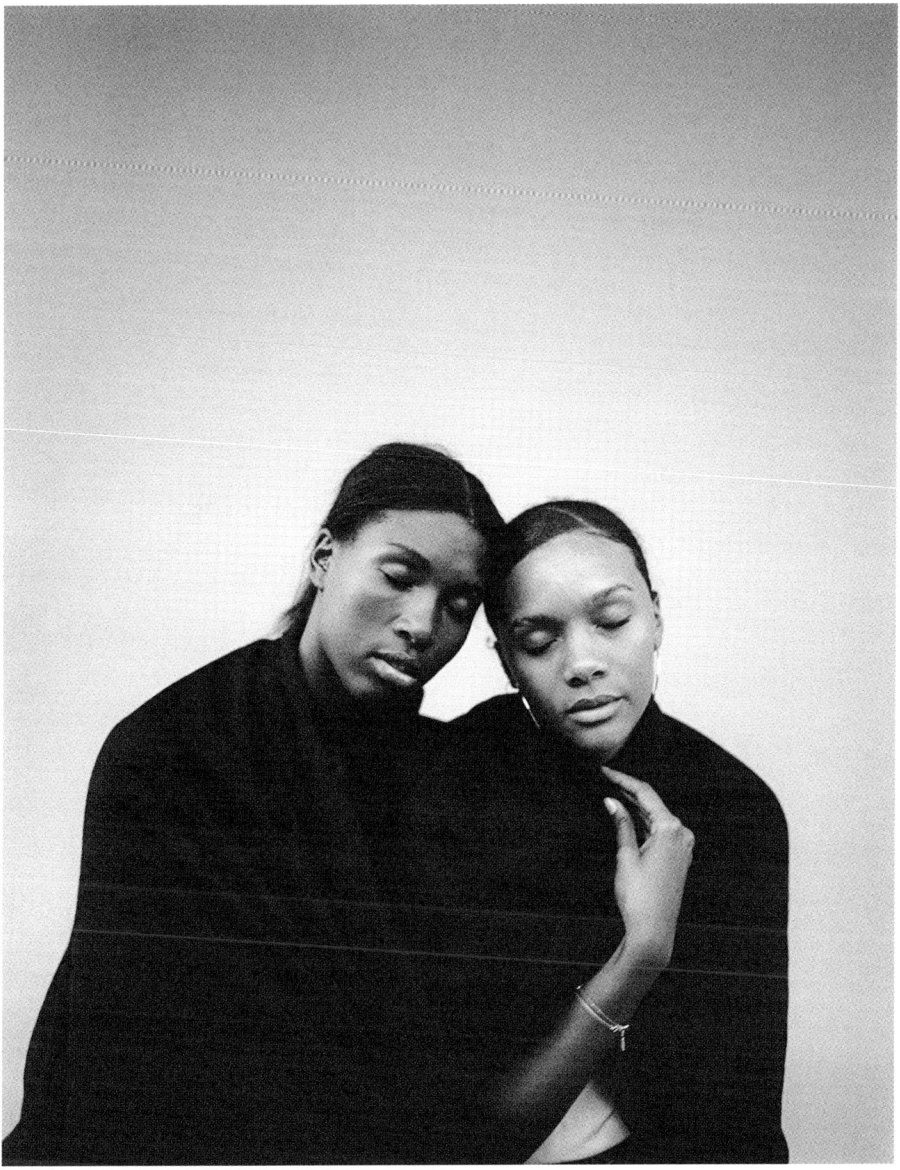

Young Twins #3

by Peter Voerman

Westervelde, The Netherlands

I put an ad in the local paper inviting twins to take part in a photography project. I photographed 50 sets of twins including these seven-year-old girls, Mayte and Amaya, who visited me with their mother. They didn't speak much but it was obvious they were very close. Mayte is not afraid of anything and Amaya acts first and then thinks.

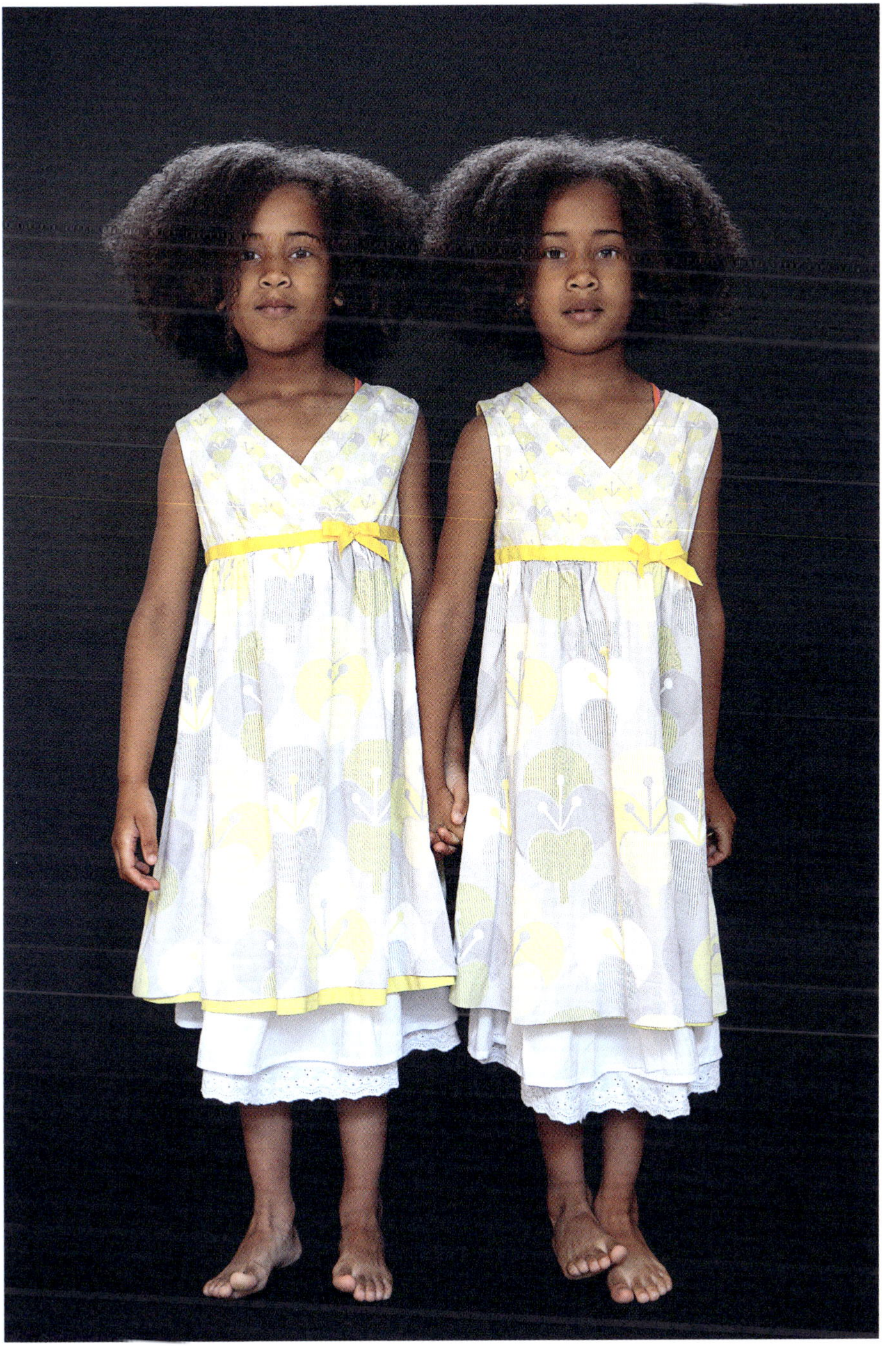

Lina Wearing Traditional Colombian Dress

by Sara Lorusso

Bologna, Italy

Lina Giselle Murillo Martinez is originally from Colombia. She left her country with her mother and sister when the family went in search of a better future.

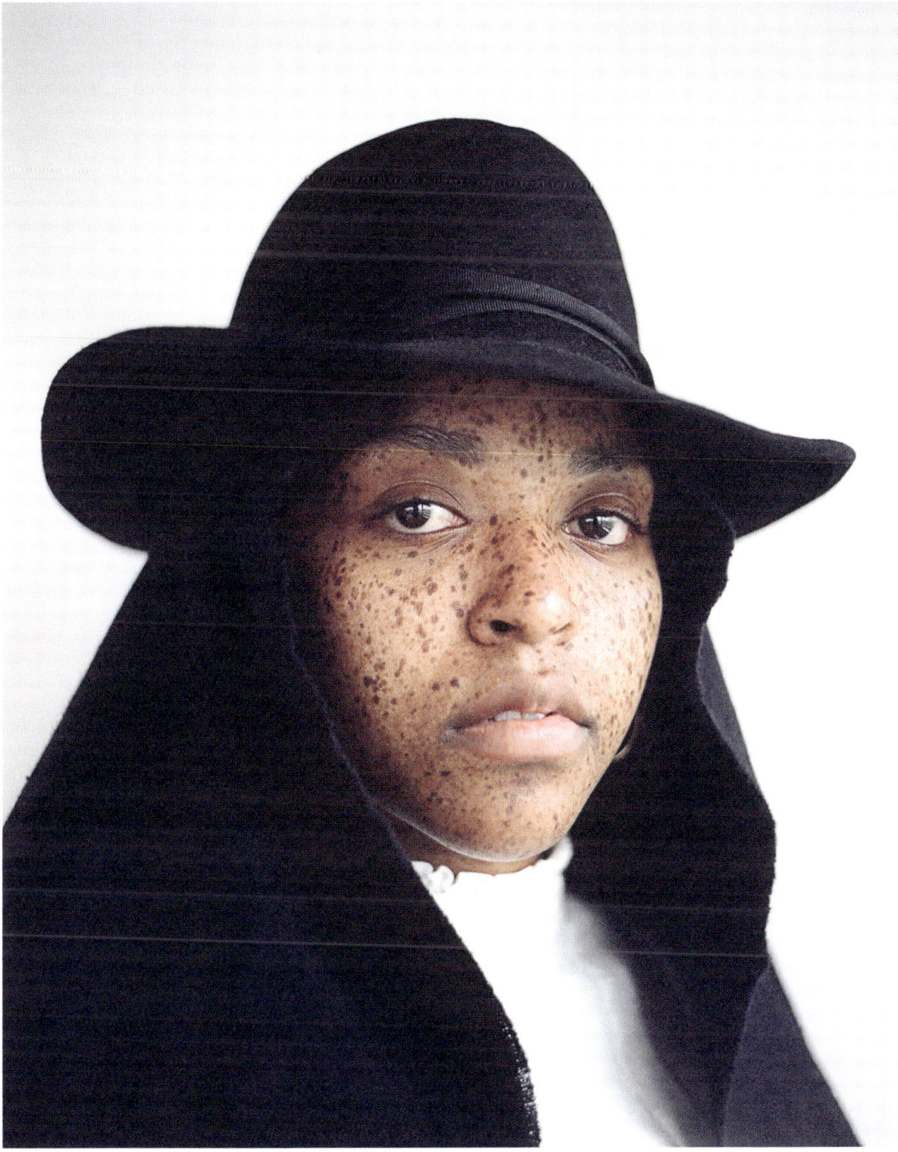

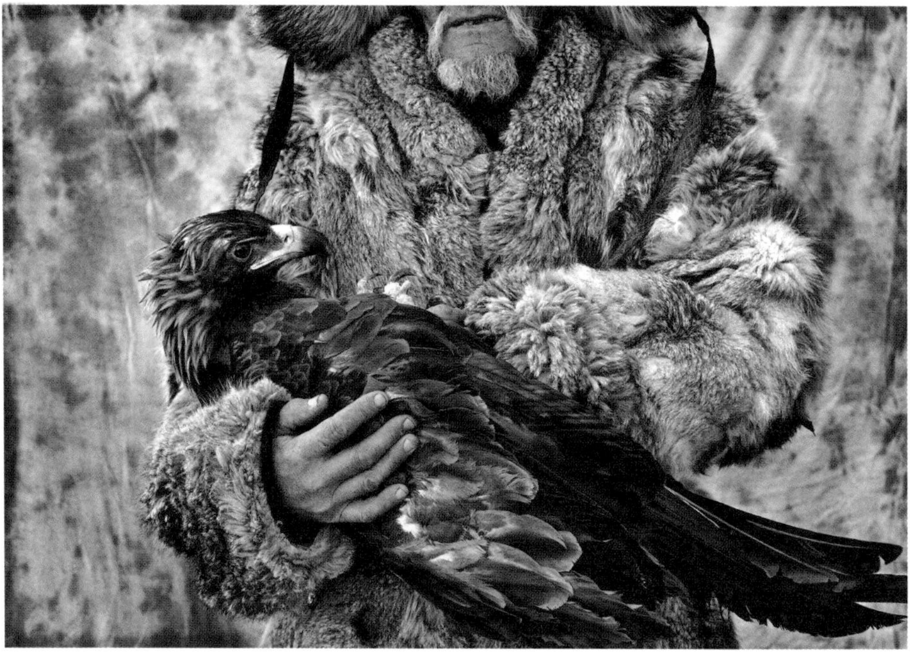

The Hunter and His Eagle

by Palani Mohan

Altai Mountains, Mongolia

Madina is a 63-year-old Kazakh eagle hunter. He tells me that the eagles are like humans. 'They love to be carried in such a way. It makes them feel loved and relaxes them.'

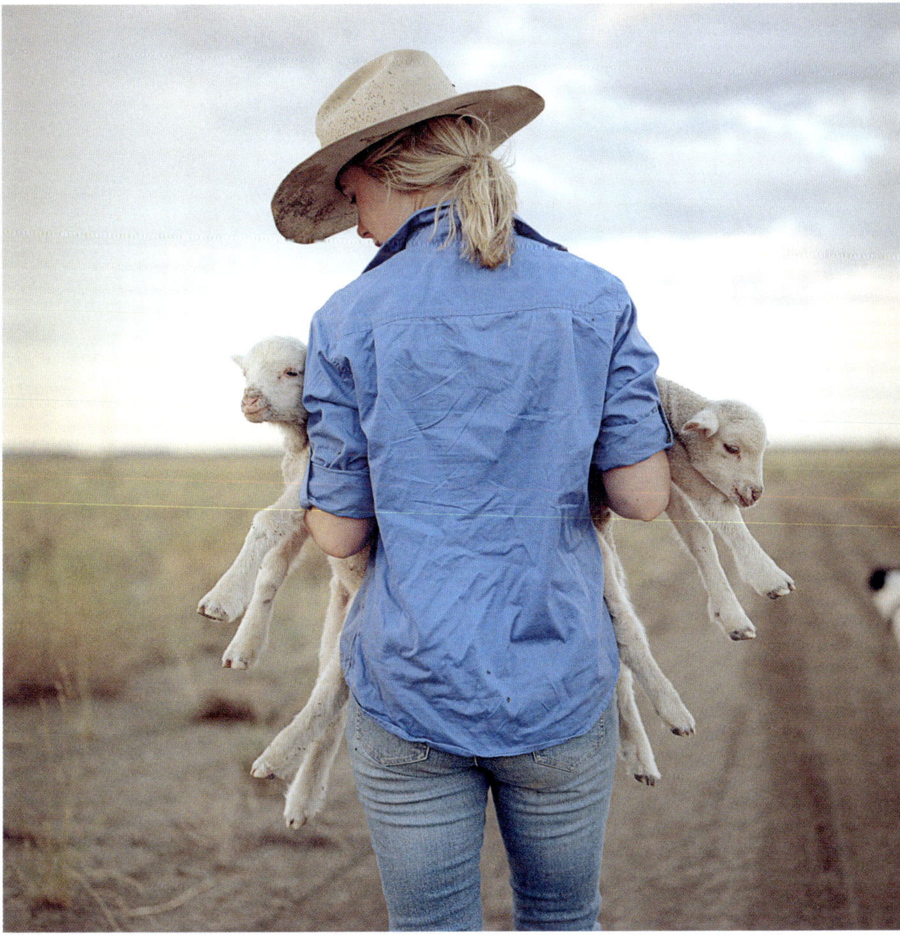

Girl with Lambs

by Barbora Tomíková

Longreach, Australia

For five months I lived and worked on a cattle station in Outback Queensland. Amy Macintosh is a 30-year-old sheep farmer who helped to run her family's sheep farm before severe drought forced the family to sell its sheep.

Letting Go, The Final Act

by Brett William

Belchertown, Massachusetts, USA

I was pulled serendipitously into the life of one of the
fathers of improv theatre, 94-year-old David Shepherd,
six weeks before his death. David suffered from dementia.
His ability to let go and allow what was happening to
him seemed challenged at times. David's expression
seemed to transition from frustration
to contemplation to meditation.

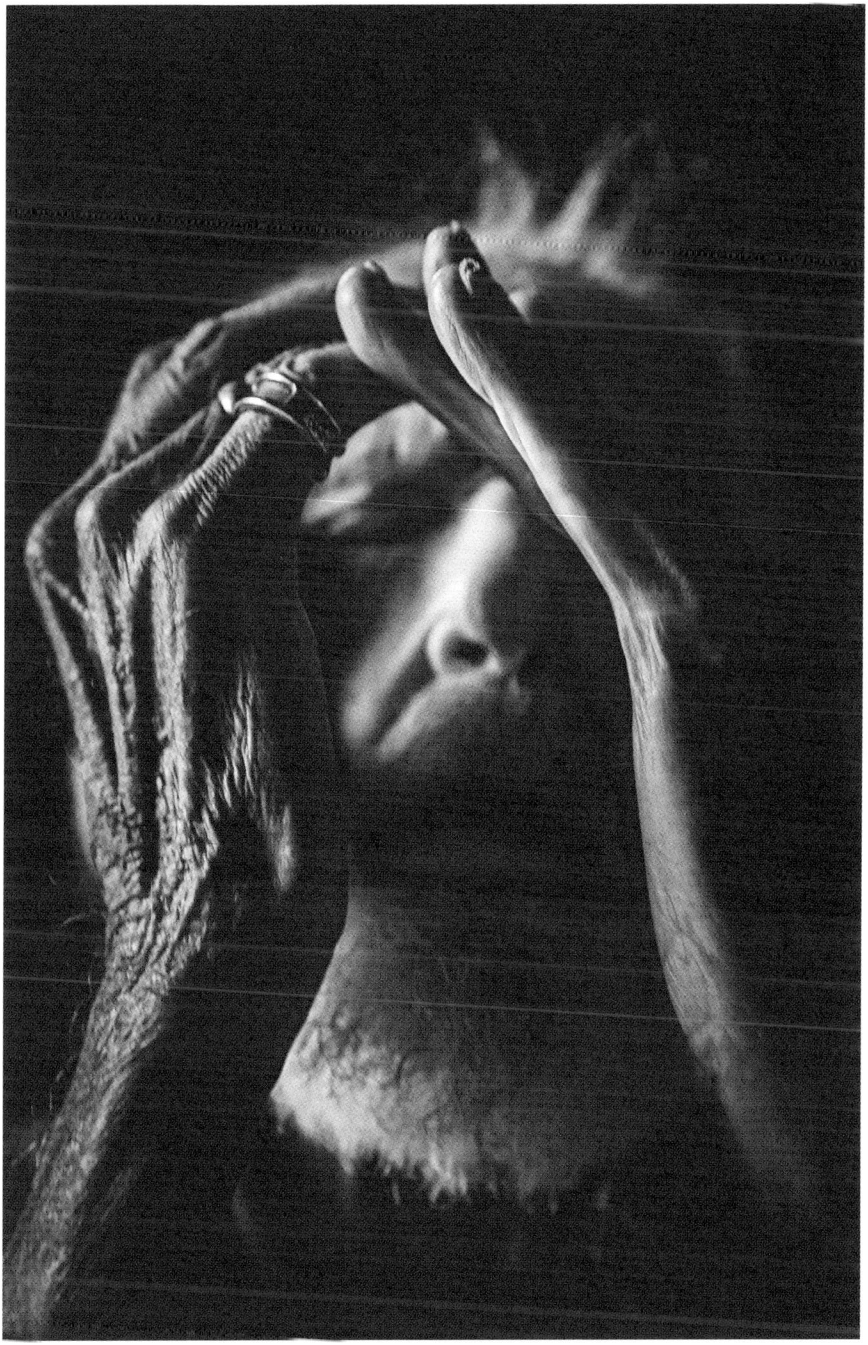

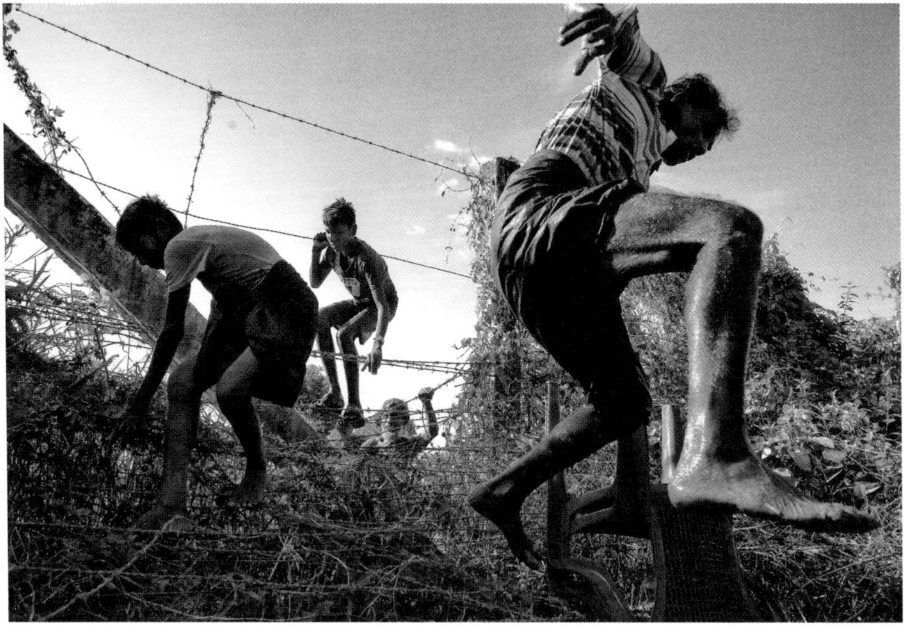

The Great Exodus

by Mushfiqul Alam

Cox's Bazar, Bangladesh

Rohingya refugees cross the Bangladesh-Myanmar border.

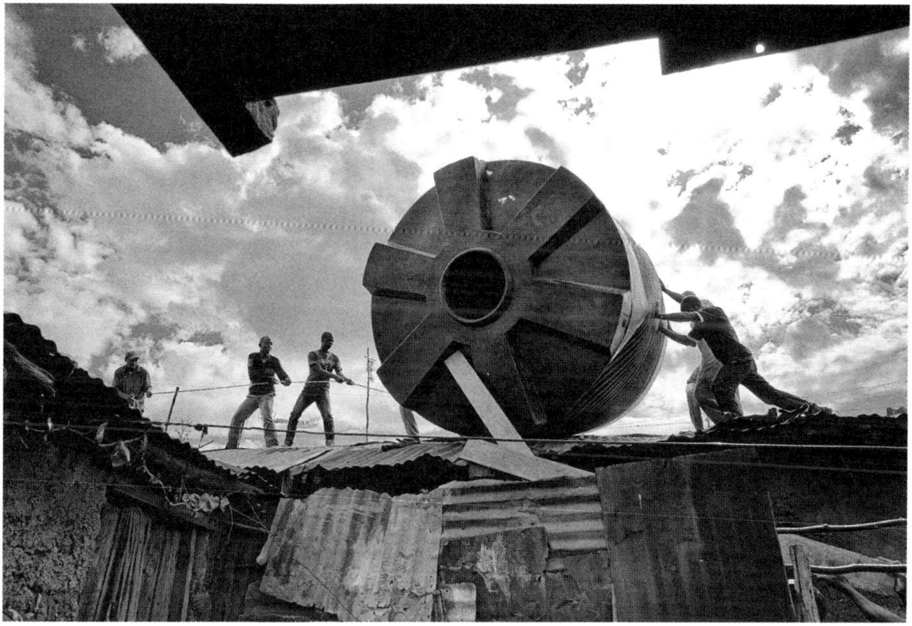

Moving the 10,000 Litre Water Tank
by Maureen Ruddy Burkhart
Nairobi, Kenya

The Kibera slum outside of Nairobi has no running water or plumbing for between 500,000 and 1 million residents. Toilets are limited to a few key areas served by these huge tanks. To get this tank to its destination many men were hired to roll the (empty) tank over flimsy metal rooftops.

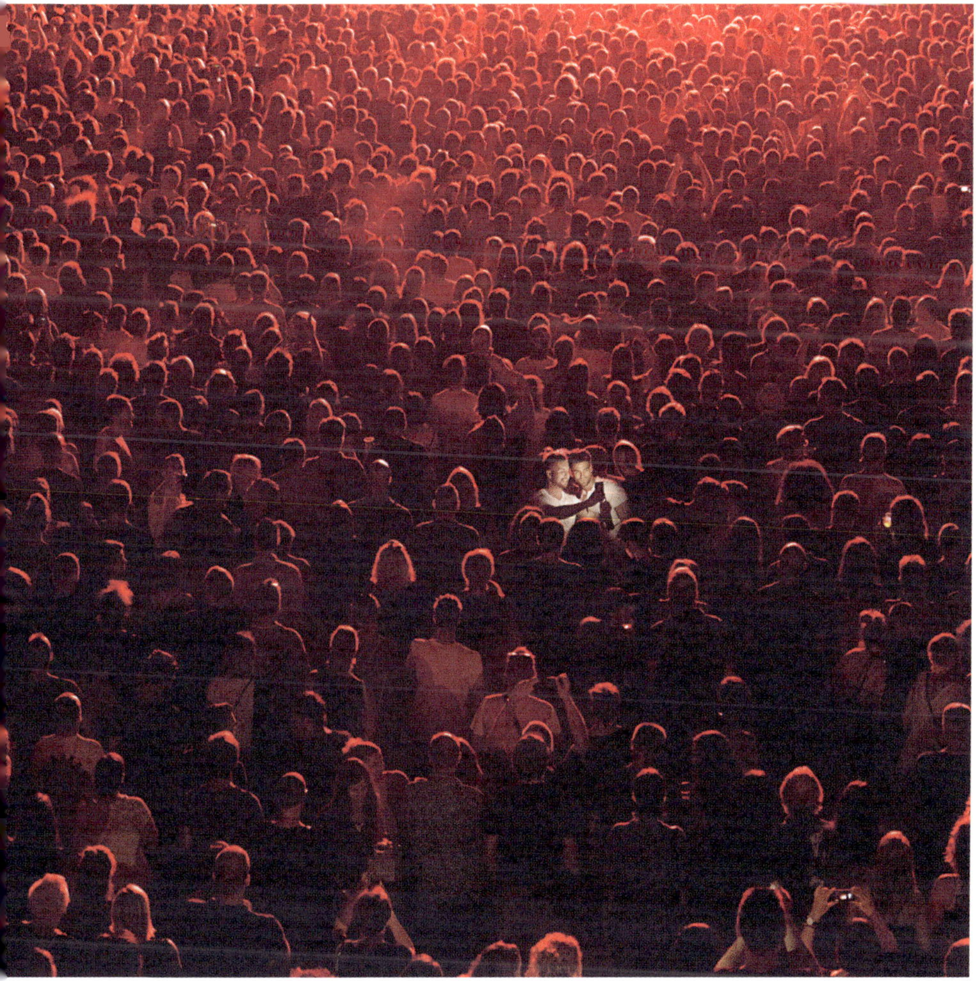

Selfie Culture
by Jelena Janković
Pula, Croatia

I spotted these men lit up in the crowd of a concert. Selfie culture has begun to dominate our existence. As a result, we often miss opportunities to enjoy the world around us.

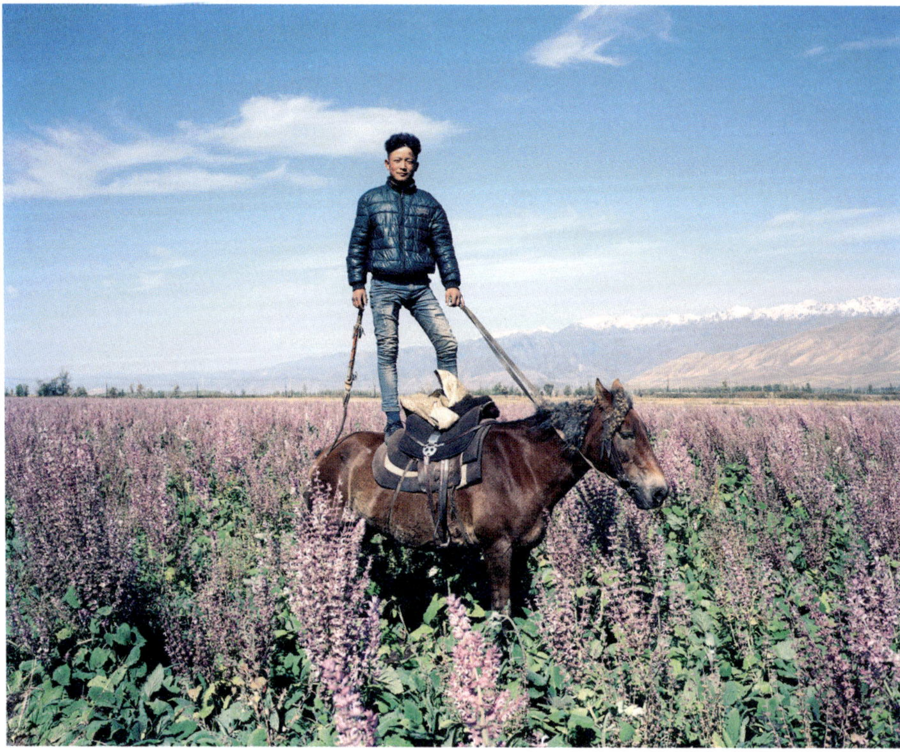

Aiger

by Li Wei

Nalati Grassland, Xinjiang, China

Eighteen-year-old Aiger rides a horse when herding sheep. He showed off his horsemanship by standing on the animal's back. The snowy Tianshan Mountains are visible in the distance.

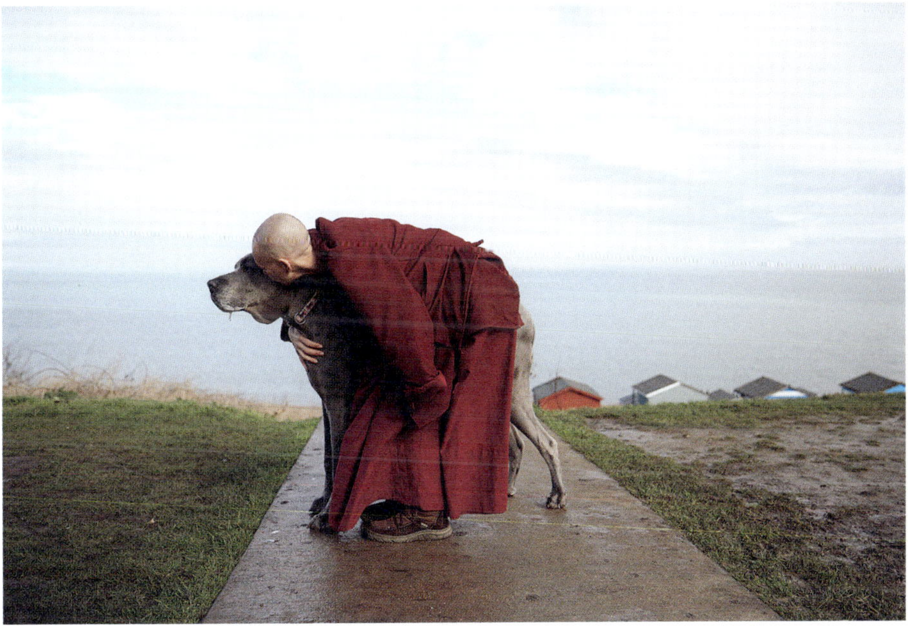

The Long Goodbye
by Wendy Carrig
Whitstable, UK

Buddhist nun Emma Slade bids her friend, Fitch, a Great Dane, farewell. Fitch was terminally ill and died a few weeks after this picture was taken.

Tara by the Window

by Alice Zoo

London, UK

Tara is a fat-positive activist and mental health advocate. I was struck by her strength, honesty and openness. She is completely unapologetic about her body, which I think is rare for a woman in today's society.

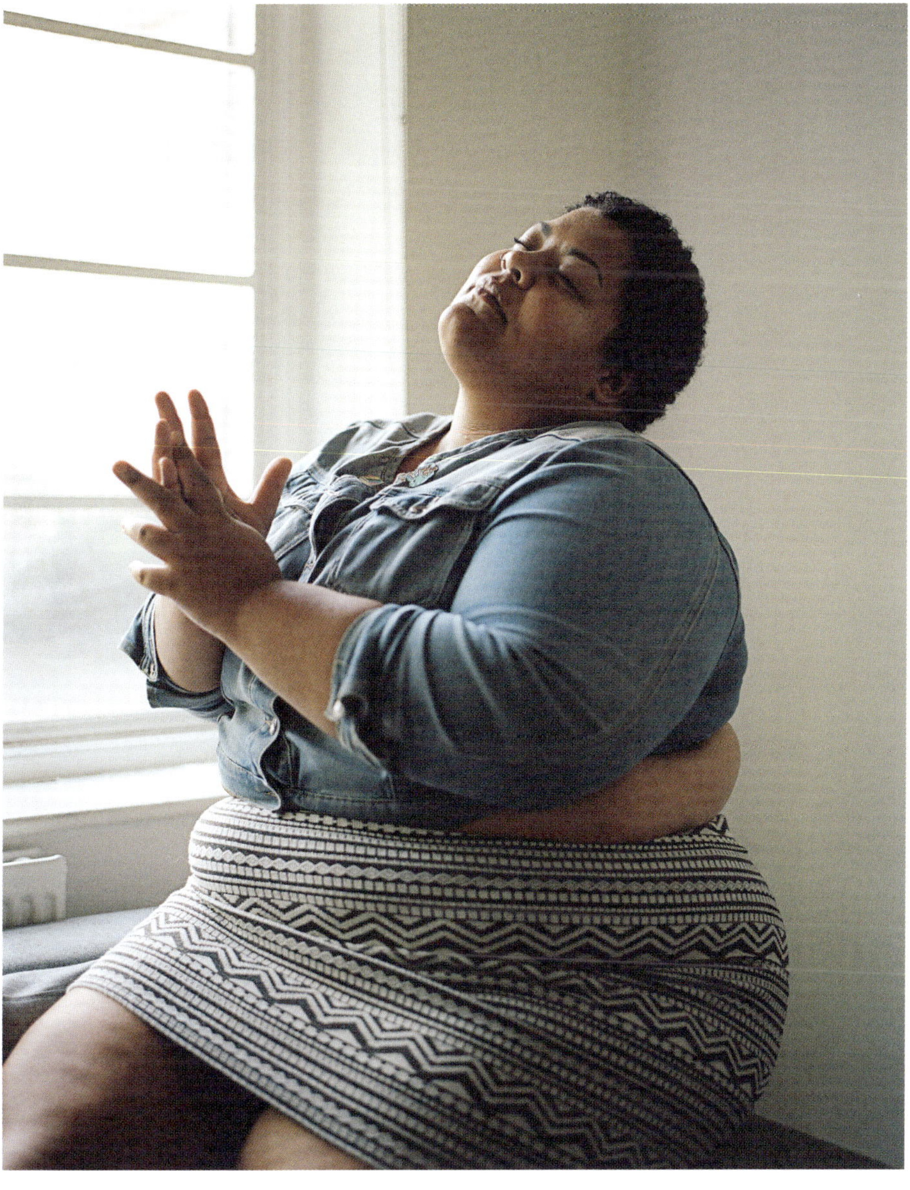

James

by Linelle Deunk

Mukono District, Uganda

When I met 16-year-old James I hoped that he and his siblings could break out of the cycle of poverty using the support I provided to attend good schools. As years passed, James changed from a boy into a confident man, learned to speak English and attended a vocational school where he trained to become a plumber.

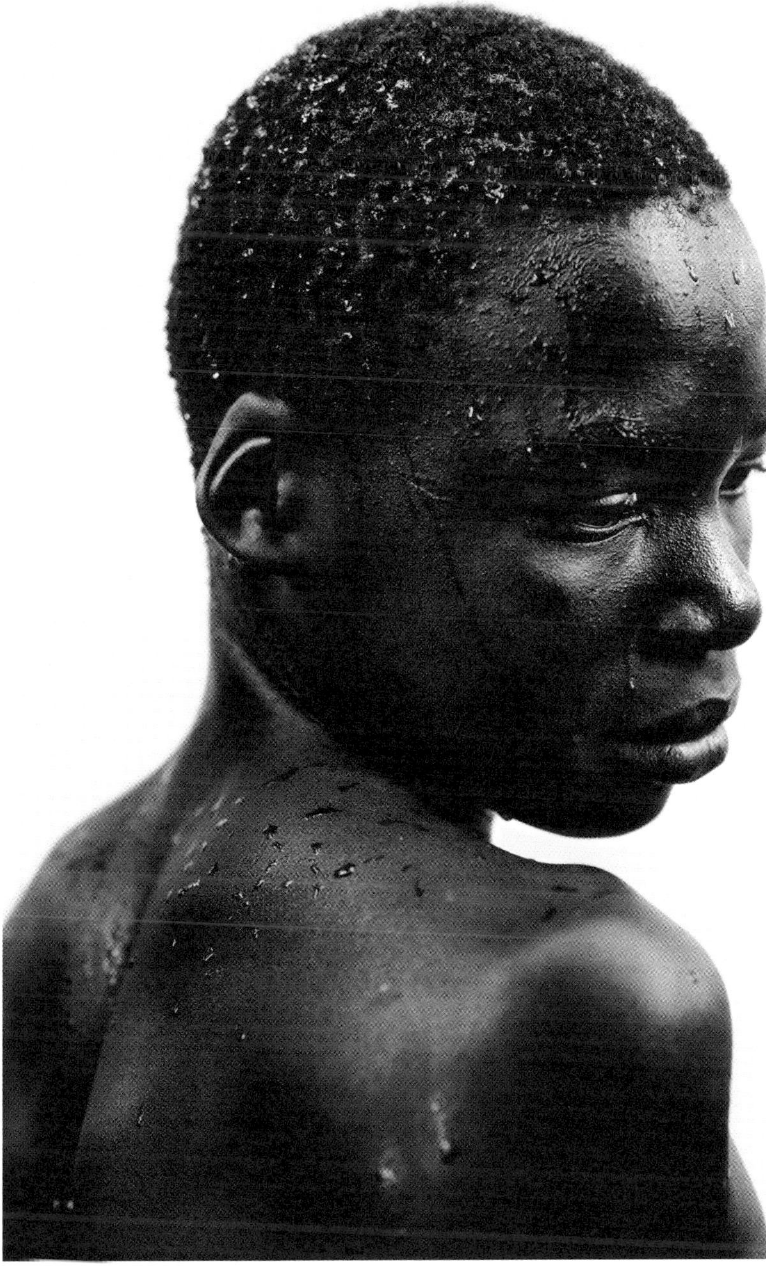

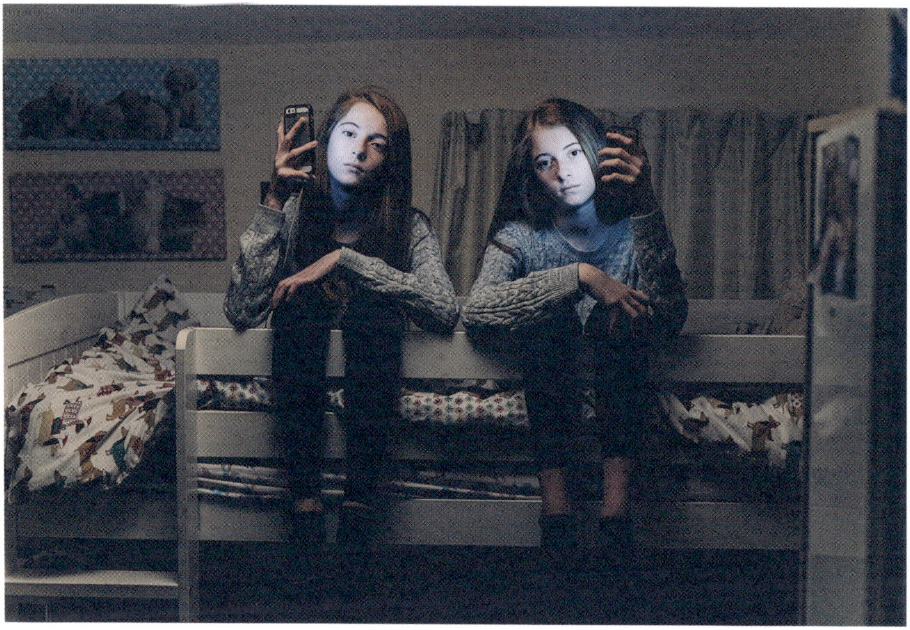

Chloe and Leah
by Mikael Buck
Ashford, UK

As a parent I'm interested in the enormous changes smartphones have made to the way children learn about the world and interact with their peers. We aren't yet at a point where we know what the full implications are.

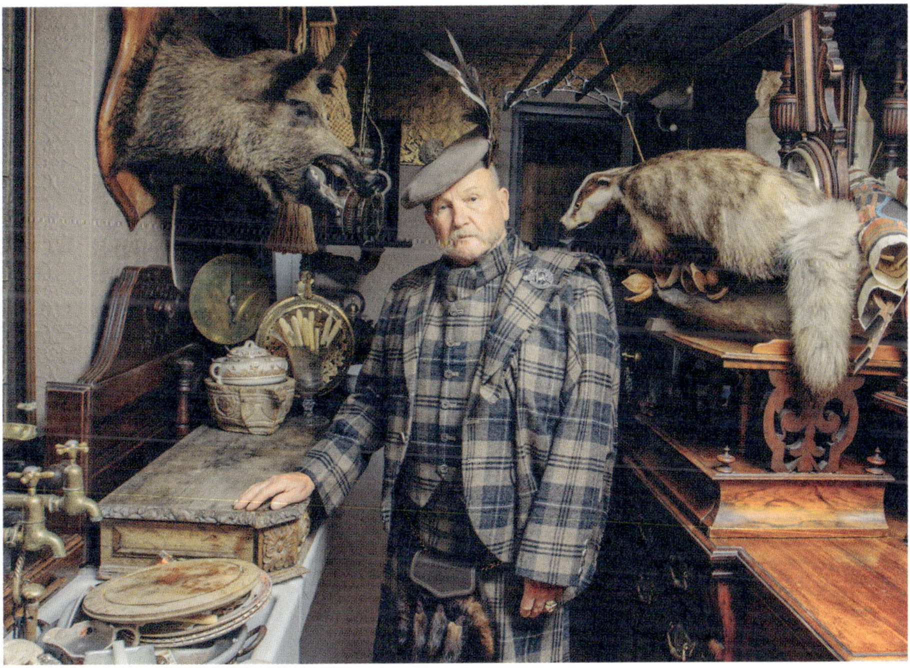

Brian 'The Duchess' in His Kitchen

by Gavin Li

Rugby, UK

Brian is an eccentric character who has a fascination for uniforms. He is also a member of Europe's oldest gay leather group which dates back to 1965 in London. I made this portrait at his home, which is full of antiques and restored furniture.

The Prepared Virgin

by Stanley Fung

Taipei, Taiwan

As a Christian pastor, I use photography to tell stories from the Holy Bible. Here, a member of my church's daughter poses to depict a story Jesus tells in the Parable of the Ten Virgins.

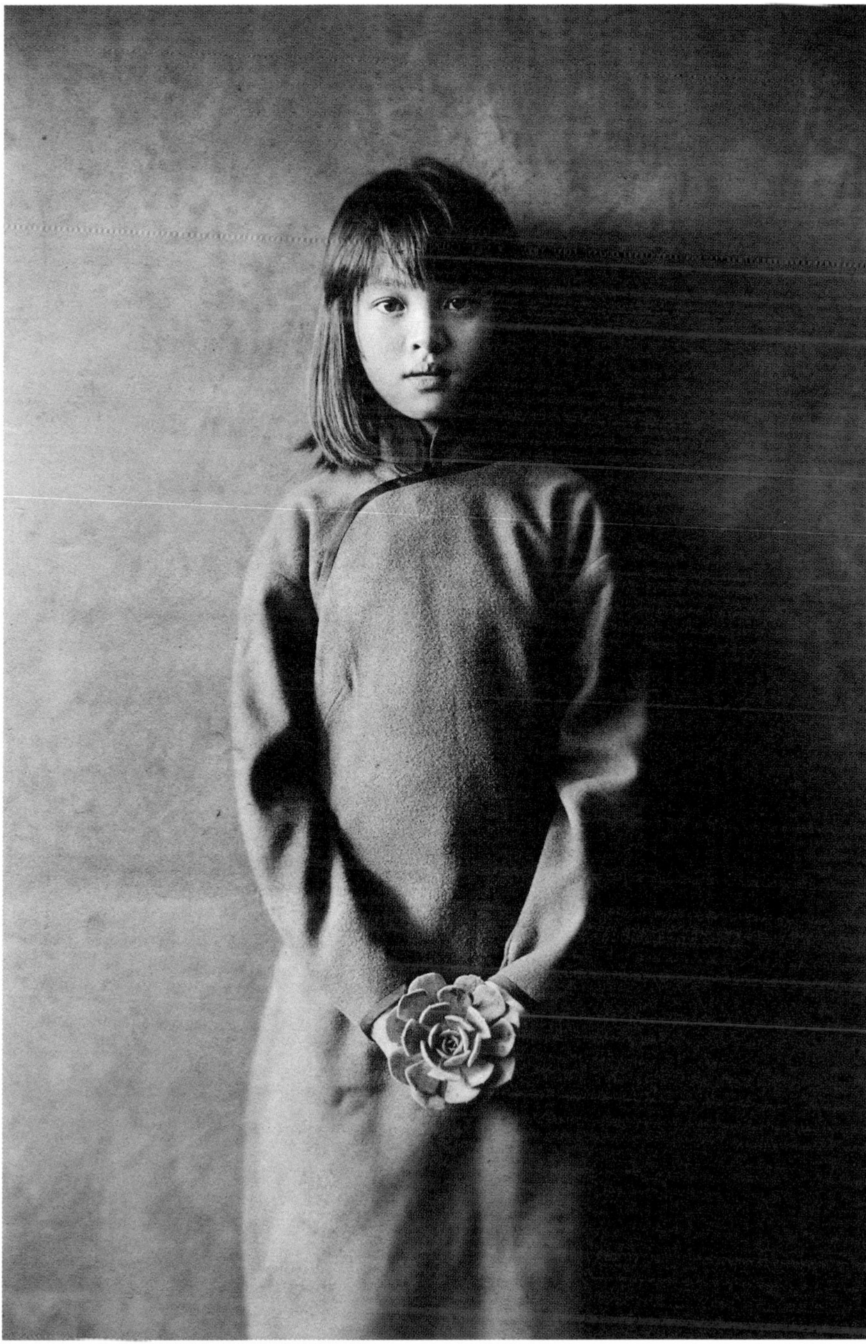

Jewish Children Celebrating Purim

by Manos Chatzikonstantis

London, UK

I photographed these children in Stamford Hill, which is known for its Jewish Hasidic community. They were dressed up to celebrate the Jewish holiday of Purim. There was a carnival-like atmosphere – people were playing music and dancing in the streets.

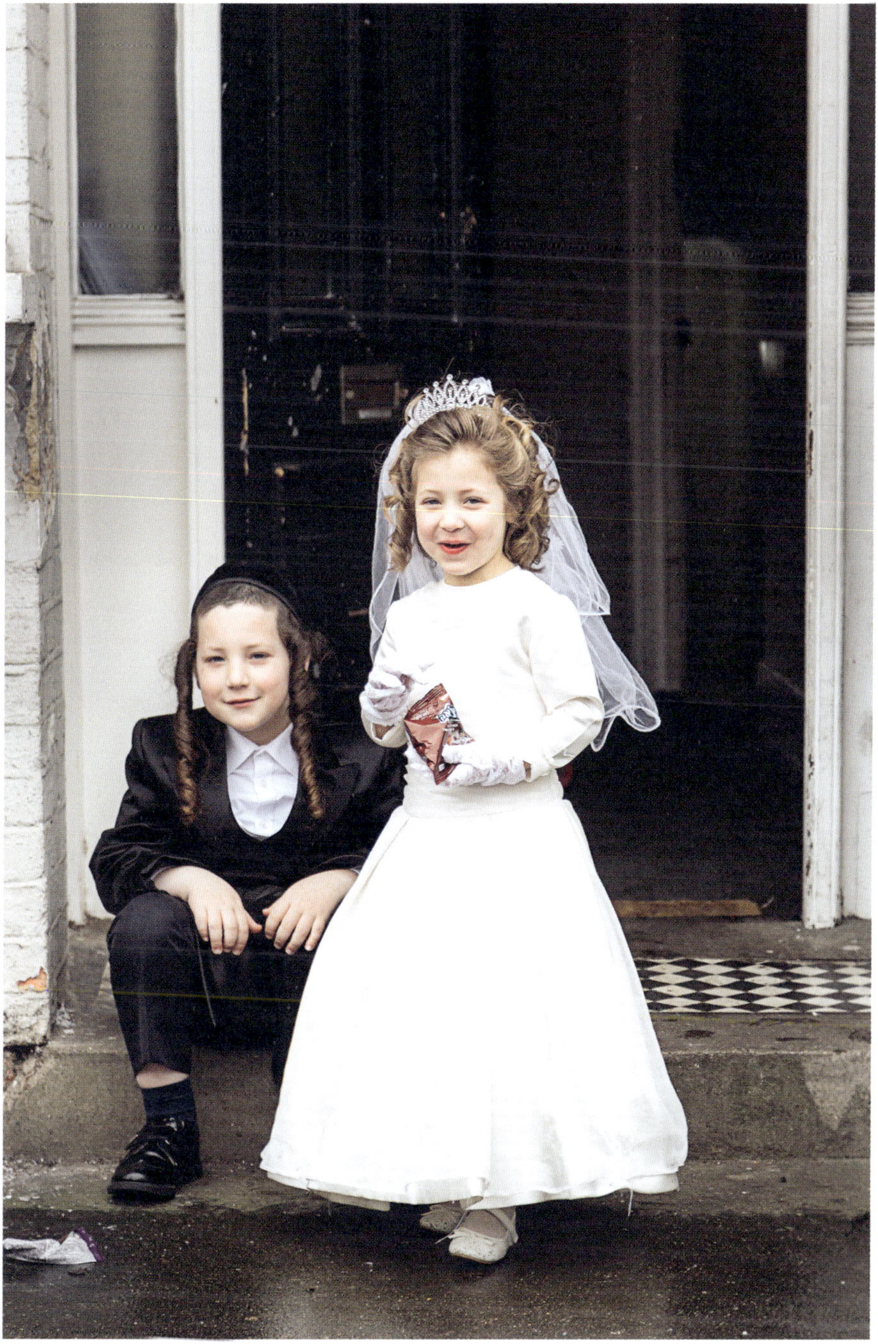

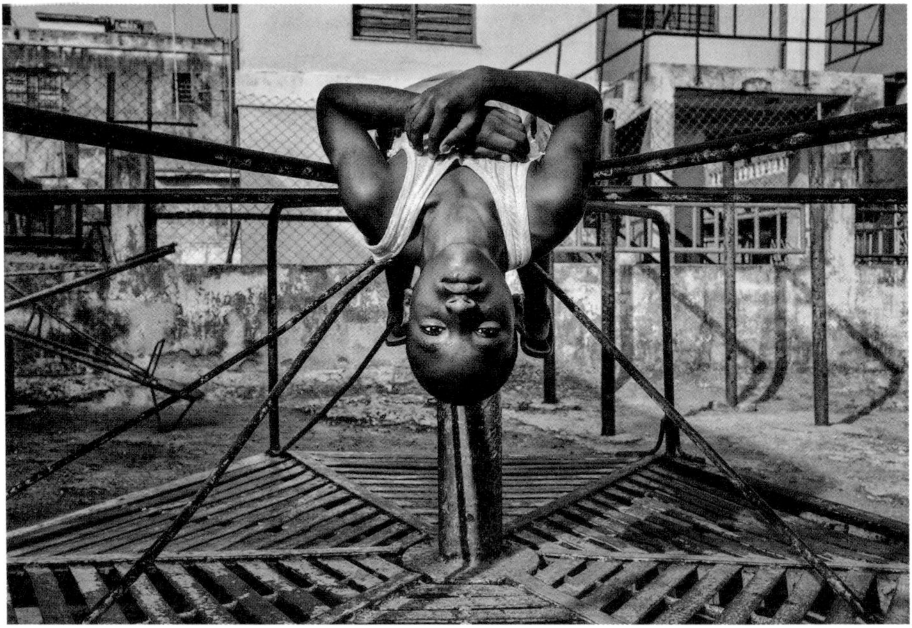

Orlando

by Priscilla Falcón Moeller

Regla, Cuba

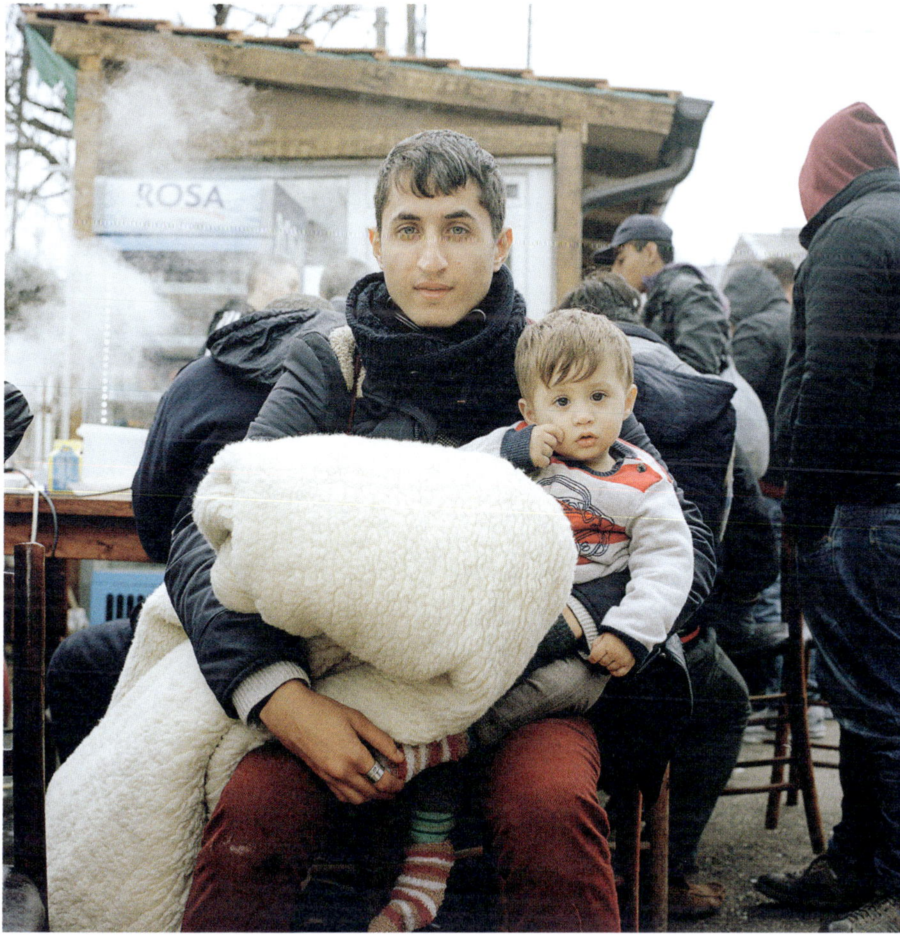

Escaping

by Claudio Rasano

Preševo, Serbia

I came across these two while they were waiting at a bus stop next to a refugee camp they had been living in. The young man told me they came from Syria and that they were heading to Croatia and then on to Germany.

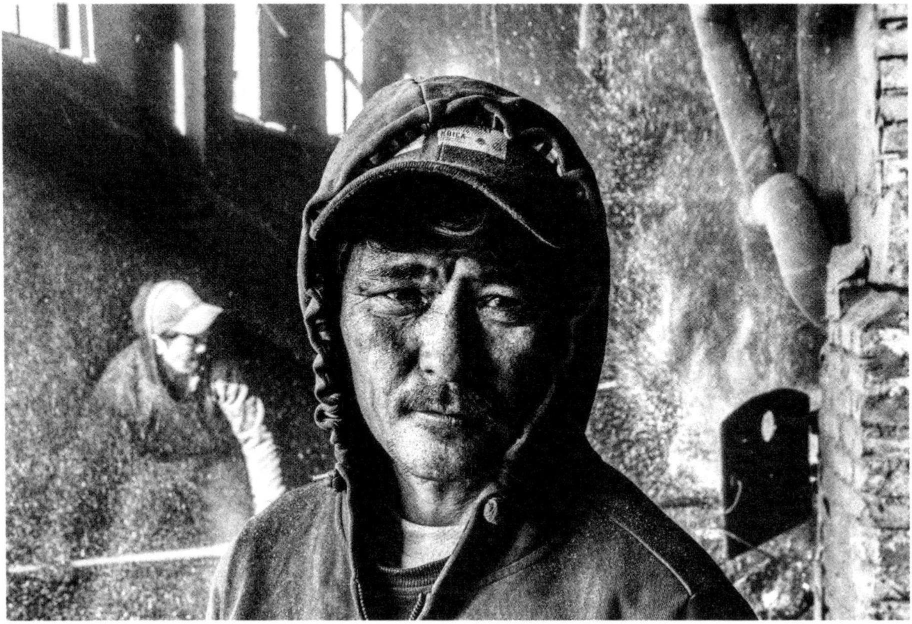

Mongolian Coal Factory Worker
by Sung Kun Hwan
Baruun-Urt, Mongolia

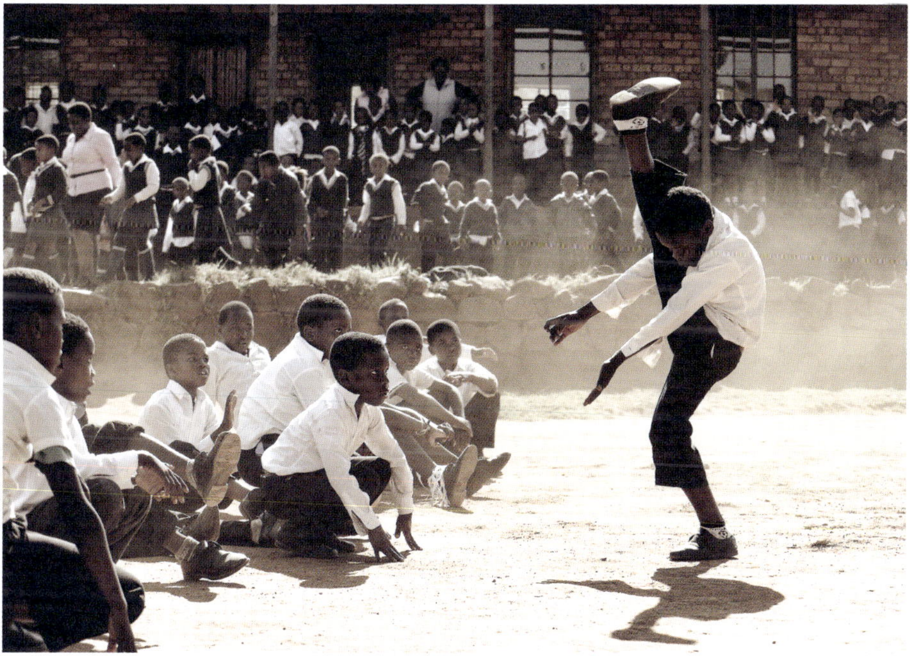

Zulu Warrior Dance

by Jay Groat

Mpumalanga, South Africa

These schoolboys are taking part in a Zulu warrior dance. The boy on the right is demonstrating the moves for his fellow dancers. To me, this photograph symbolises strength, agility and leadership. Everyone was in awe of the boy's style.

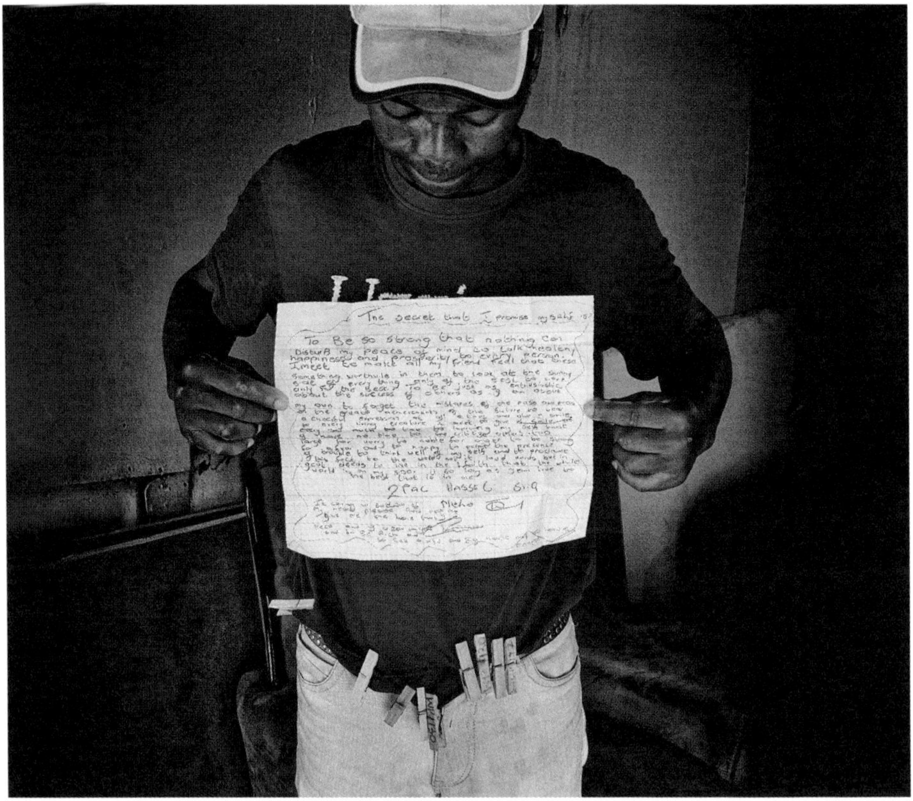

The Secret

by Darcy Brown

Cape Town, South Africa

During my quick tour of Meko's home, which was made from corrugated iron and cardboard, he produced a 'mission statement' detailing the things he sought for himself and others. These were as universal as goals can be: peace, health, happiness and prosperity.

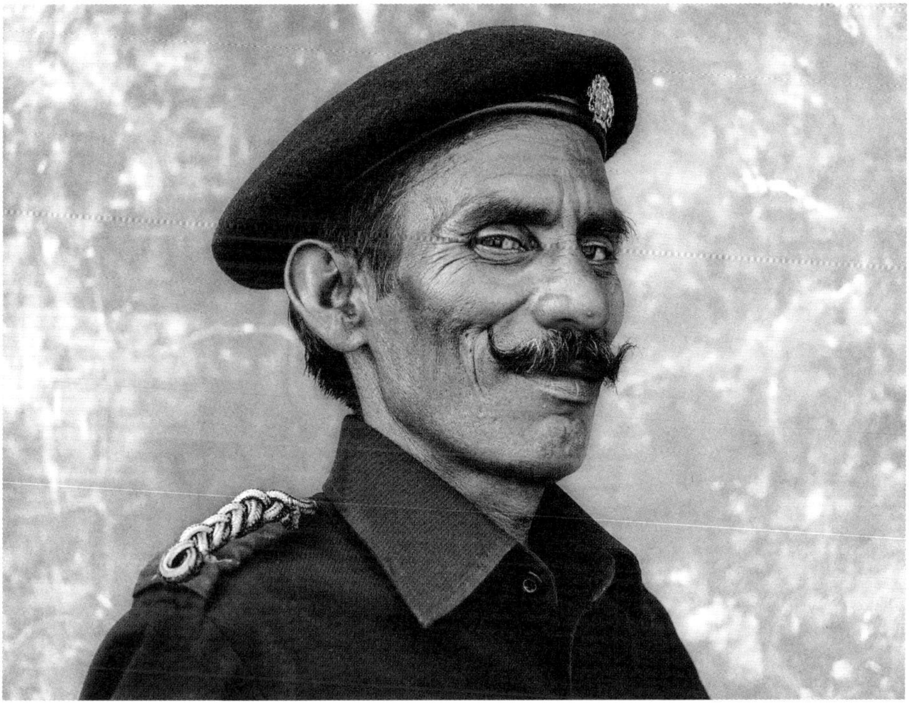

Security Guard
by Gerard Sexton
Amber Fort, Jaipur, Rajasthan, India

Karamojong Child Carrying Water

by Desiree Engelage

Near Moroto, Uganda

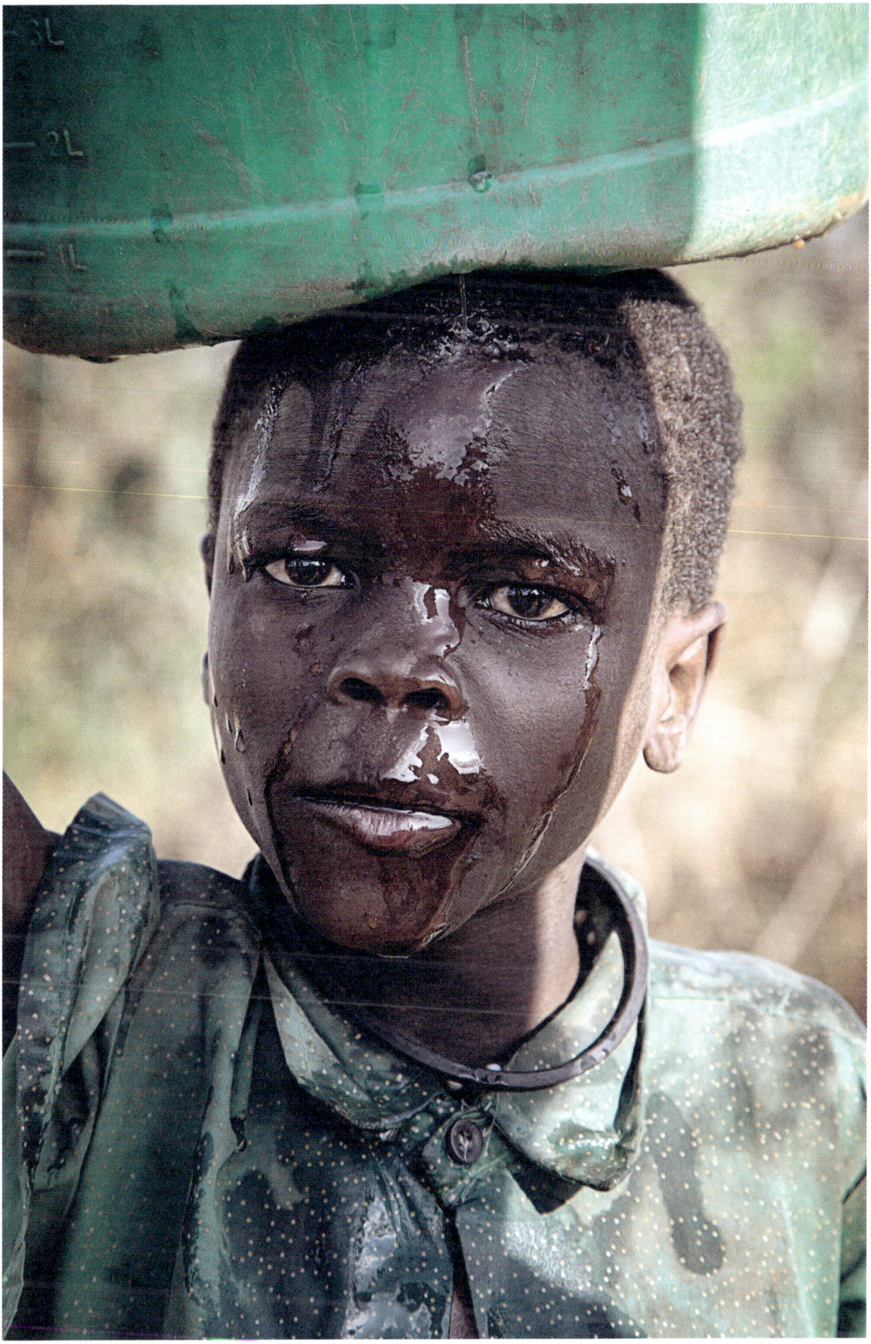
2L
1L

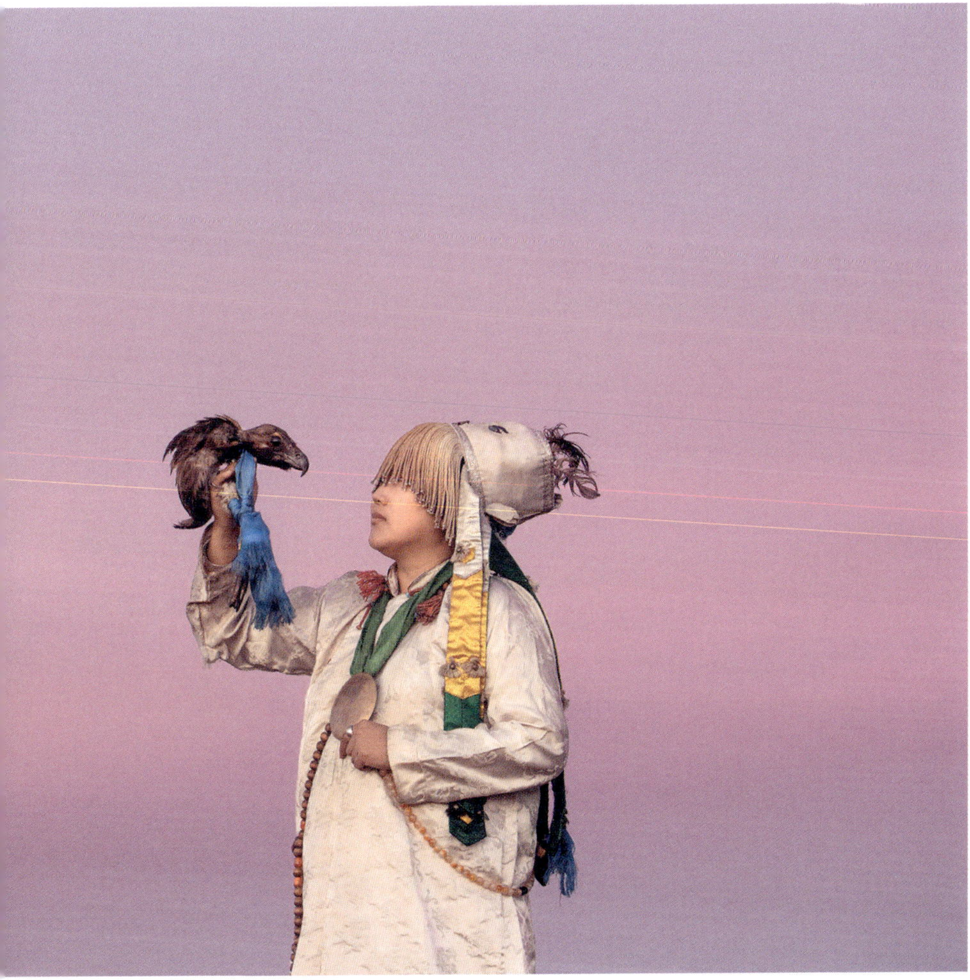

Walker Between Worlds

by Marie van der Heijden

Darkhan, Mongolia

Urtnasan Ankbayar, 35, wears a typical shaman costume. Her spirit animal – the eagle – protects her soul when she enters a trance and helps her to connect with her ancestors.

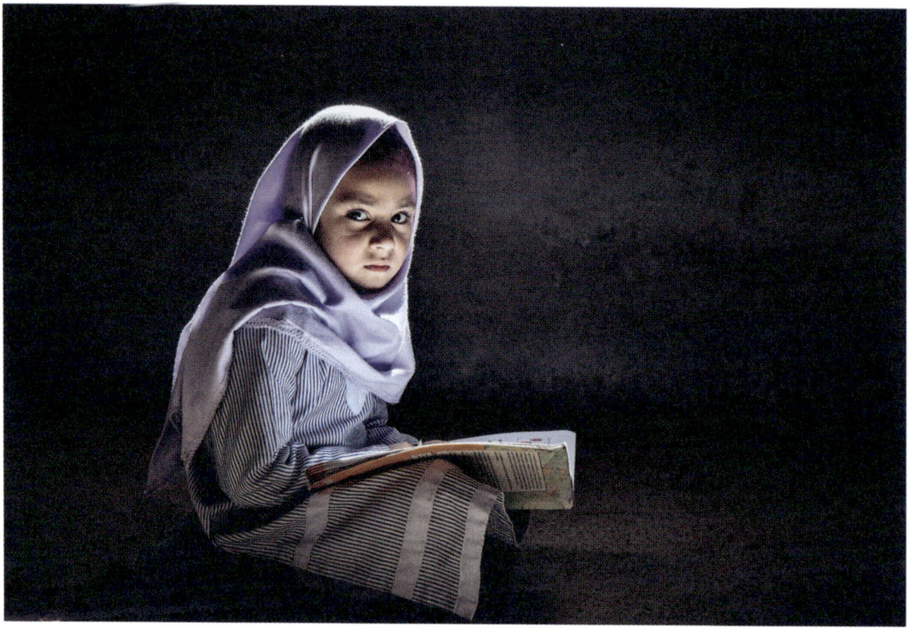

Electricity Shortage
by Andrea Francolini
Akber Abad, Pakistan

Seven-year-old Abieeha is one of many students in a school that has no electricity. The kids have to either sit outside or follow the sunlight so they can read their books or see the blackboard.

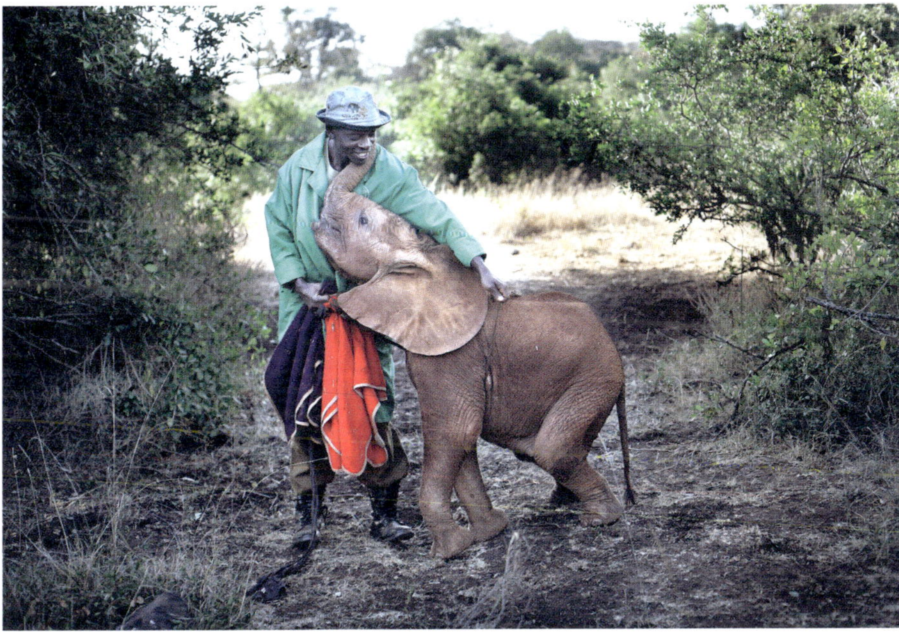

Surrogate Mum
by Rosie Hallam
Thabiti, Kenya

A carer looks after a young, orphaned elephant at the David Sheldrick Wildlife Trust. The elephants have lost their mothers to poaching and form close bonds to their human 'mums'.

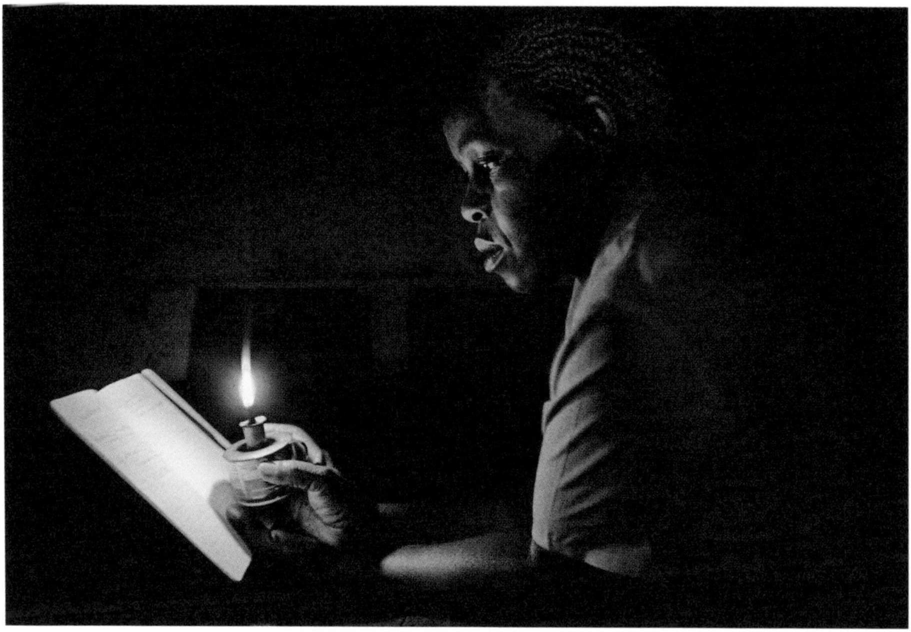

Mother of Pearl

by Leslie Alsheimer

Kyotera, Rakai District, Uganda

Nakanyike Agenina is a 36-year-old widow and mother of four. Her husband died of malaria, his immune system compromised by HIV/AIDS. Many Ugandan women like Nakanyike shoulder the primary economic and social responsibility for households left fatherless due to disease, civil unrest, polygamy and economic migration.

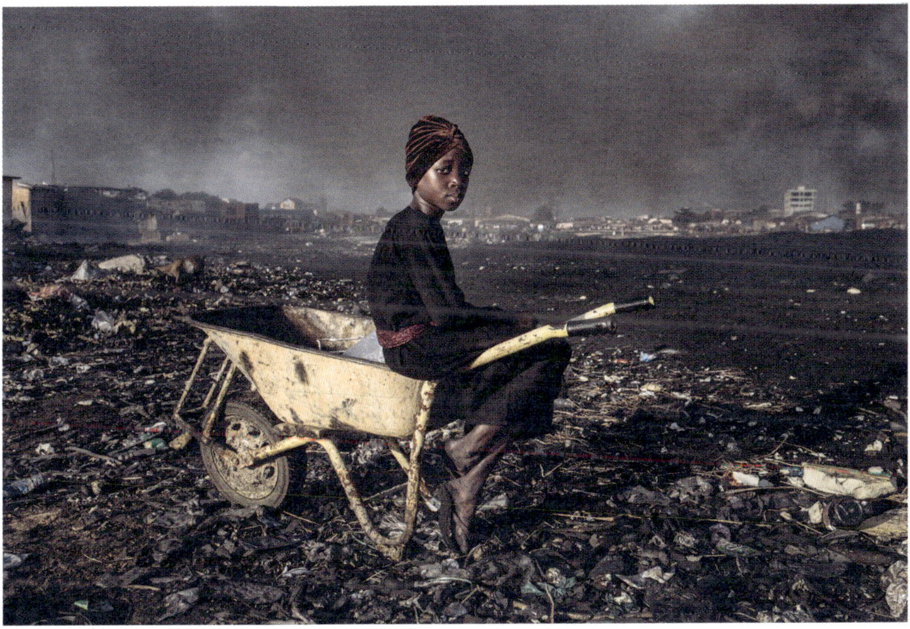

Rashida

by Carolina Rapezzi

Accra, Ghana

Rashida is a water seller in a scrapyard in Agbogbloshie, a former wetland. The site is now an e-waste dump, where workers are paid a pittance to strip metals from discarded appliances.

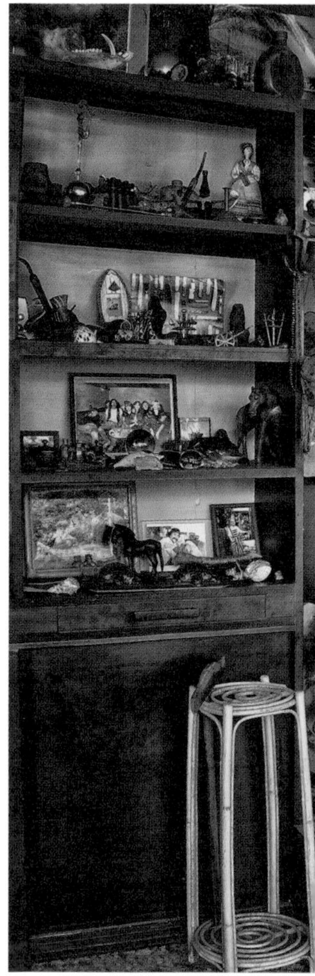

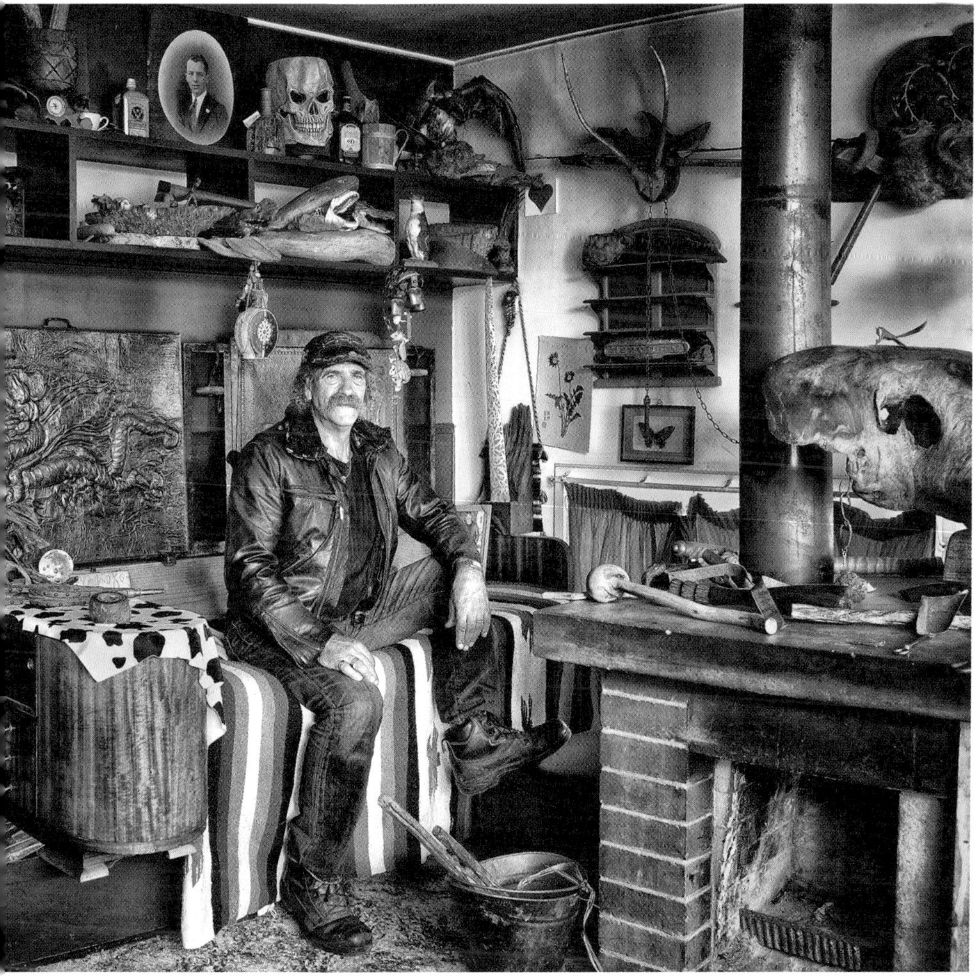

Man with Leather Jacket

by Ilan Wittenberg

Auckland, New Zealand

I met Ken Trelic at a Sunday market where he was selling bric-à-brac. I photographed him in his home, surrounded by memorabilia.

Ela and Ania

by Zuza Krajewska

Warsaw, Poland

Ela and Ania are long-time friends of mine. We're all from Gdańsk but live in Warsaw. Ela was in a pretty low state after her divorce and Ania helped her to rise back up.

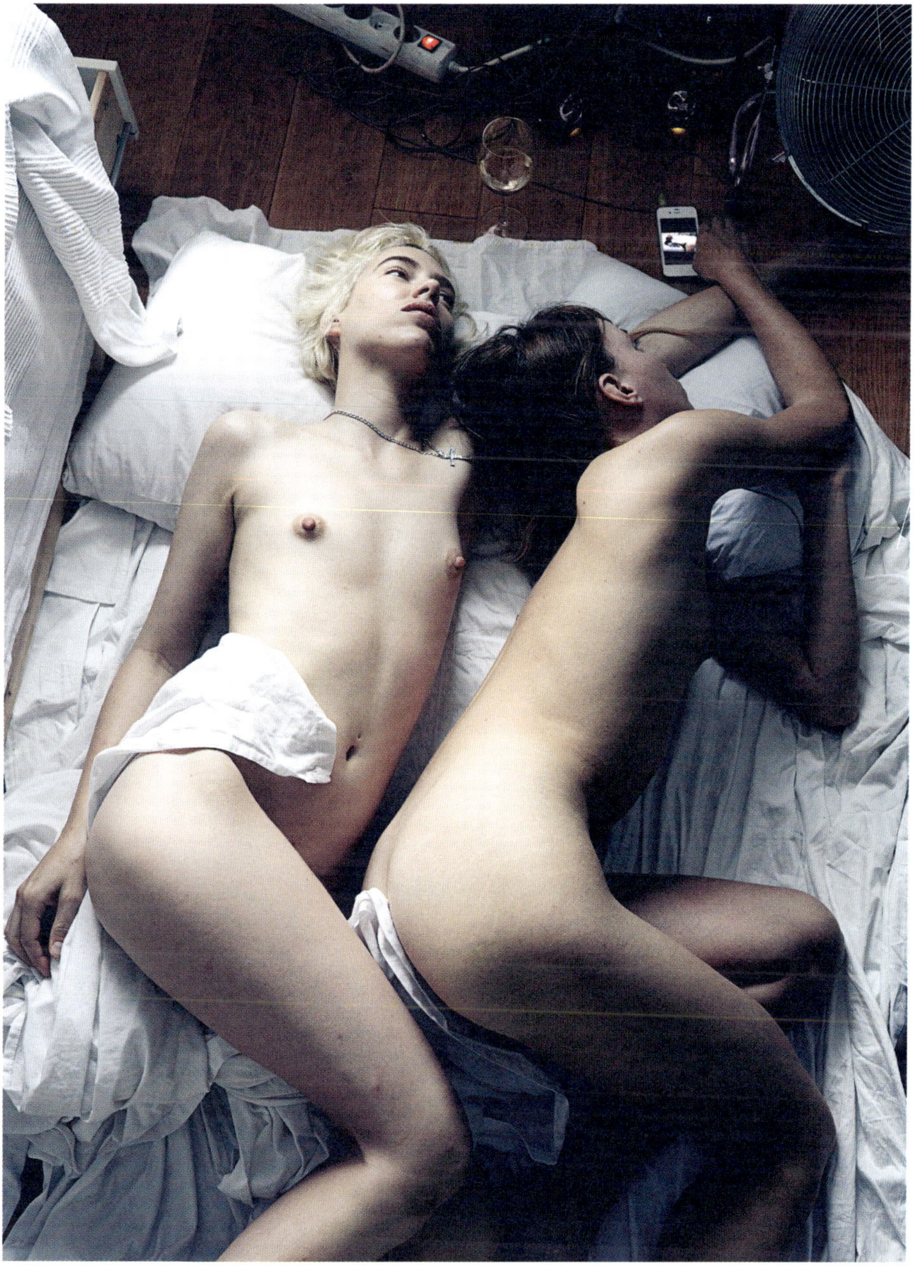

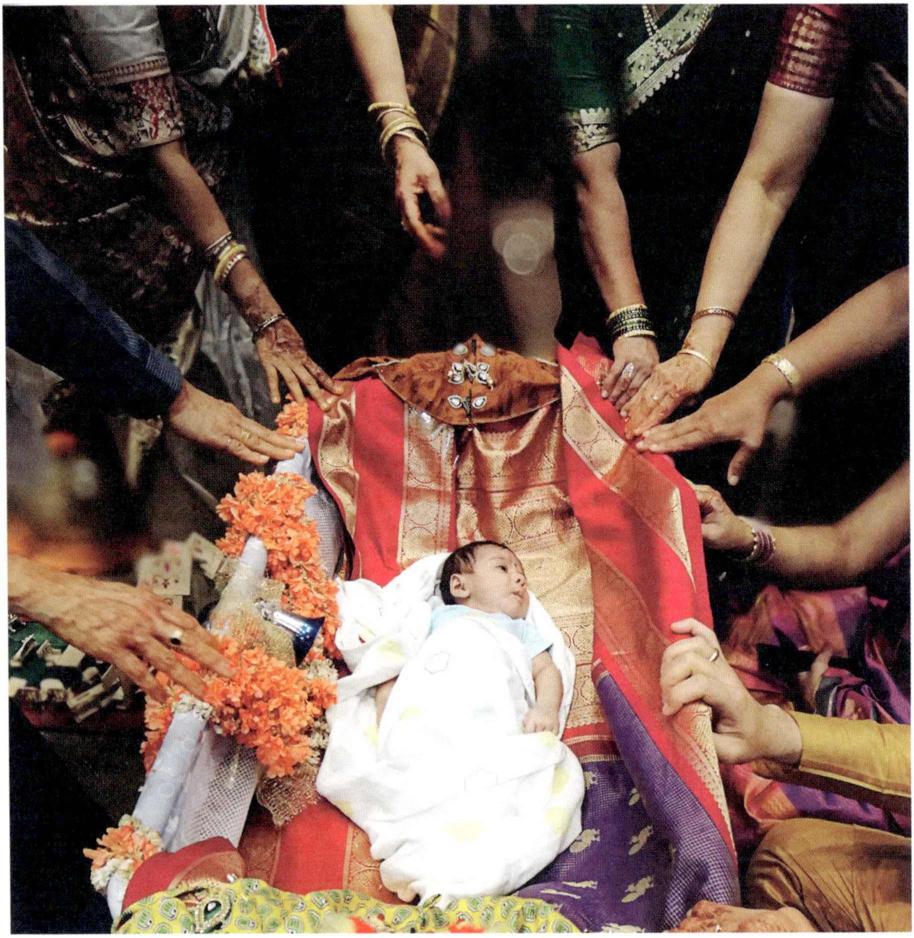

Beloved

by 王艳萍

Bangalore, India

Family and friends say prayers and bestow blessings upon a baby boy at a name-giving ceremony on the occasion of his '100th day' birthday.

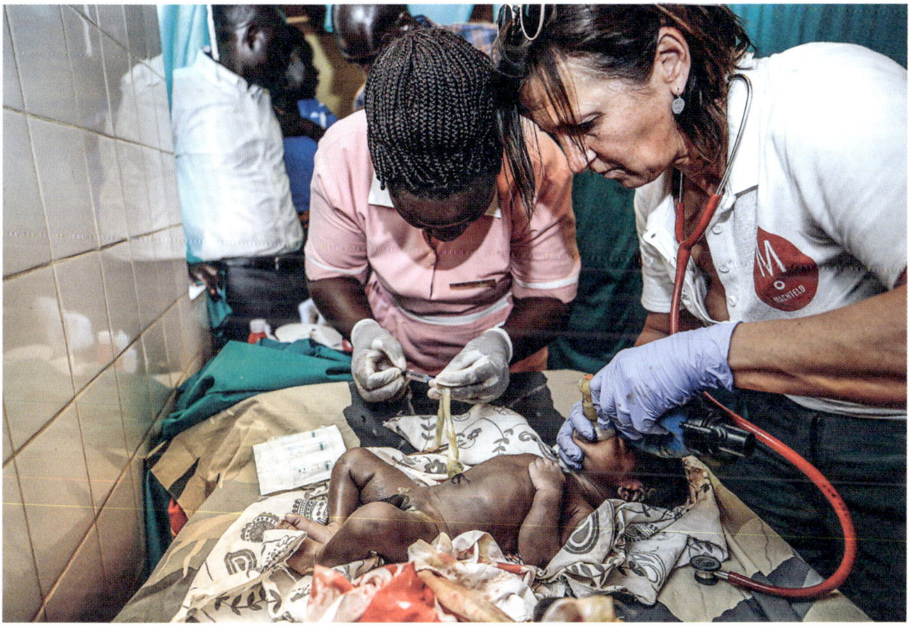

Fighting for Life

by Marie-Pascale Vandewalle

Lira, Uganda

A doctor and nurse fight to save the life of a newborn baby who has been without sufficient oxygen following a complicated birth.

Gardener

by Ewoud Bon

Khajuraho, India

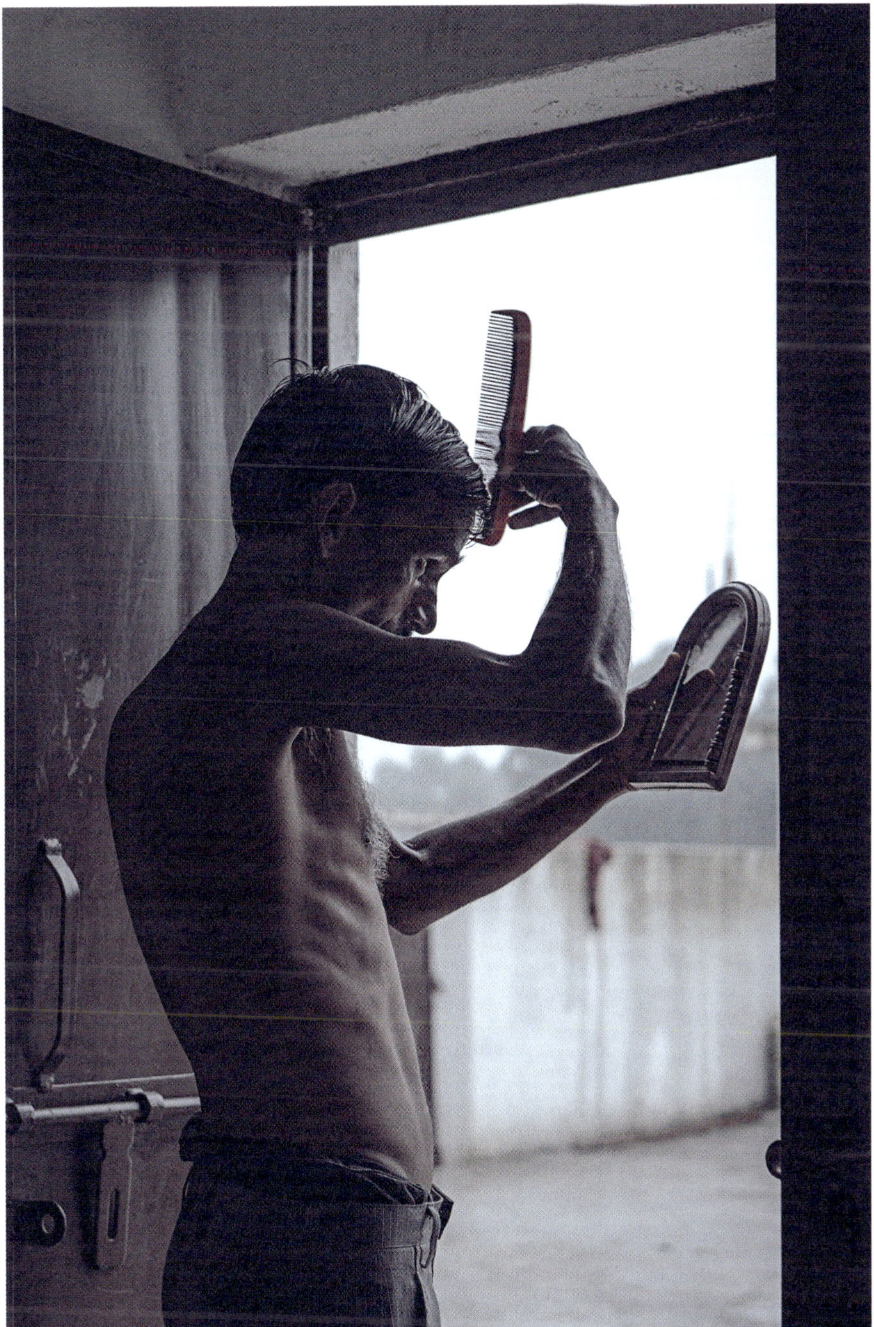

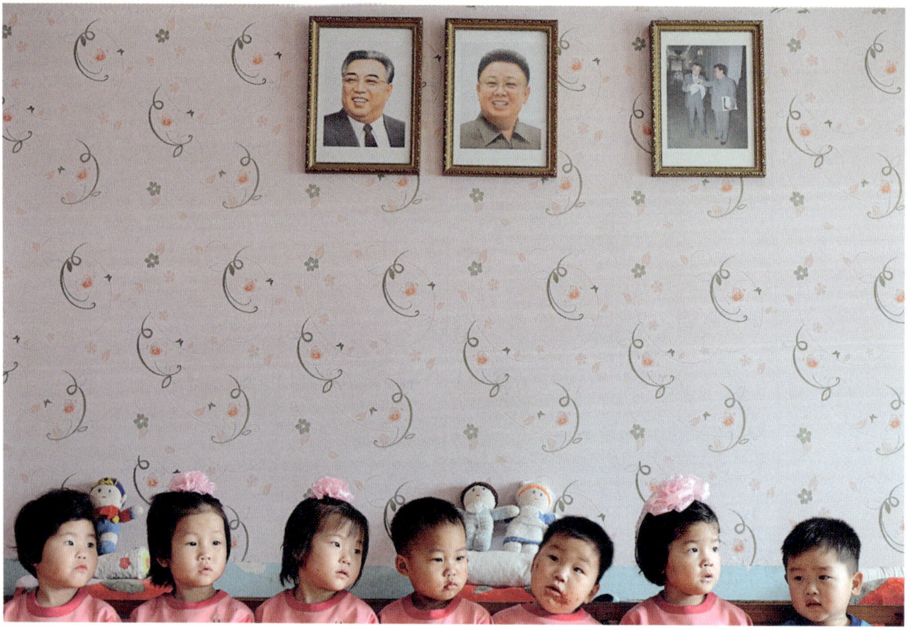

The Hands that Rock the Cradle

by Fabian Muir

Nampo, North Korea

These children live in an orphanage. They make me think not only of their own future but also of their country's future. I hope they will grow up in a North Korea that opens up and emerges from the time capsule within which it has been locked for well over half a century.

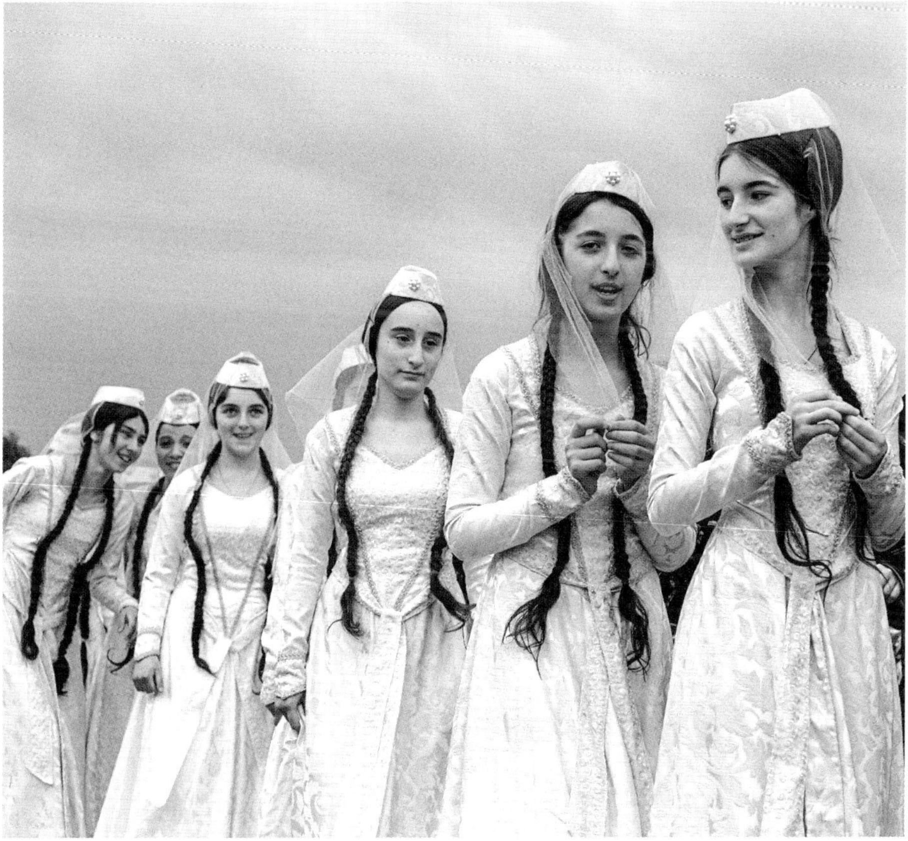

The White Parade

by Hossein Fardinfard

Tbilisi, Georgia

Every May, people in Georgia celebrate a national holiday by dressing up in traditional garments. Here, young ladies wear a popular Georgian folk costume.

Bayamandai

by Jeroen Toirkens

Bayan-Ölgii, Mongolia

Bayamandai is an eagle hunter, one of just a handful of Kazakhs who keep the ancient tradition alive.

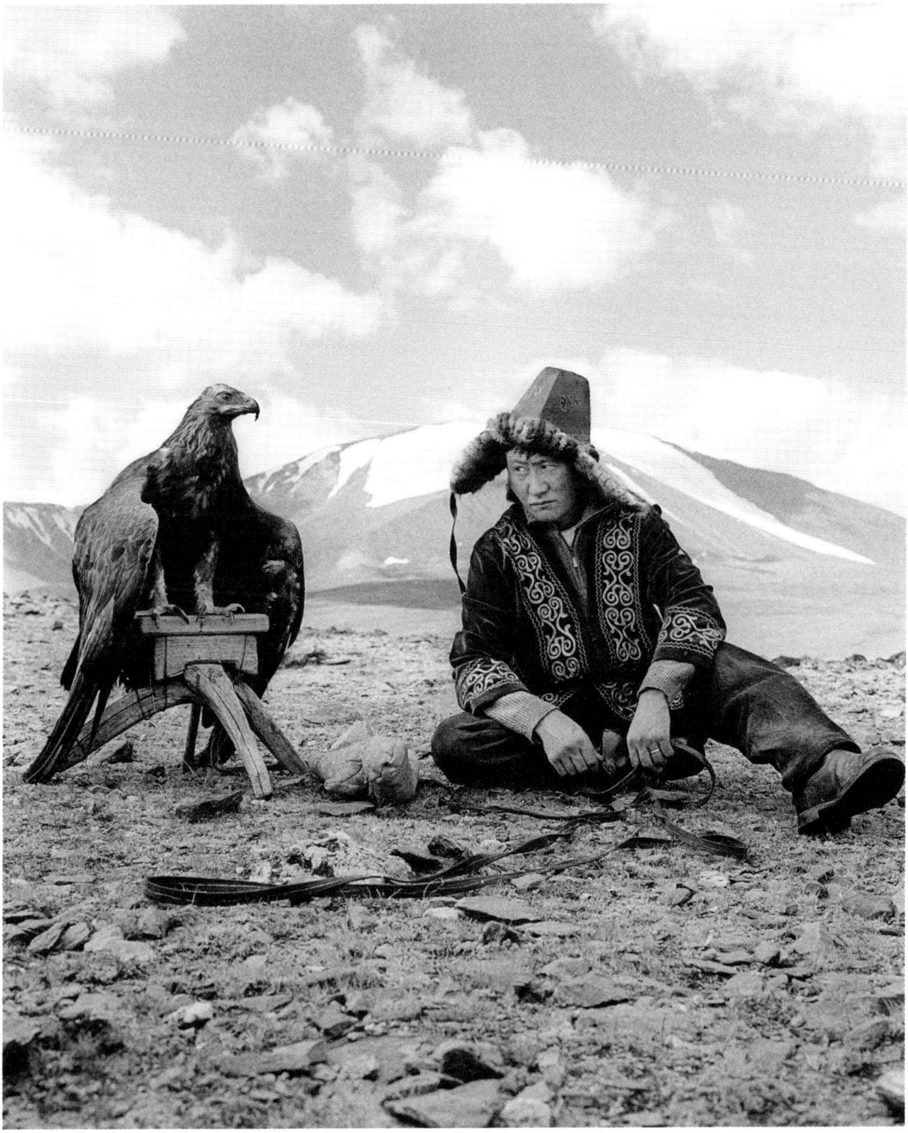

The Art of Aging

by Arianne Clément

Montérégie, Quebec, Canada

A deep tenderness exists between couple Paul, 101, and Christine, 87. They are always affectionate towards each other.

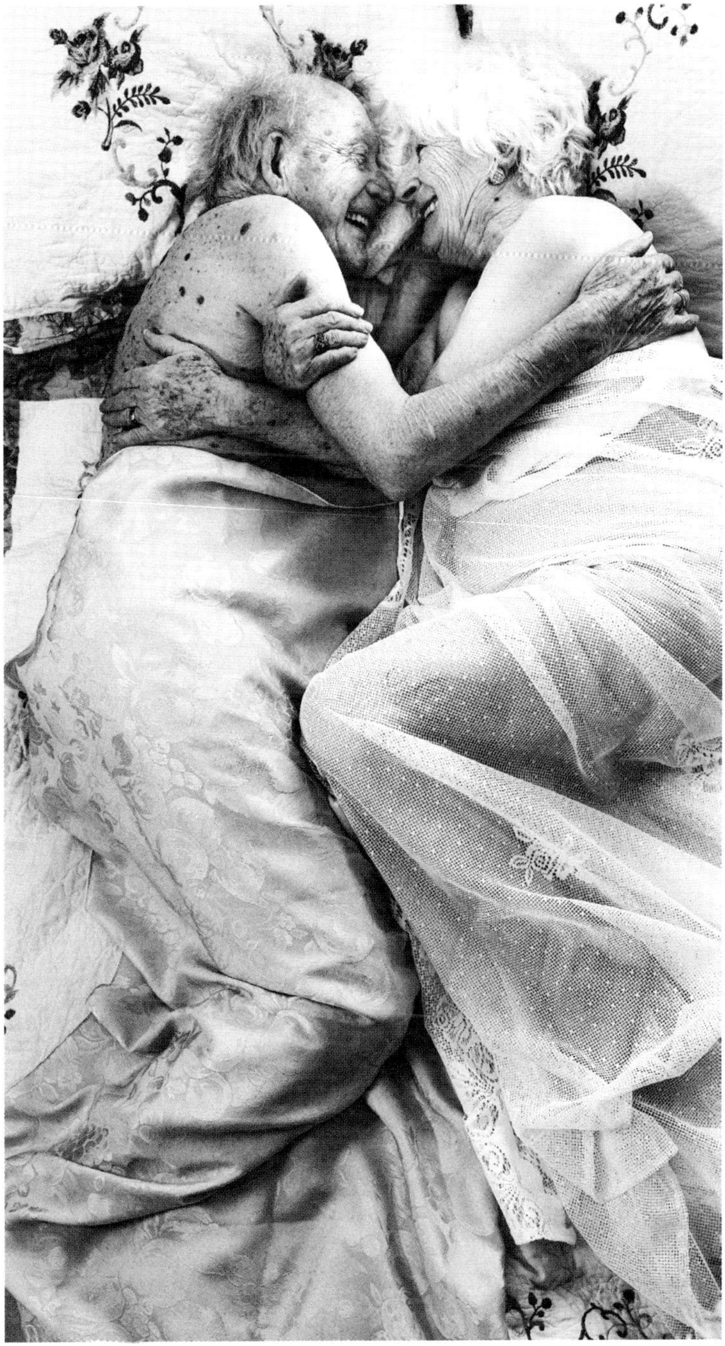

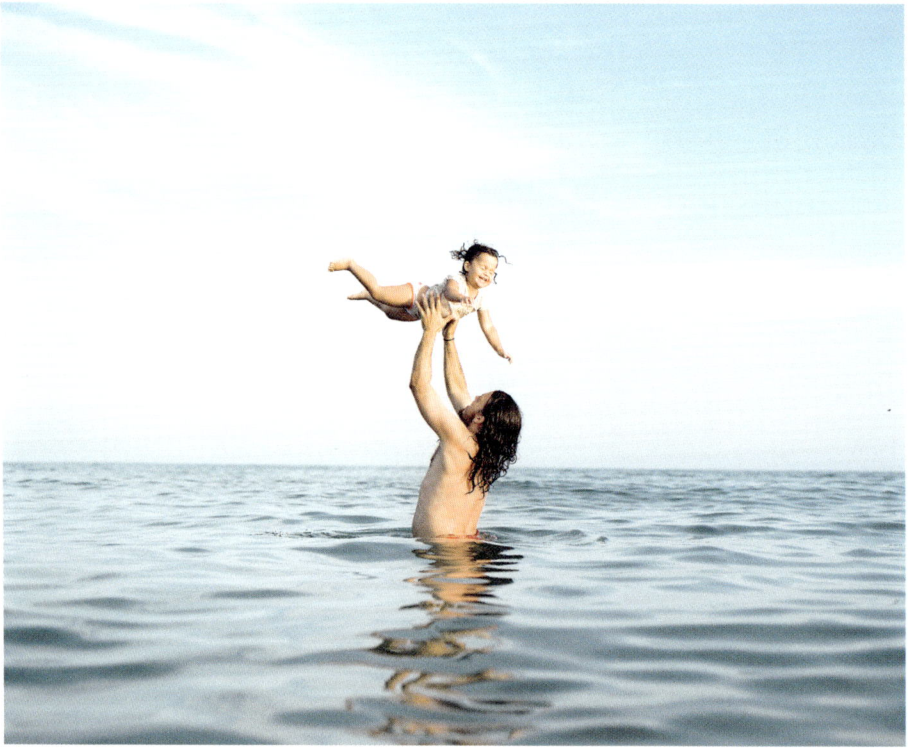

Adrian and Sofia at the Beach

by Javier Caso

Barcelona, Spain

The artist and political activist Adrian Monzón, his wife Yordi and their daughter Sofía are a young Cuban family living in a little beach town a few miles away from Barcelona. I had the opportunity to document a truly beautiful moment of love, happiness and connection between Adrian and Sofia.

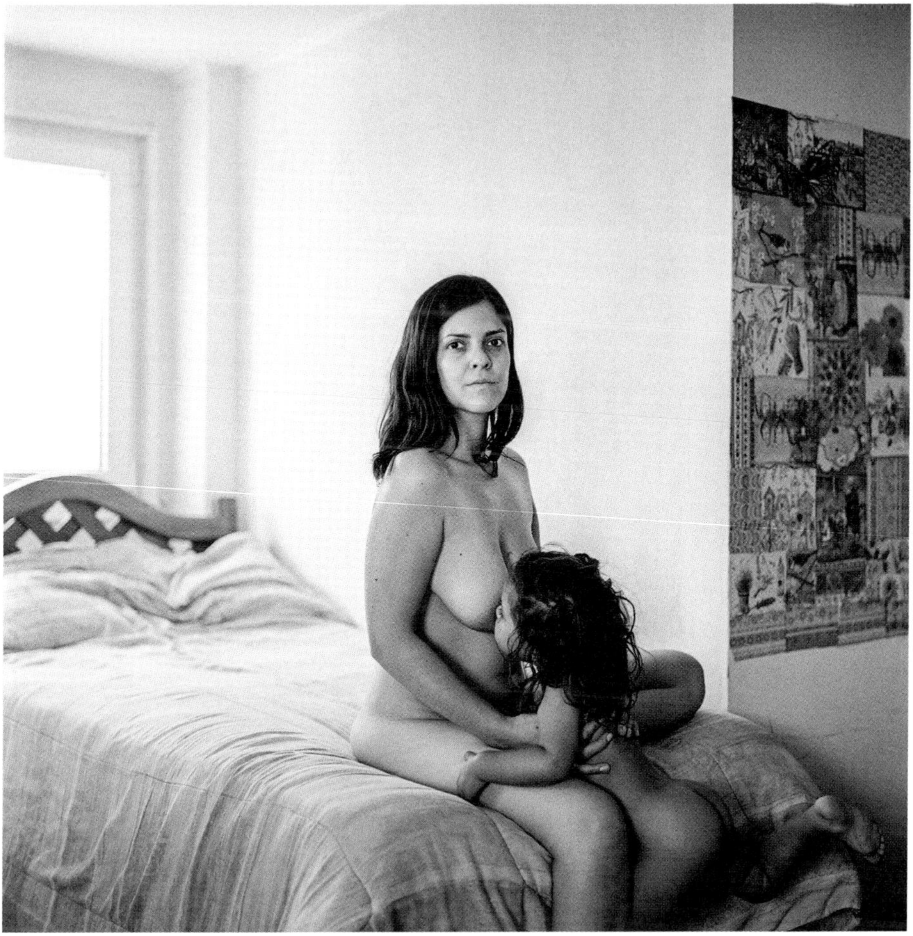

Mother and Daughter at Home

by Catalina Juger Cerda

Santiago, Chile

Antoni

by Kevin Faingnaert

Matavenero, Spain

A remote ecovillage in the isolated mountainous region of northwest Spain, Matavenero is home to a group of strong, independently-minded people who want to live in harmony with nature. Antoni grew up in a nearby city, but now calls Matavenero home.

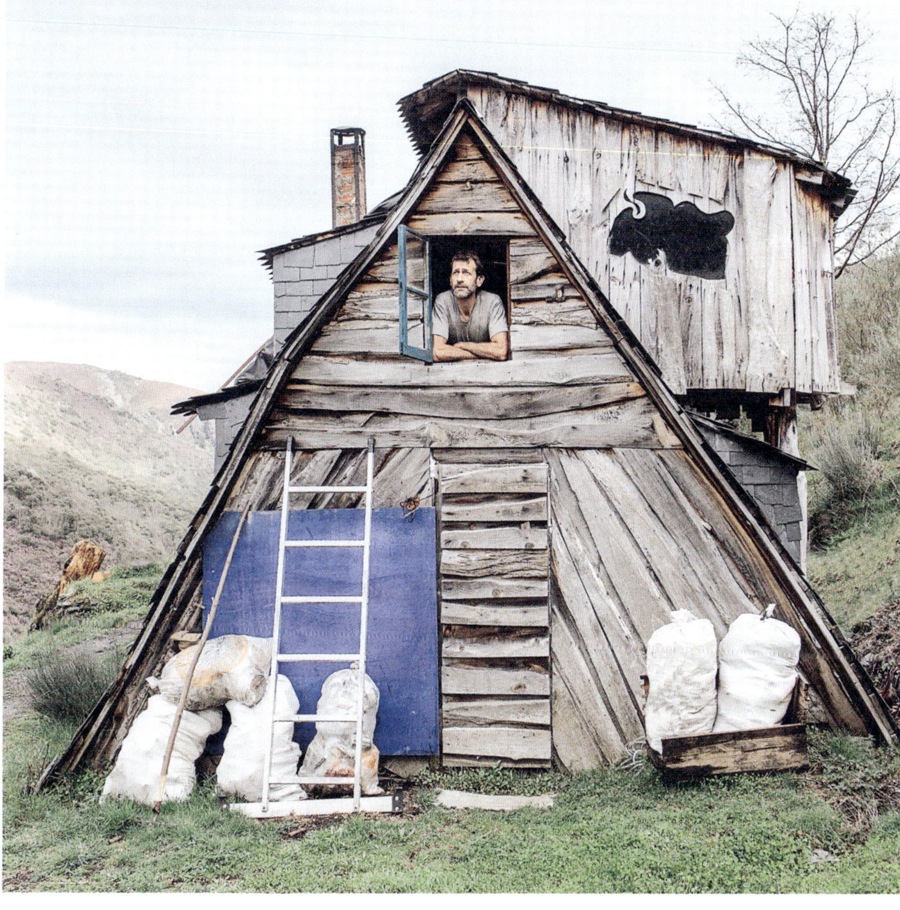

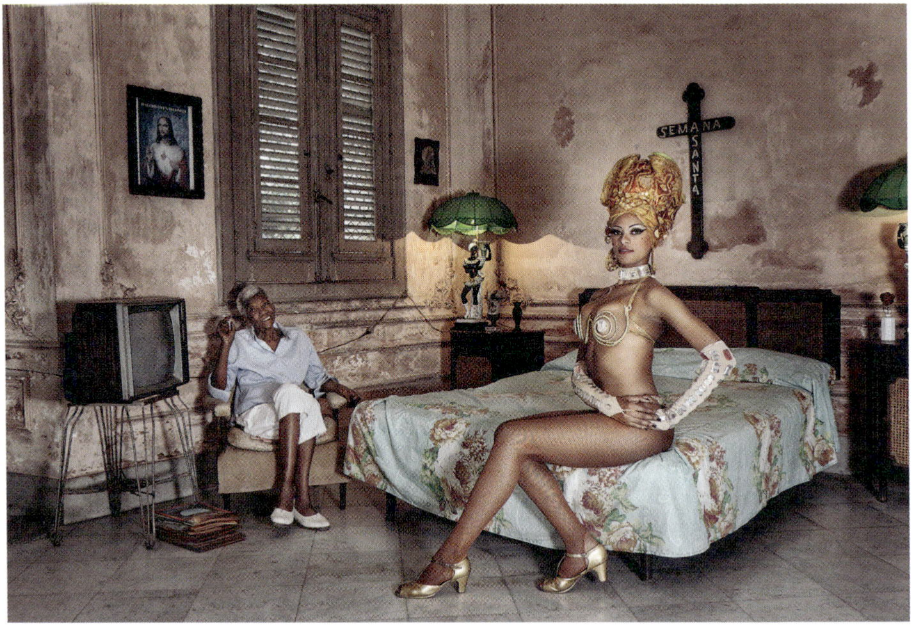

Joana
by Katinka Herbert
Havana, Cuba

Joana, a dancer at Havana's Tropicana Club, poses with her maternal grandmother.

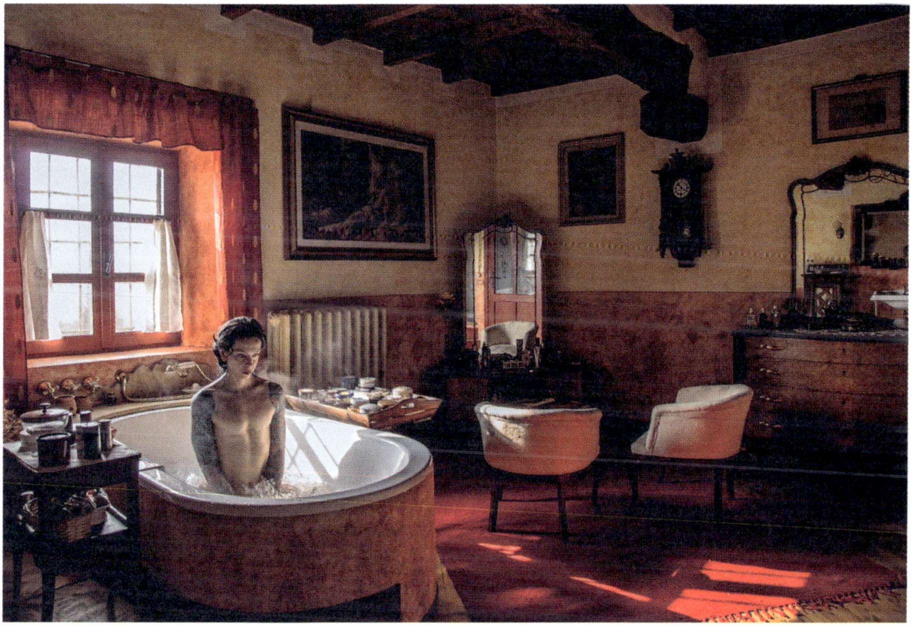

Pat's Rebirth

by Graziano Perotti

Milan, Italy

Pat is transitioning to male. When I took this picture, Lucio, as he is now known, had just told me about the physical suffering he had endured while transitioning, but the happiness and relief of getting rid of his 'burden' was so great he didn't want people to know about the pain.

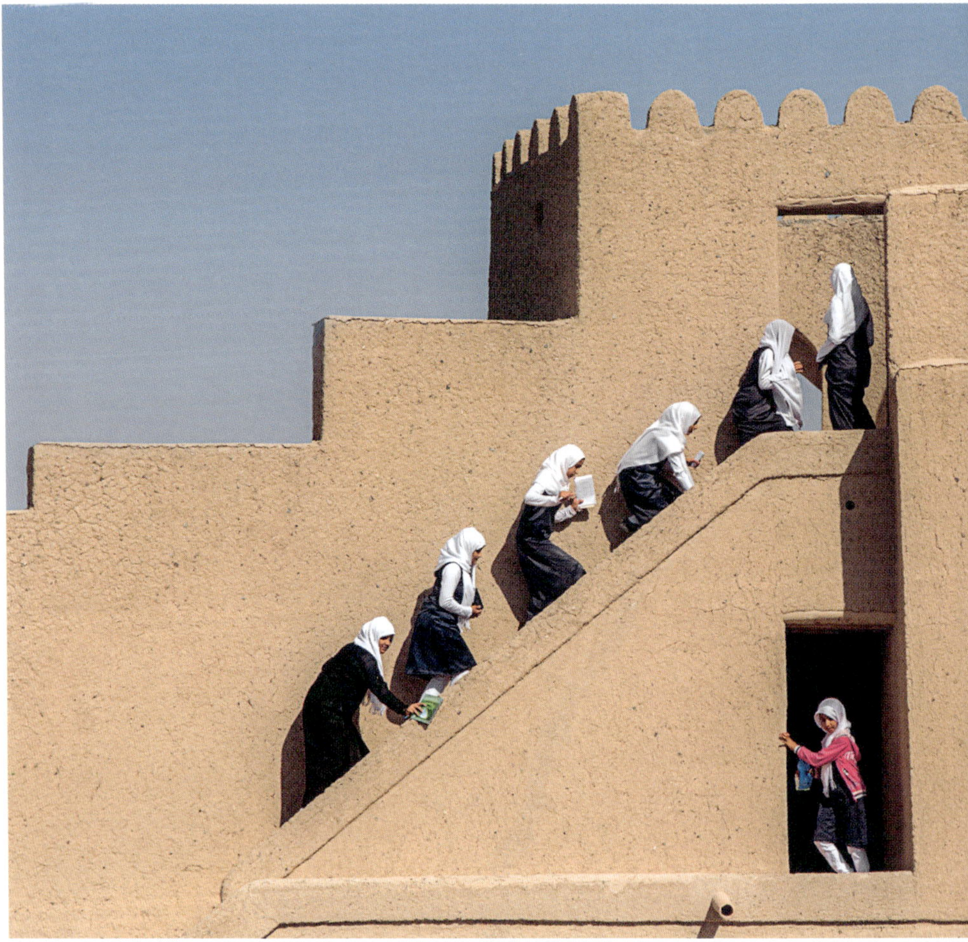

School Trip
by Alberto Mesirca
Nizwa, Oman

It was a windy day when I visited Nizwa Fort. I spotted a line of girls on a school trip climbing the stairs, bending in the wind while clutching their notebooks. The choreography of the scene struck me immediately.

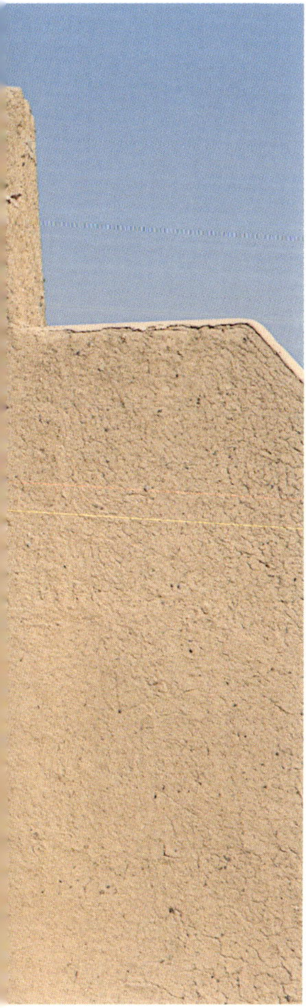

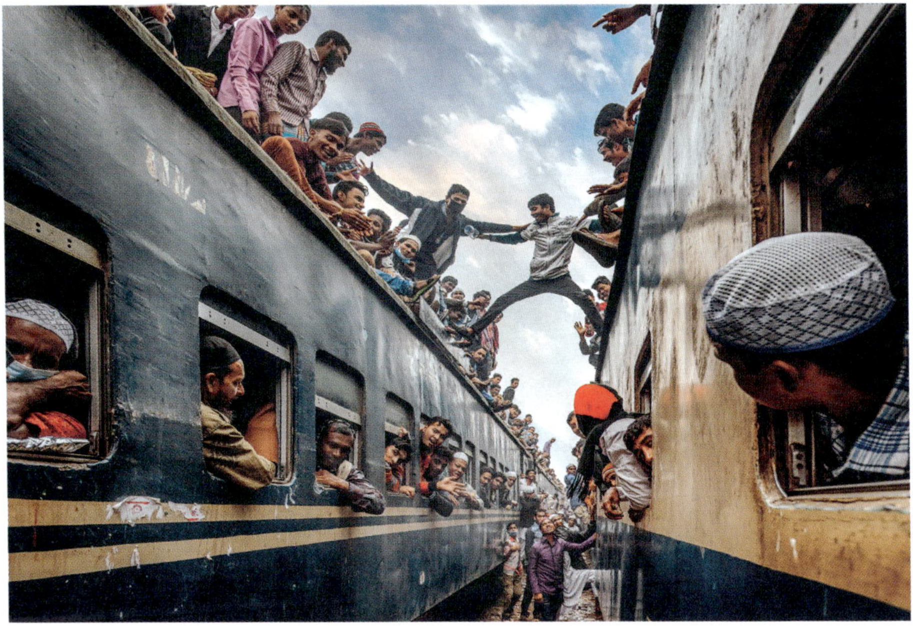

Time to Go Home
by David Nam Lip Lee
Bangladesh

Visitors to the muslim annual gathering of Bishwa Ijtema at Tongi in Bangladesh catch trains home. Demand for public transport is high and consequently passengers sit on train roofs.

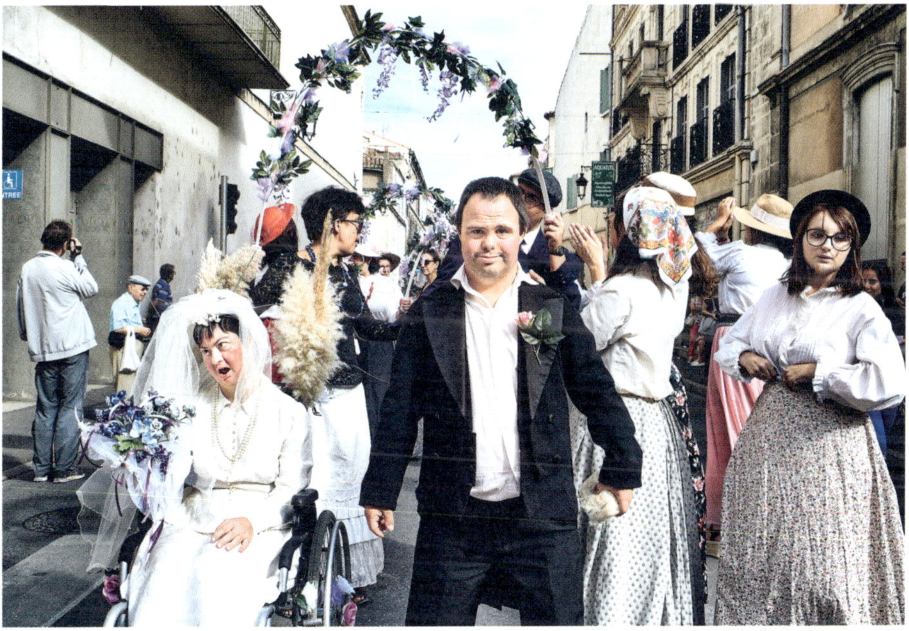

Dignity

by Rob Lavers

Arles, France

The energy of this procession was intoxicating.

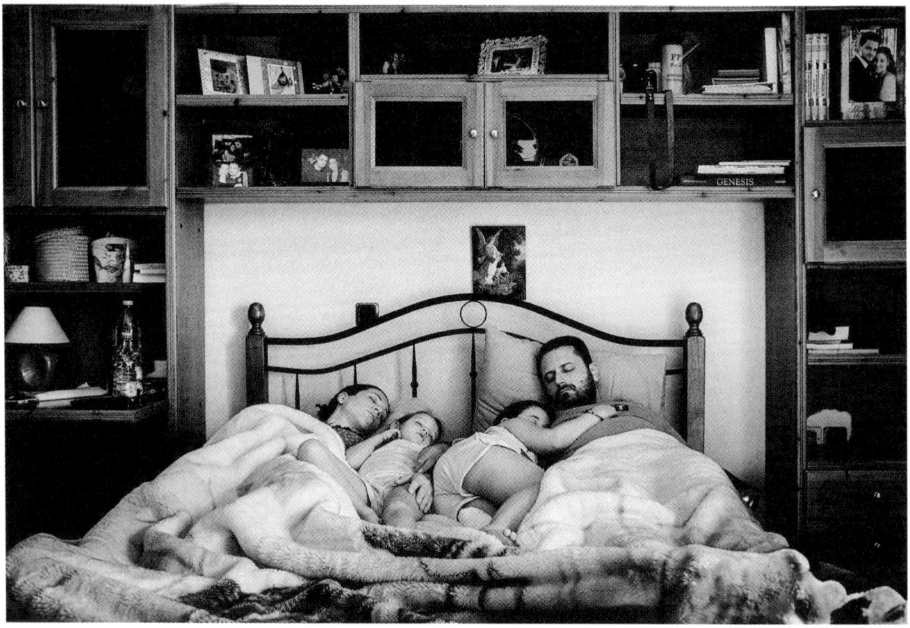

My Family Portrait
by Alexandros Tsiolis
Corfu, Greece

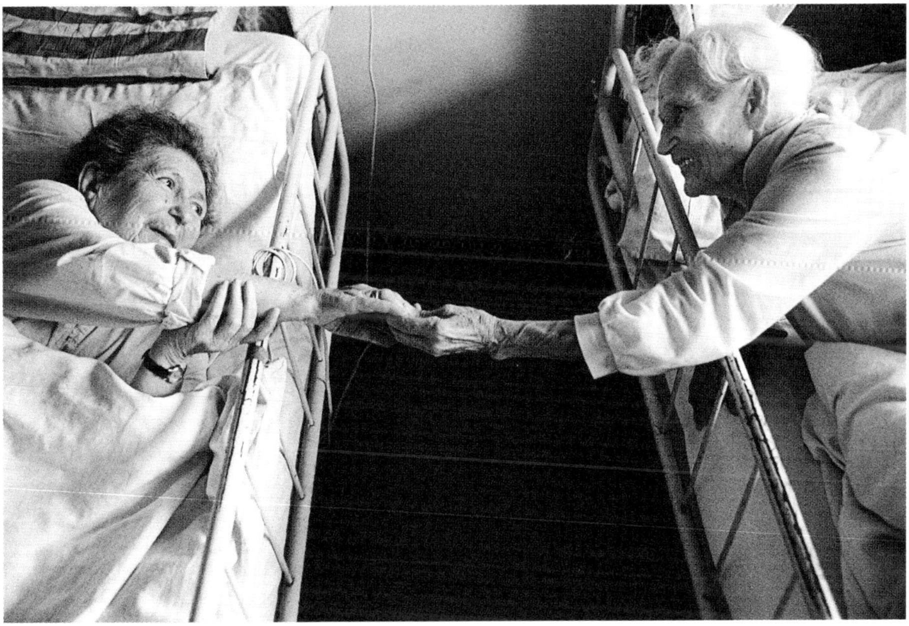

Hospital Friends

by Yuri Dojc

Bratislava, Slovakia

This is my mother, Regina Dojcova, on the left, with her newfound friend, Isabella Majska. They talked about the past and how my mother was a teacher. Isabella had been a cleaning lady and was very impressed by my mother's intelligence. They made a promise to meet up once they got out of hospital.

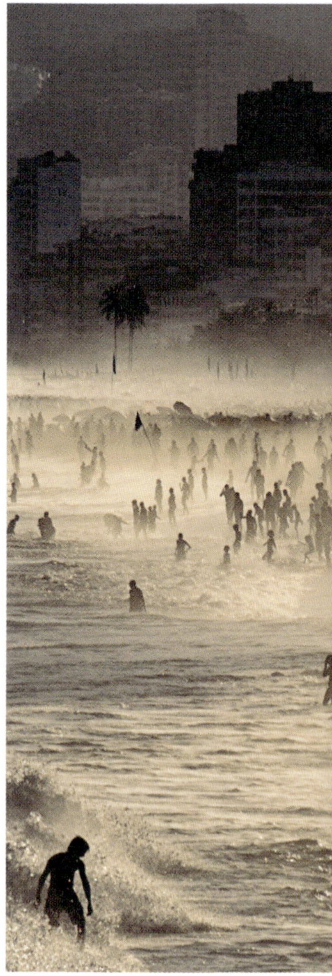

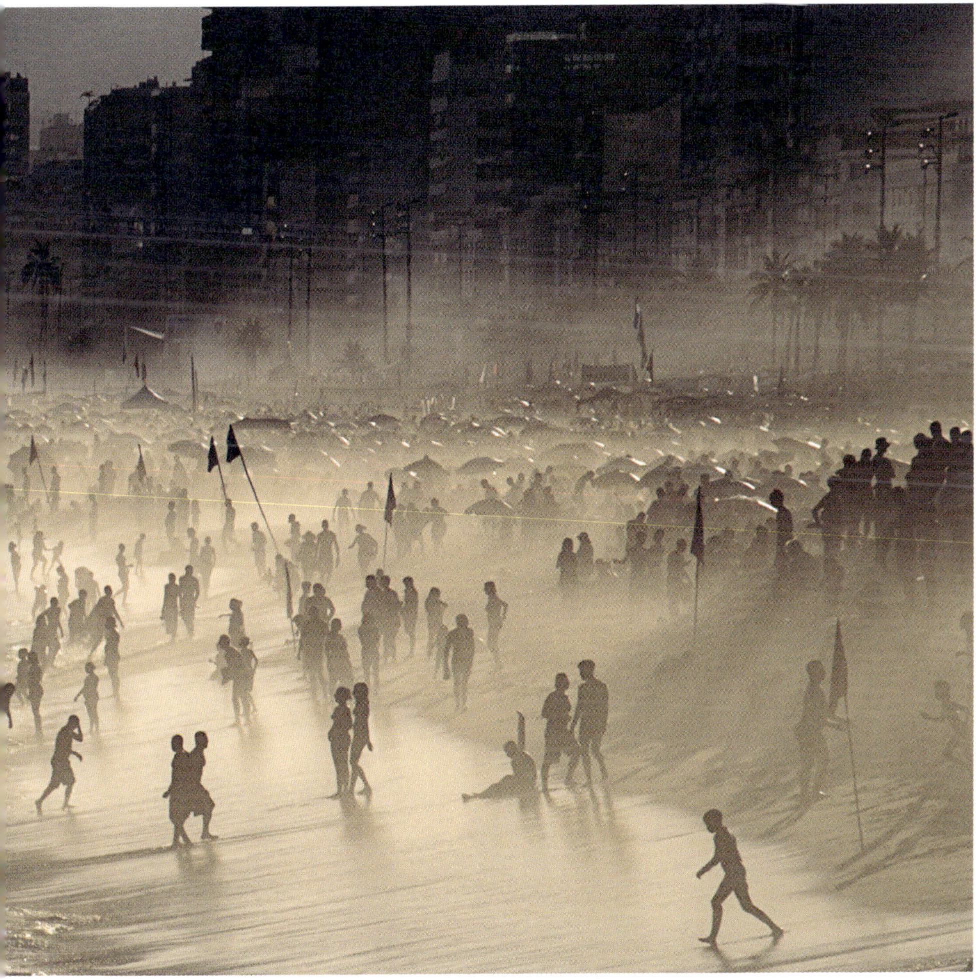

A Strange Day in Ipanema

by Sandra Cattaneo Adorno

Rio de Janeiro, Brazil

Famed for its beaches, Rio de Janeiro is often referred to as 'cidade maravilhosa' or 'the wonderful city'. On this day, the sea was very rough as the sun set.

Tuniwuni Kirijini Kukuni:
Black Boy Water

by Wayne Quilliam

Tiwi Islands, Australia

As one of only a few professional photographers working among Indigenous communities in remote rural and urban areas of Australia, I feel it is my responsibility to record the history and culture of our people. I have been visiting Tiwi Islands in the Northern Territory for more than 30 years, creating visual narratives that represent a proud and culturally strong people. Here, a young man washes down after a ceremony to cleanse his spirit and cool off in the extreme heat.

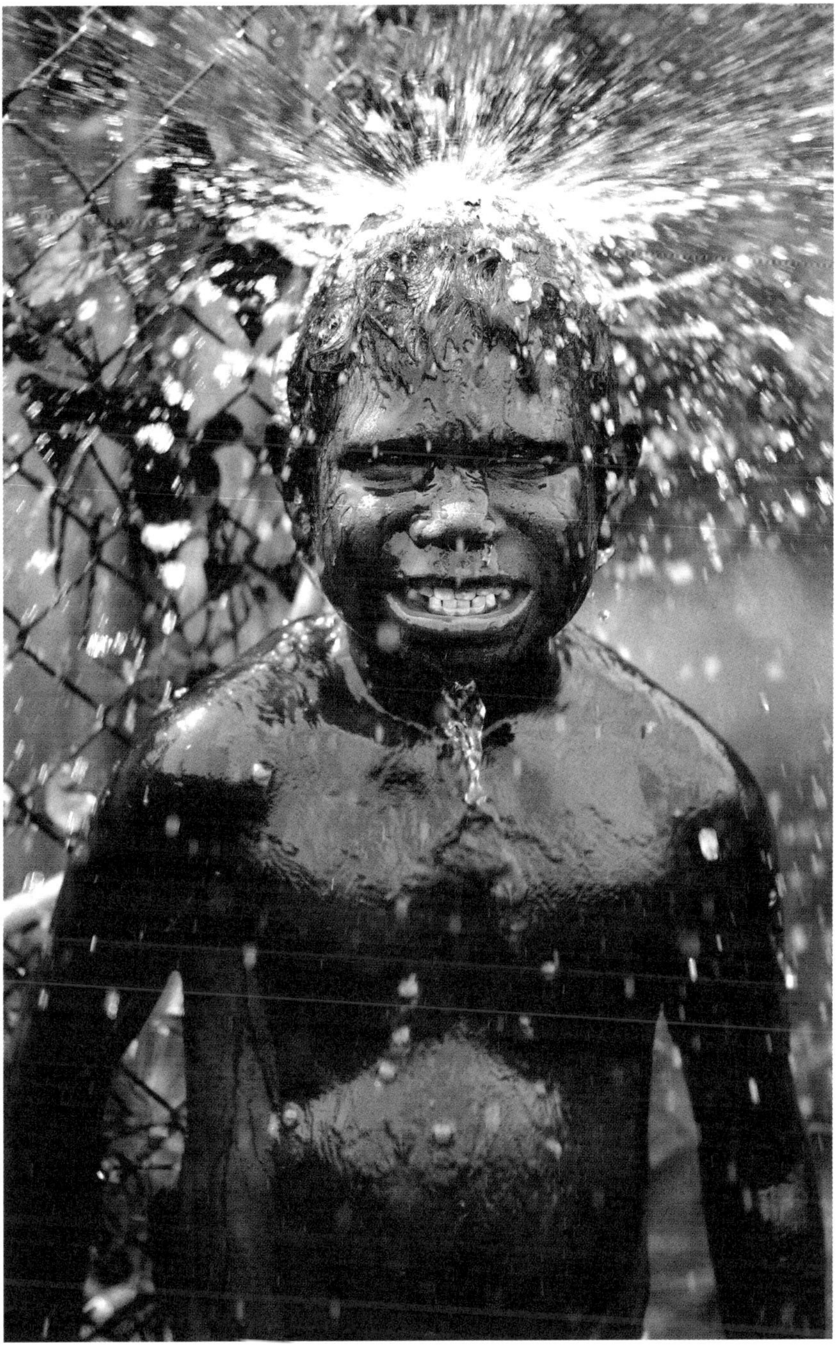

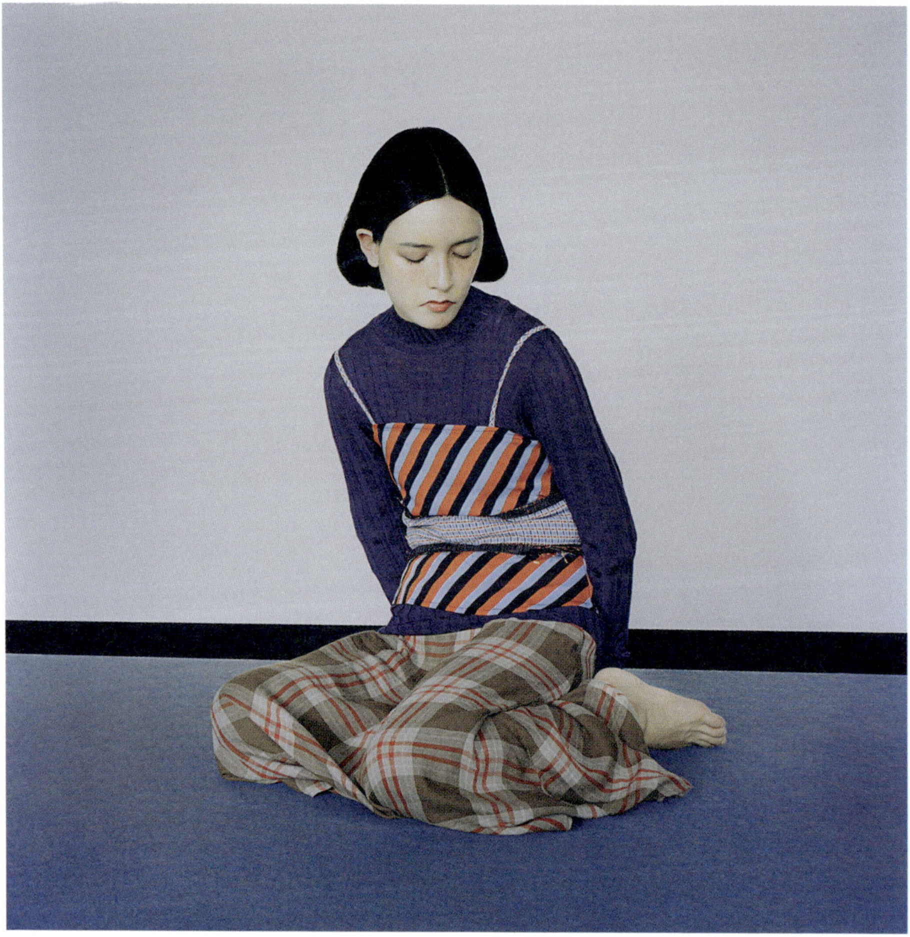

Blue

by Hui Choi

Guangzhou, Guangdong, China

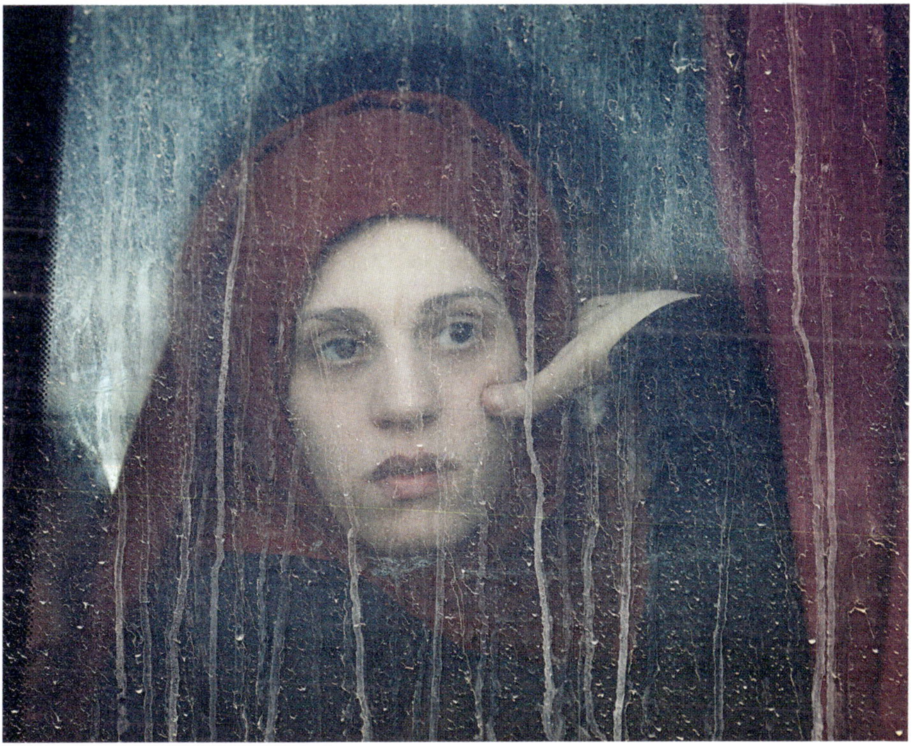

Fleeing Mosul

by Abbie Trayler-Smith

Hasan Sham refugee camp, Iraq

After a nine-month battle, ISIS was expelled from Mosul in early 2017. I noticed Sara looking out of a window as the bus she was on pulled into the refugee camp. The look on her face summed up the global uncertainty that seemed to be everywhere. And yet, despite the death and destruction, the human spirit is resilient and lives on.

Diarretou and Hawa

by Sam Armstrong

Paris, France

I find it hard to describe the connection between the people at the Pigalle Duperré basketball court in Paris. It was like nothing I'd experienced before – there was a unique air of affection, respect, passion and happiness. It really felt like one big family.

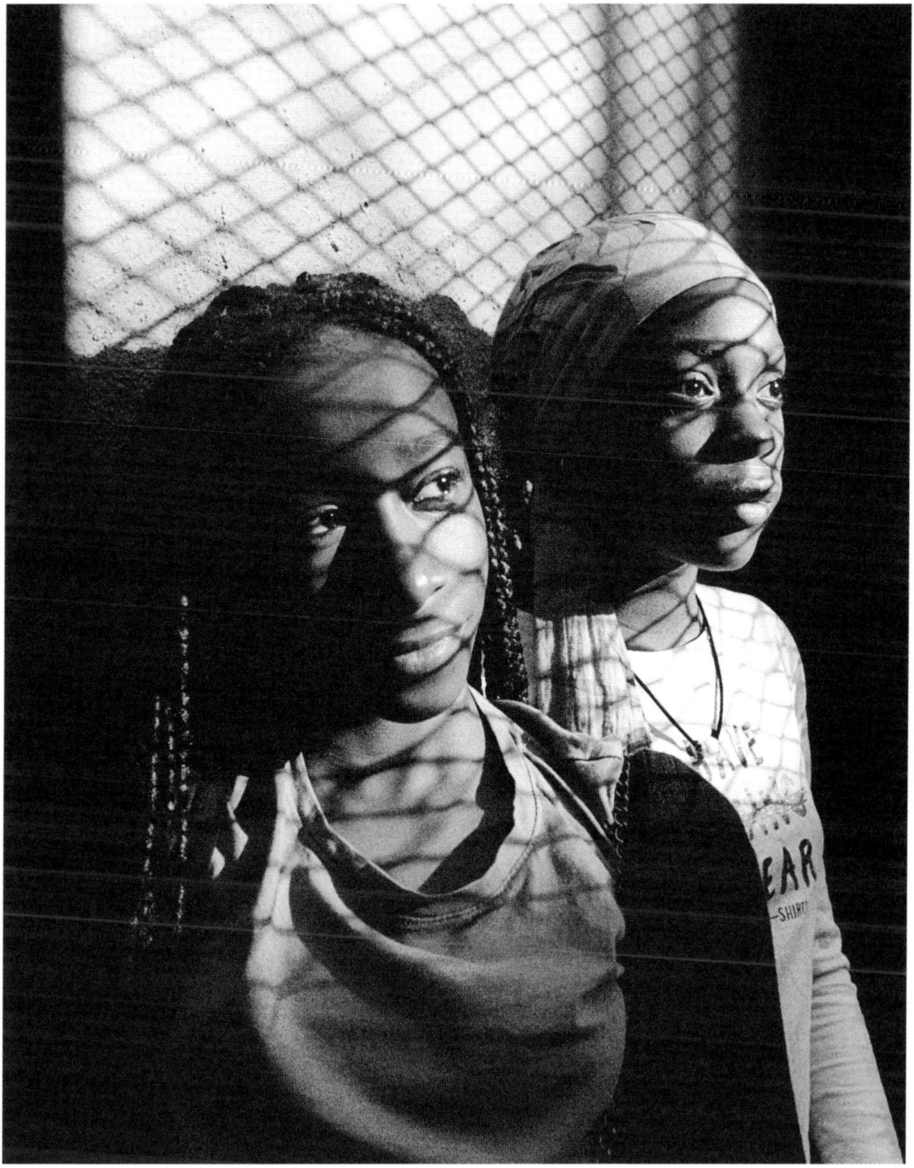

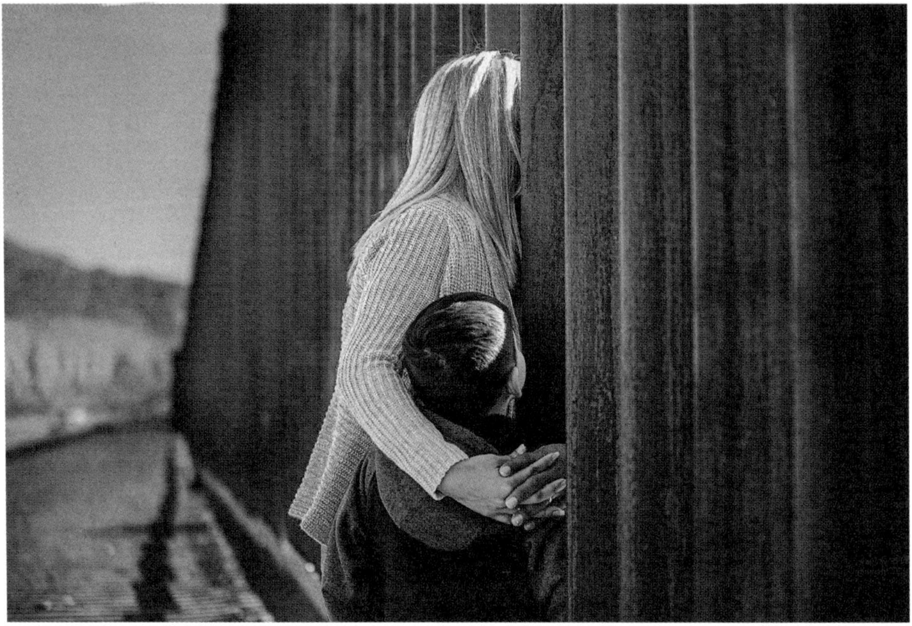

Just Married

by Monica Lozano

US-Mexico border

A newly-wed woman, seen here with her son, is allowed a three-minute hug with her husband, the father of her son, during the Hugs Not Walls event. The woman and young boy live legally on the American side while the boy's father is in Mexico. He doesn't have a passport and cannot cross over to the United States.

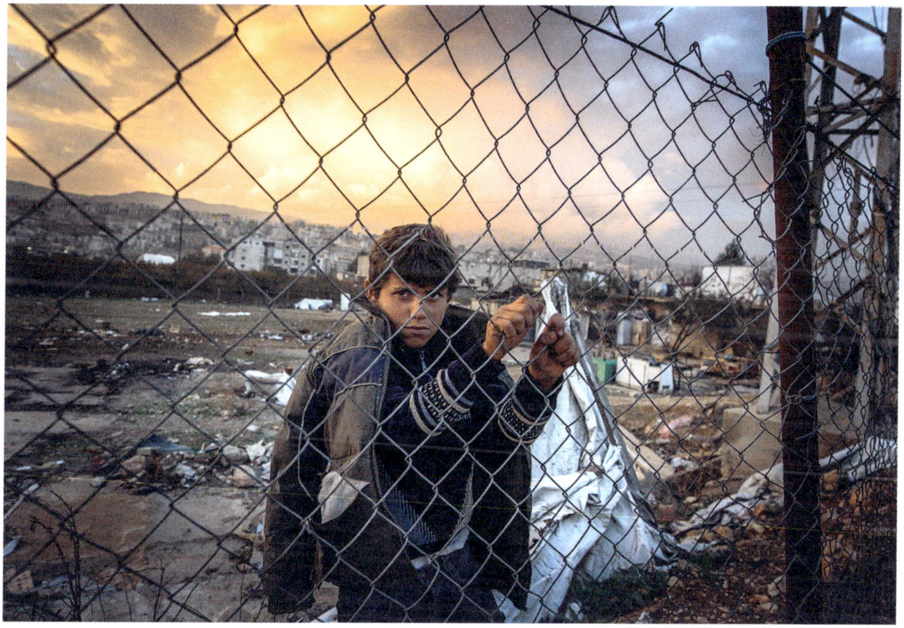

Silent Frustration

by Sølvi Iren Wessel-Berg

Zahlé, Lebanon

This little boy struck me right in my heart.
His family didn't have any food, he said.
I gave him the water I had on me.

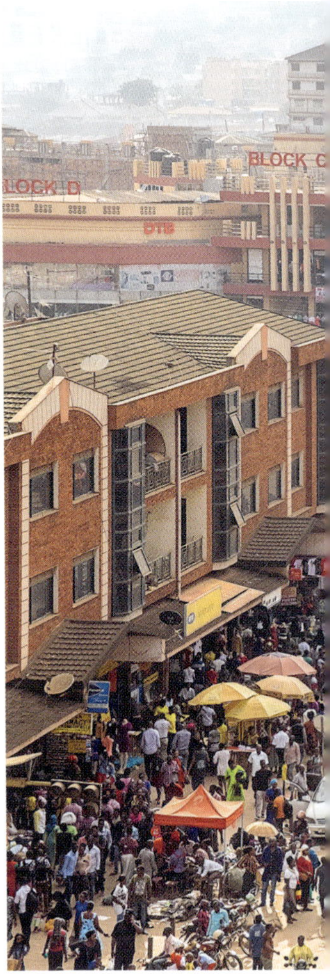
BLOCK C
BLOCK D
DTB

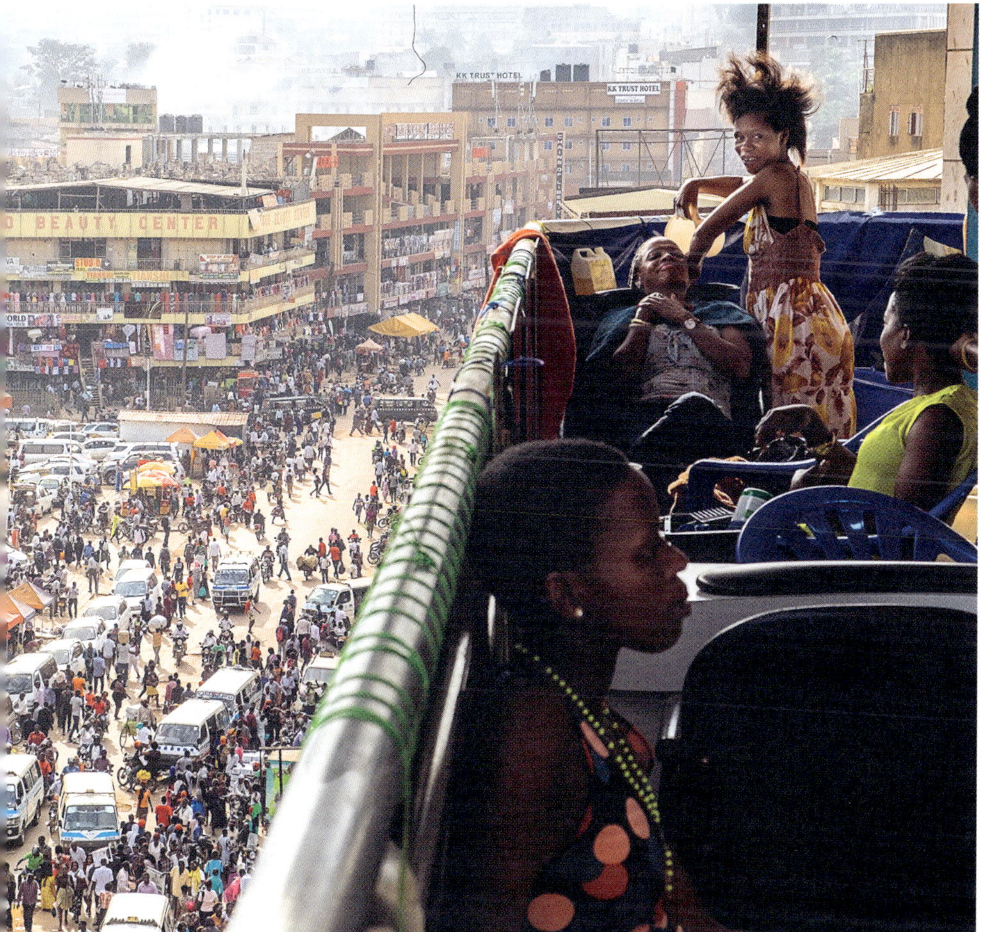

Beauty Centre

by Federico Redin

Kampala, Uganda

A hairdresser works on the balcony of a commercial building while her clients relax. Competition for trading space in central Kampala is fierce.

The Ghanaian Astronaut

by Jørn Tomter

London, UK

Wunnam is a pupil at Kingsmead Primary School in Hackney. The photo is part of a series of portraits of children dressed as astronauts. There is no more powerful fuel on the planet than a kid's imagination.

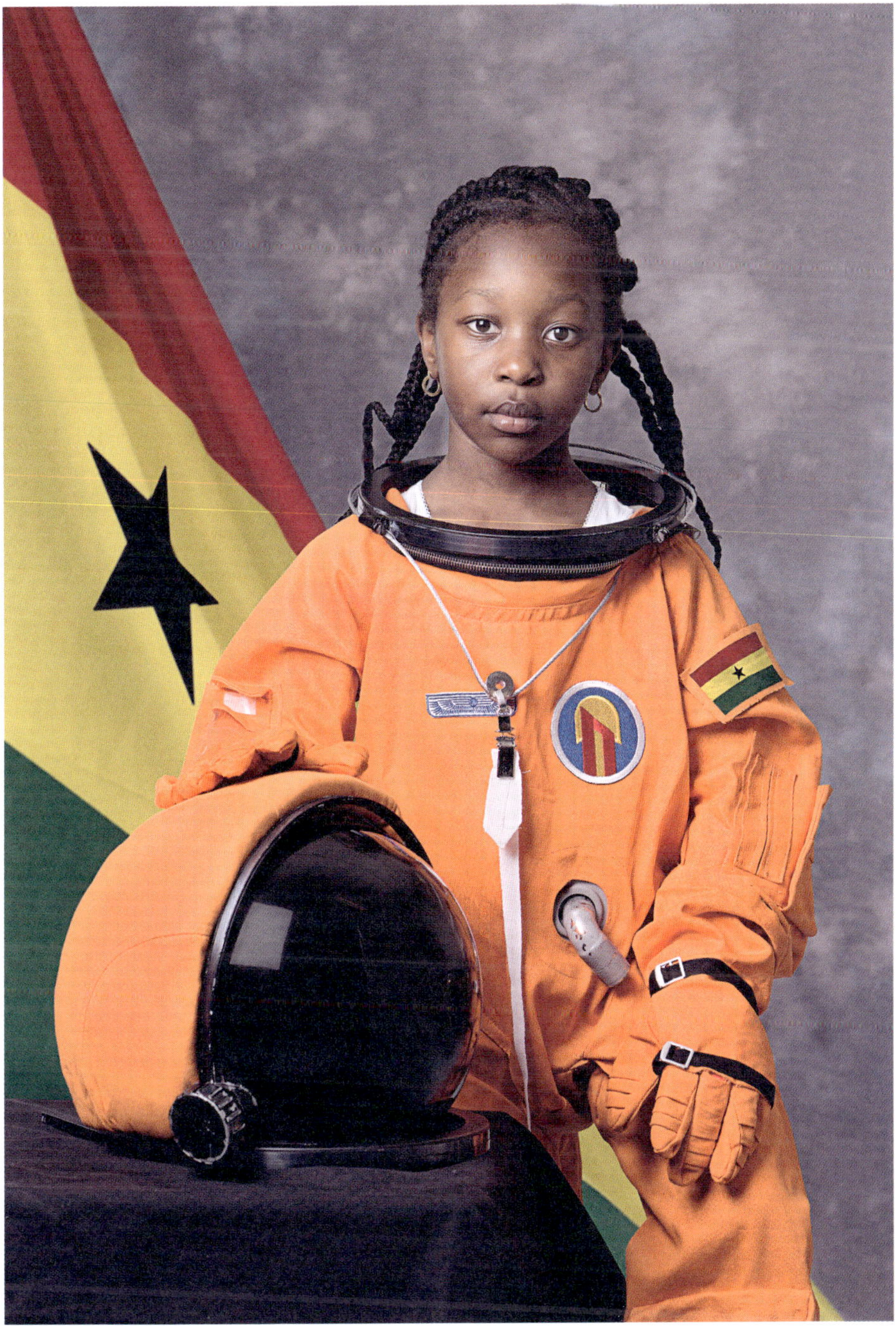

Doña Mechita

by Ric Kokotovich

Mérida, Mexico

Doña Mechita is almost 90 years old and lives in a tiny house. For a few months every year her floor and ceiling are covered in turkey piñatas, which she's been making for over 35 years. Doña started doing these for Christmas originally but since there is a growing expat community of Americans living in Mérida she now gets requests for Thanksgiving too.

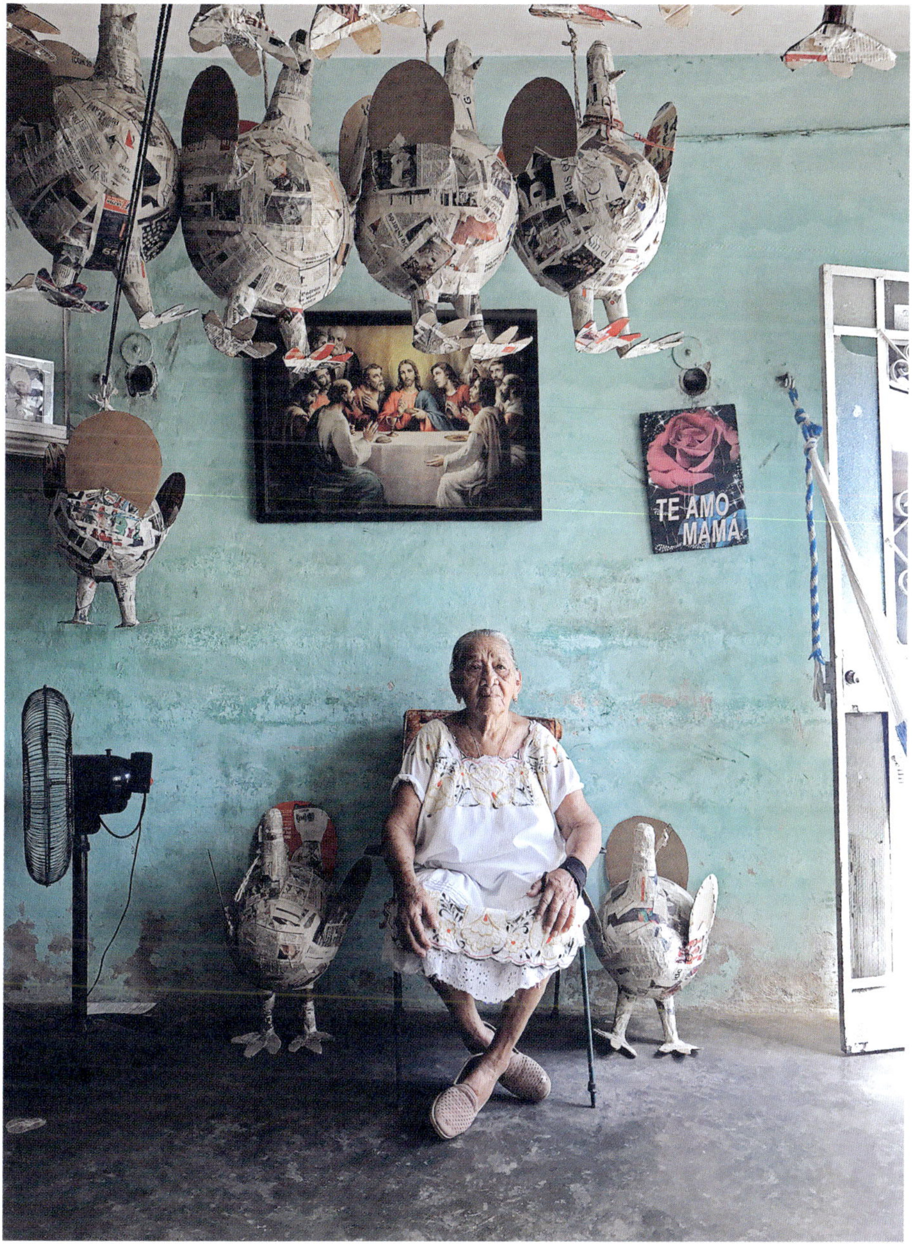
TE AMO
MAMA

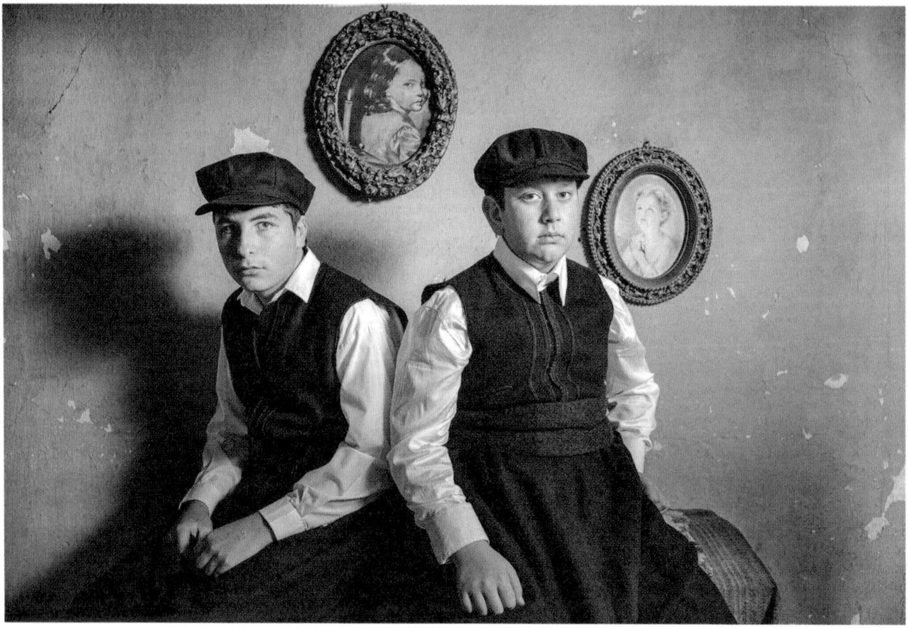

Bell-Bearers
by Nikos Vavdinoudis
Drama, Greece

Teenagers dress in traditional garments during bell-bearing celebrations. The ancient festival, which has roots in eastern Macedonia, involves dressing up in costumes and wearing masks to ward off evil spirits and welcome in the new year.

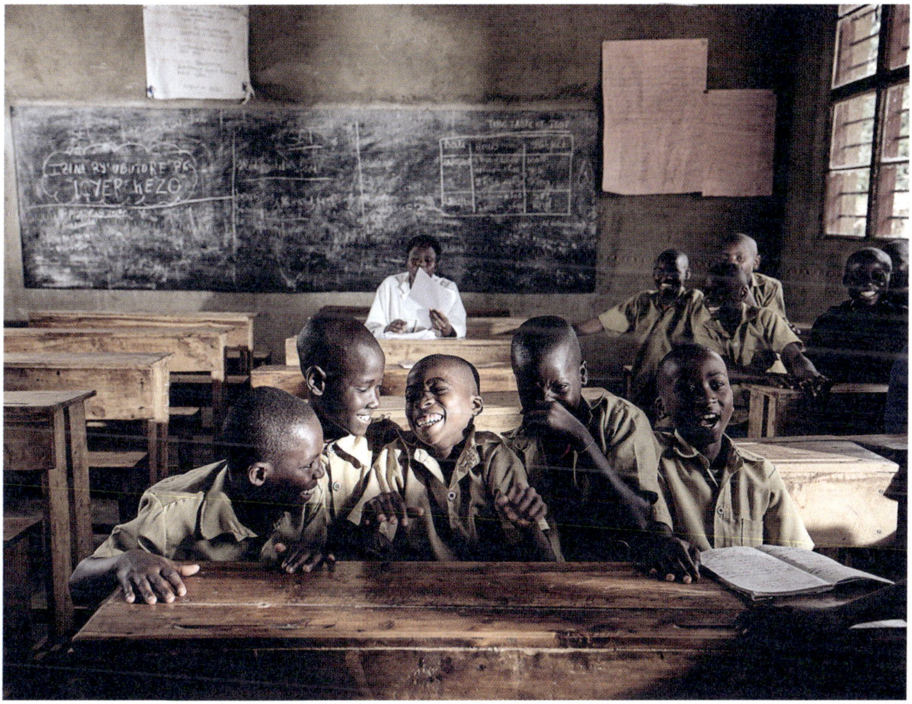

Classroom

by Nick Kontostavlakis

Muvungu, Rwanda

Dad with Dementia

by Lucy Williams

Chepstow, UK

I started photographing my dad when he was diagnosed with a rare form of dementia in 2014 at the age of 68. Even in the most challenging times the love between my mum and dad was so beautiful and tender. Dad died 10 days after their 50th wedding anniversary.

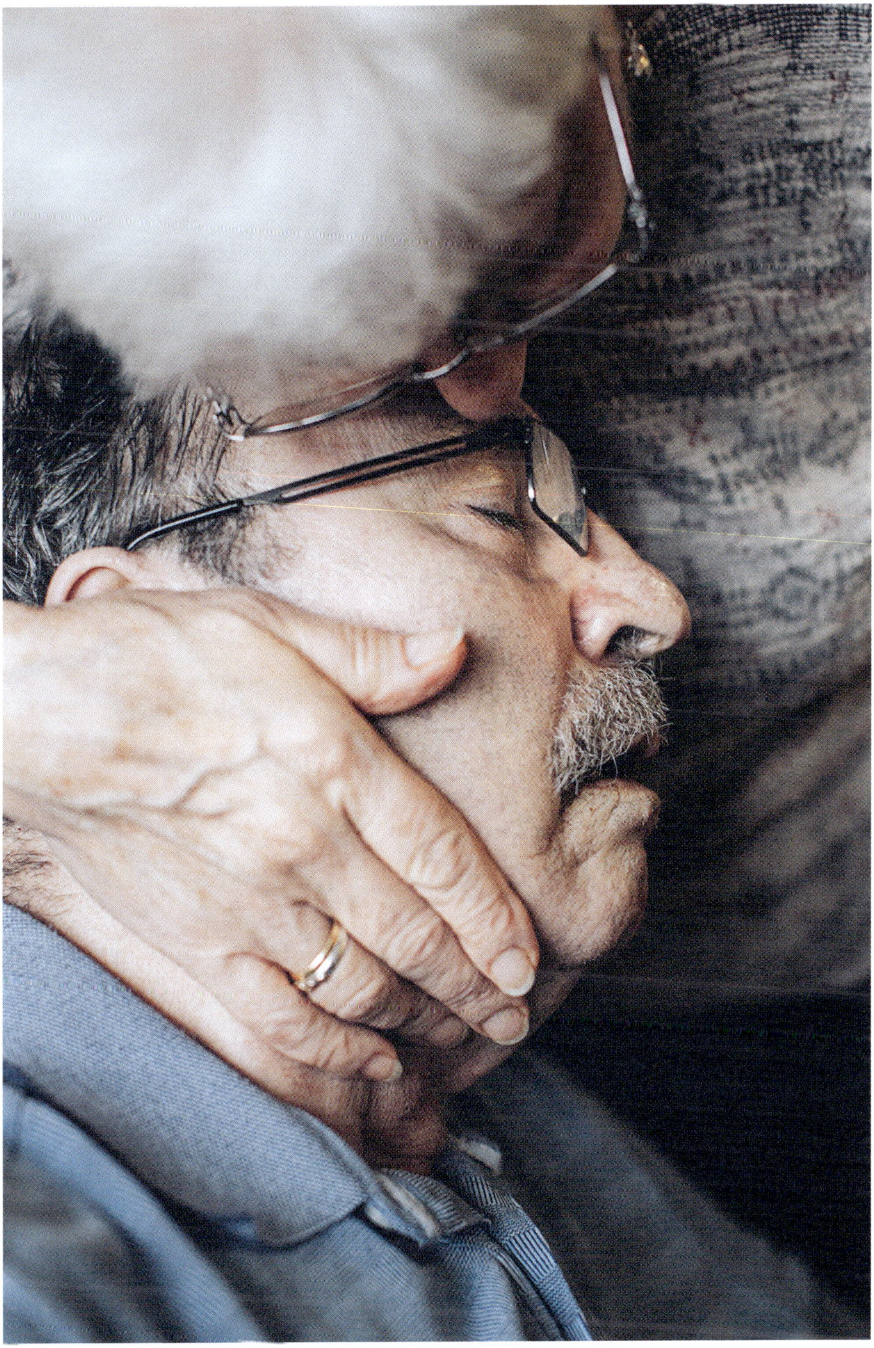

The Seer

by Kevin O'Sheean

Varanasi, India

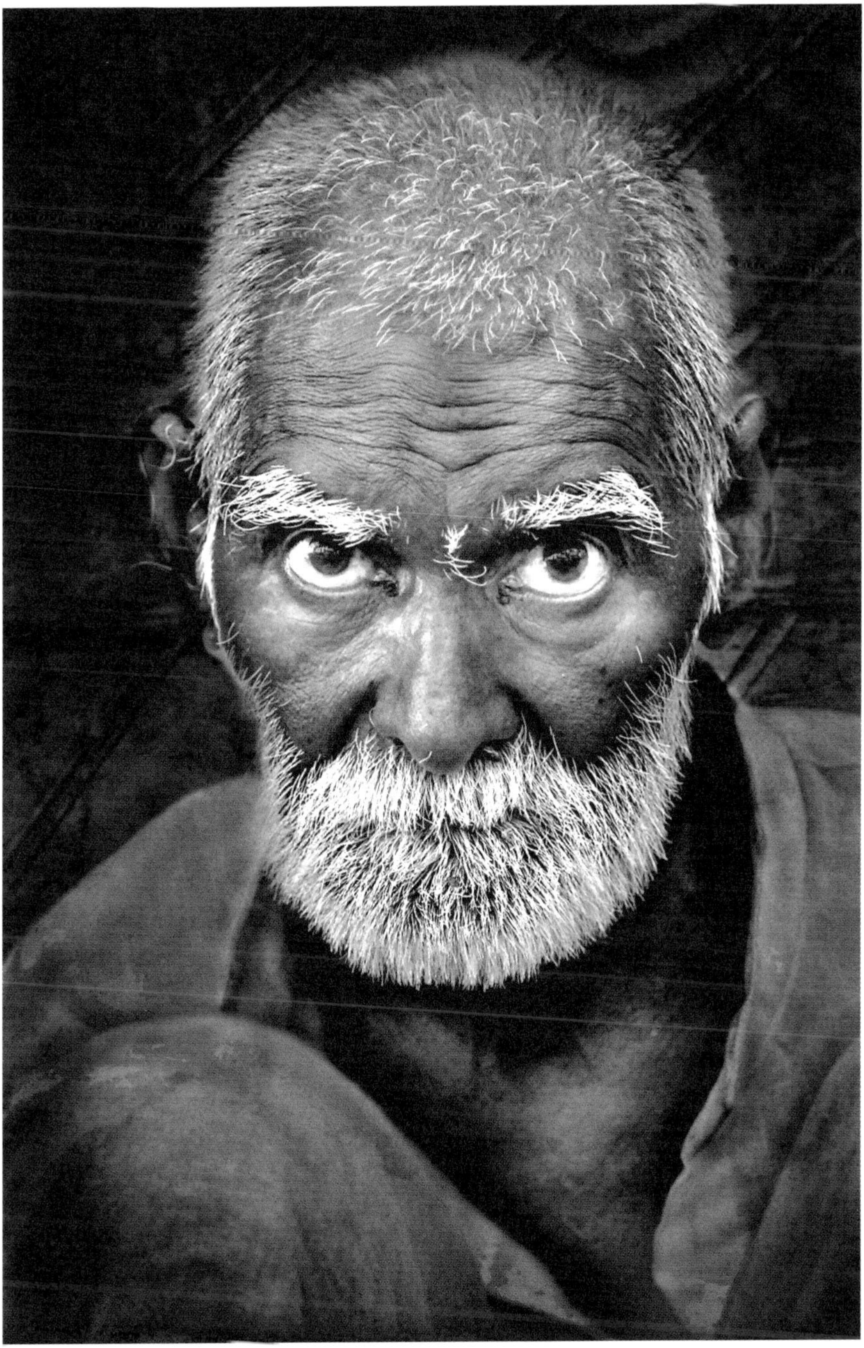

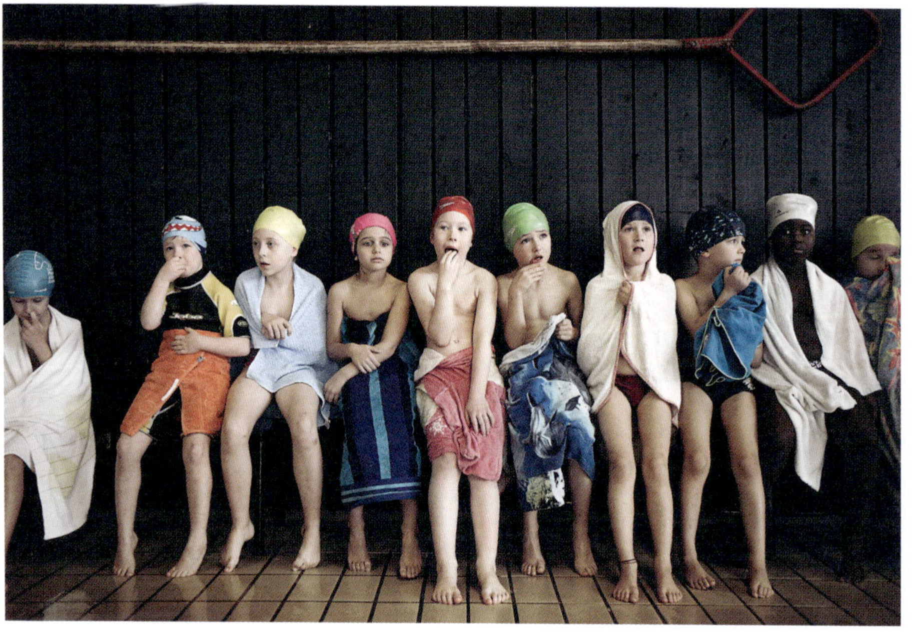

Childhood Once More
by Simon Chang
Ljubljana, Slovenia

Students of Waldorf School captured after a morning swimming lesson.

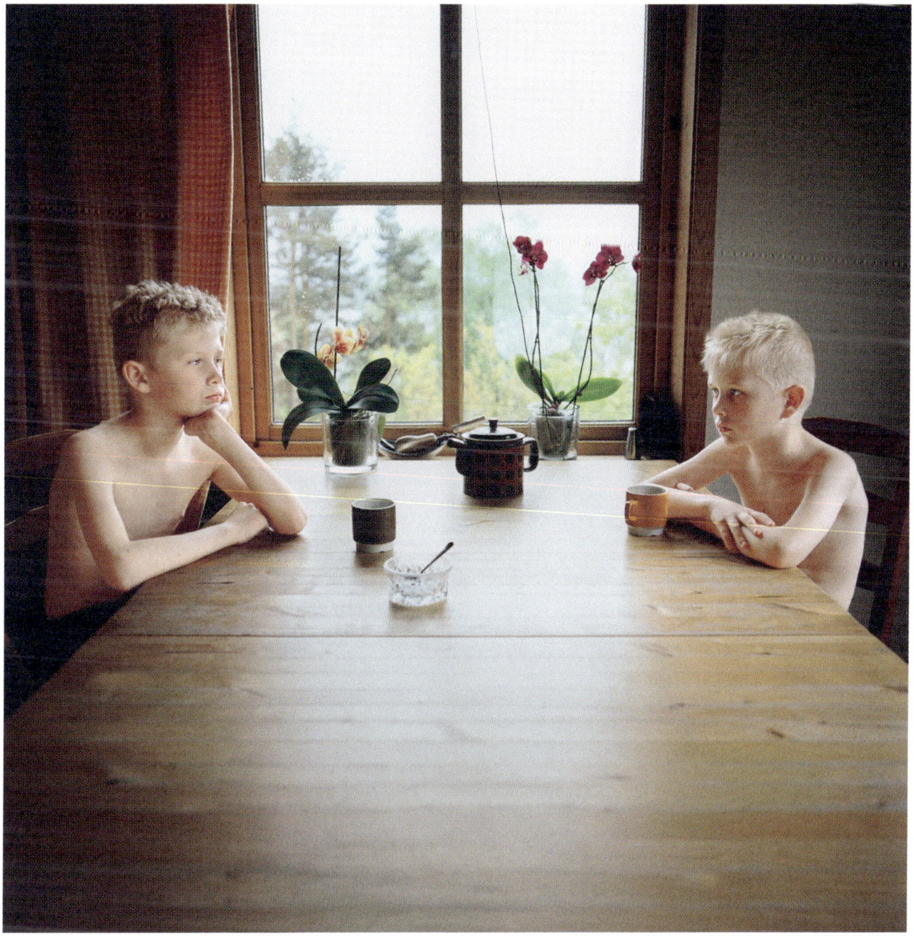

Magnus and Brage
by Viktoria Sorochinski
Halsnøy, Norway

I could sense the closeness of these brothers, even in silence. They were eager to be photographed and seemed happy to share their world with me, perhaps due to the lonely and secluded nature of the island on which they live.

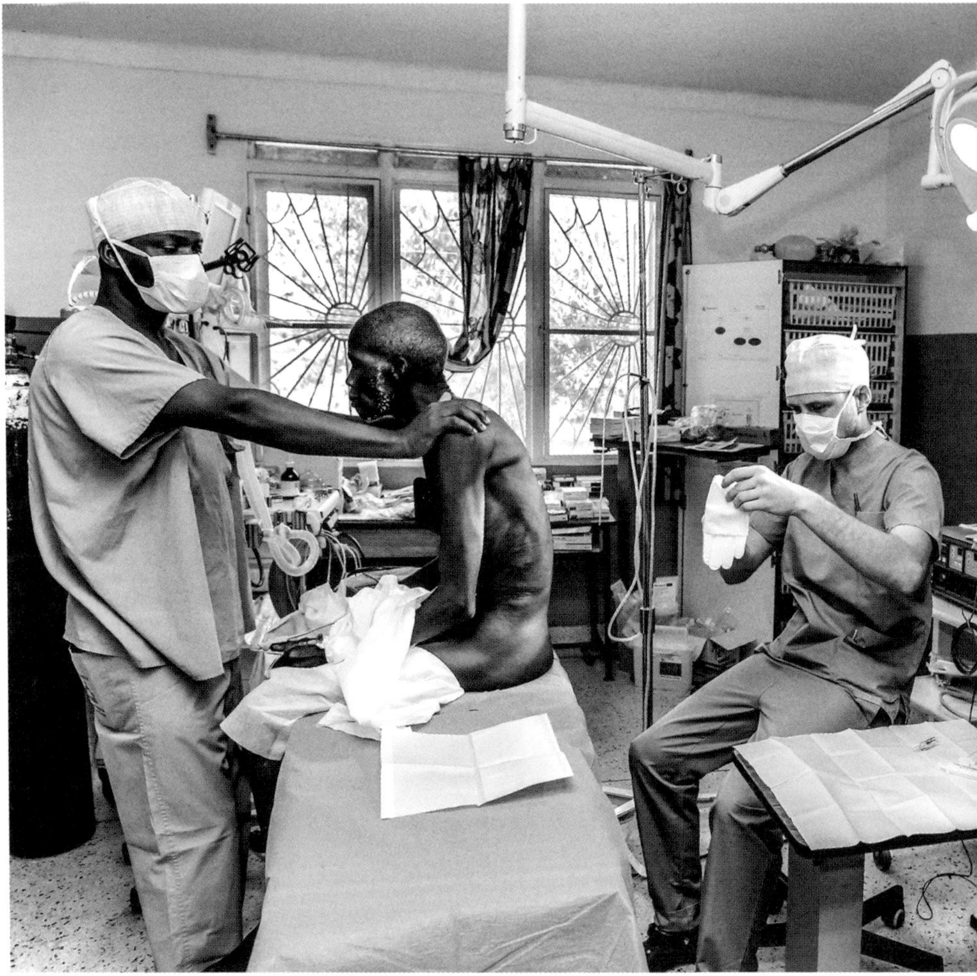

Together We Are Strong
by Marie-Pascale Vandewalle
Mbale, Uganda

An African doctor and two Flemish doctors prepare a patient – a local Ugandan man – for surgery. It's the first time the man has been cared for by professional doctors.

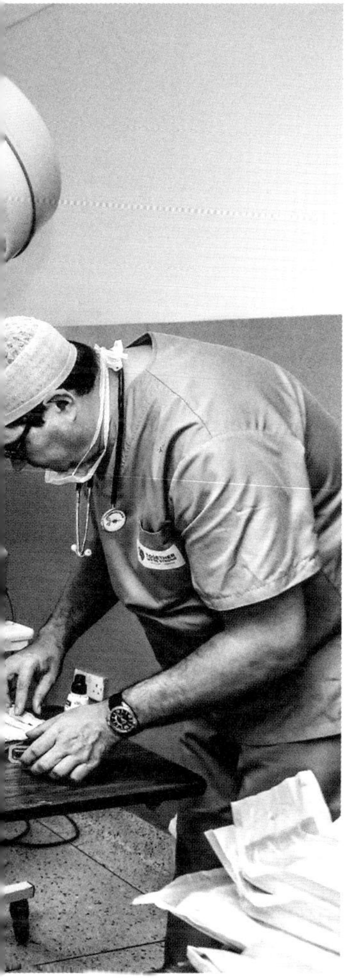

Jacob

by Laura Pannack

Brighton, UK

Jacob was a boy I scouted in Brighton. I looked around parks and met him and a group of friends. He was incredibly suspicious and refused to be photographed until the very last minute. This was part of an assignment for *TIME* magazine about the vulnerability of young men.

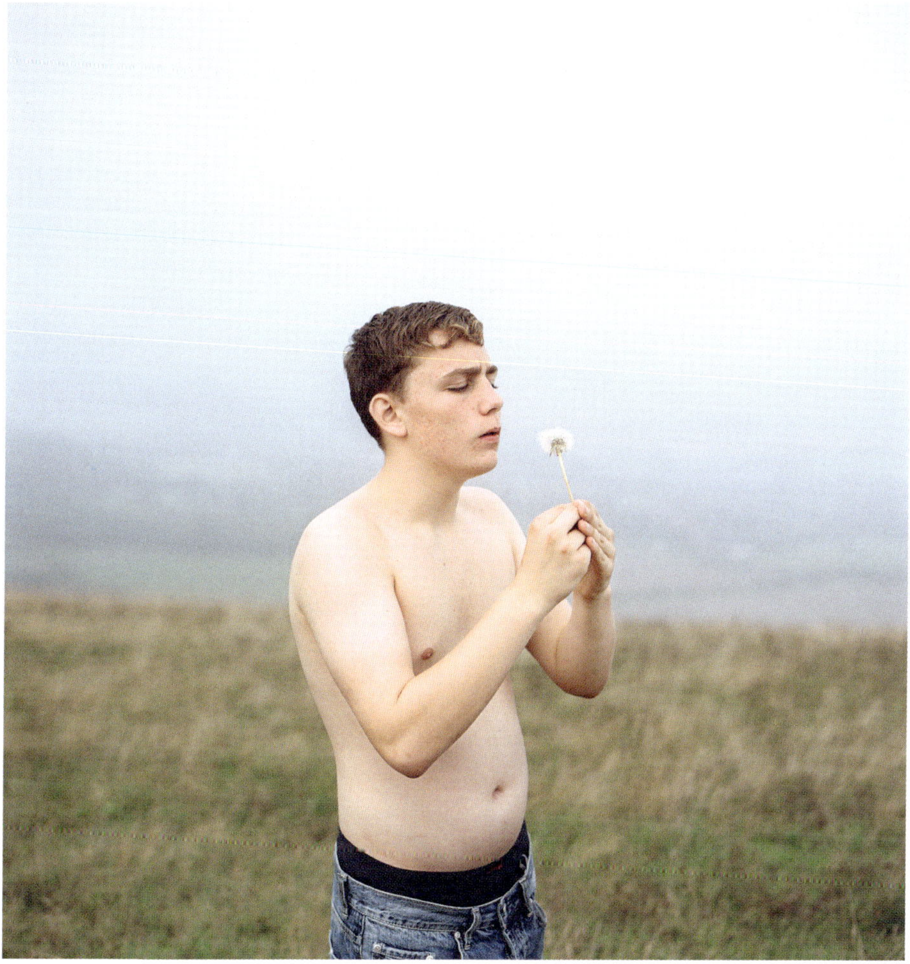

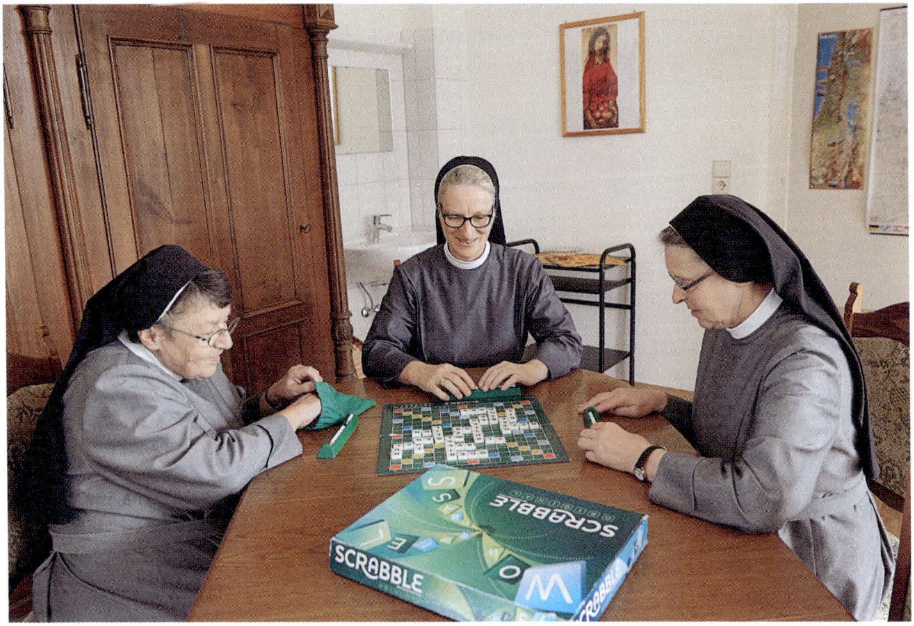

Sisters in Spirit

by Ulrike Froemel

Schramberg, Germany

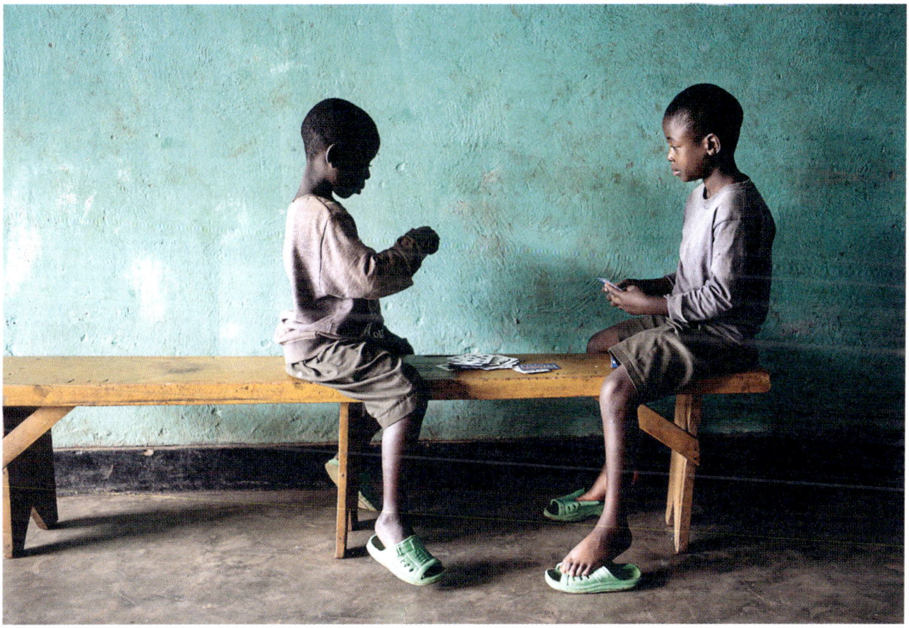

Eric and Claude

by Patricia Gutiérrez

Kabarondo, Rwanda

Eric and Claude have lived at the Streets Ahead Children's Centre Association from birth. As the youngest kids at the boys' centre they have formed a special bond. Resources are scarce, but when children feel safe they find joy in the small things such as a game of cards.

Mustafa Can Be Happy

by Milad Gorgin

Vienna, Austria

When I met Mustafa Tavakoli, who is originally from Afghanistan, he was waiting to hear if his asylum application to stay in Austria had been accepted. After living for a time in Iran, he had moved to Europe in 2015. Mustafa enjoys playing football with friends who have taught him some tricks.

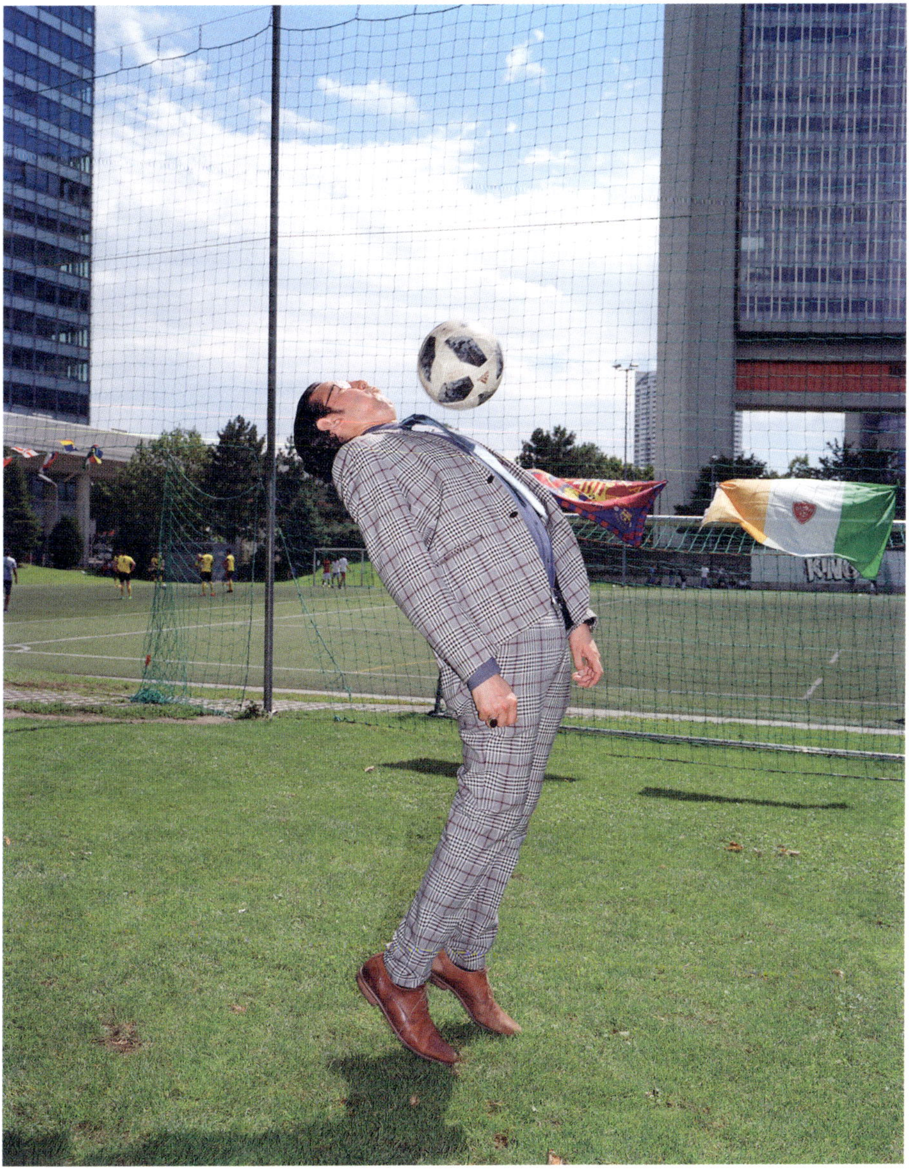

Boxer Brothers

by Luca Sage

Accra, Ghana

Fighting is a way of life in Bukom, a busy, noisy neighbourhood that has produced several champion boxers. These two young brothers belong to a street boxing club attended by kids between four and 18 years old. Every week, local people gather to watch the fights.

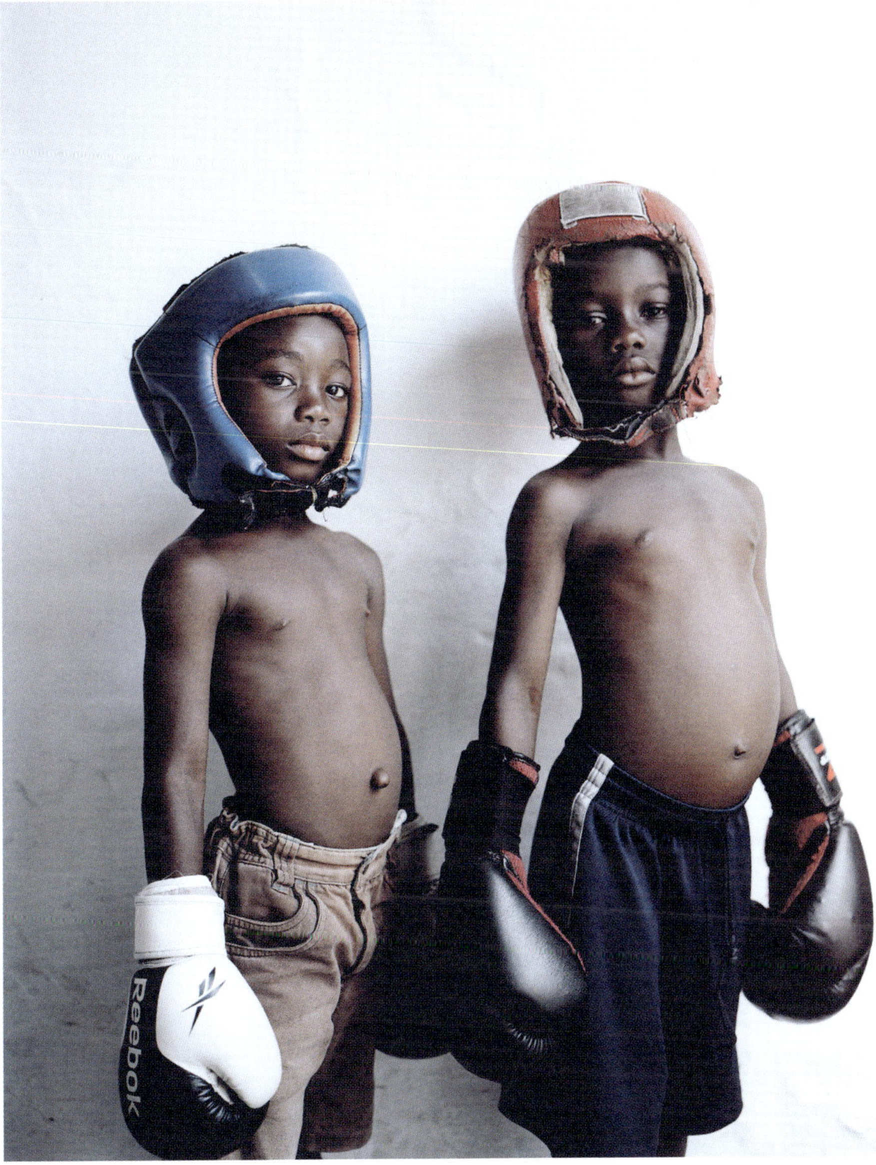
Reebok

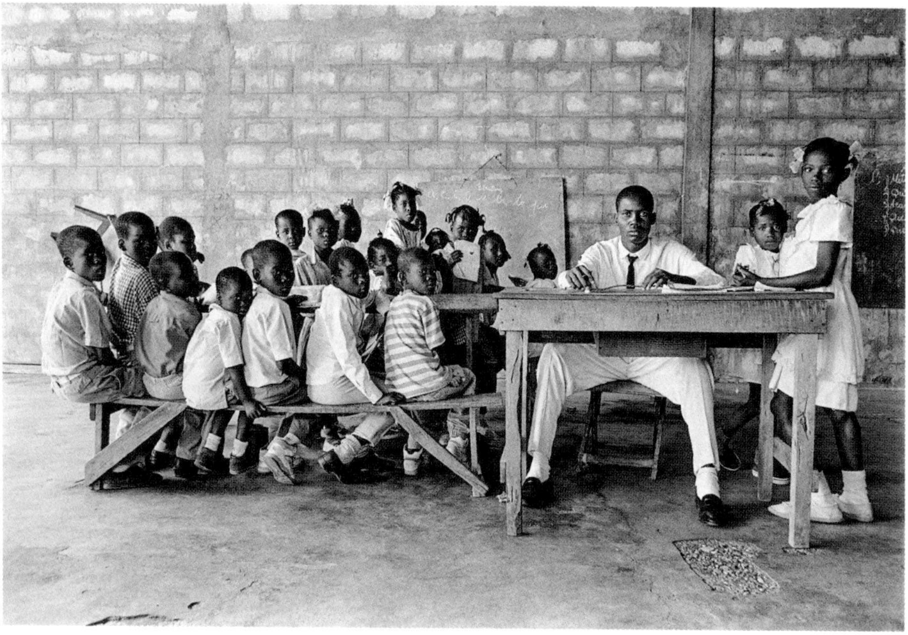

The Classroom

by Matias Recart

Port-au-Prince, Haiti

The classroom was substandard but the teacher and students were well dressed which evoked a sense of dignity that resonated with me.

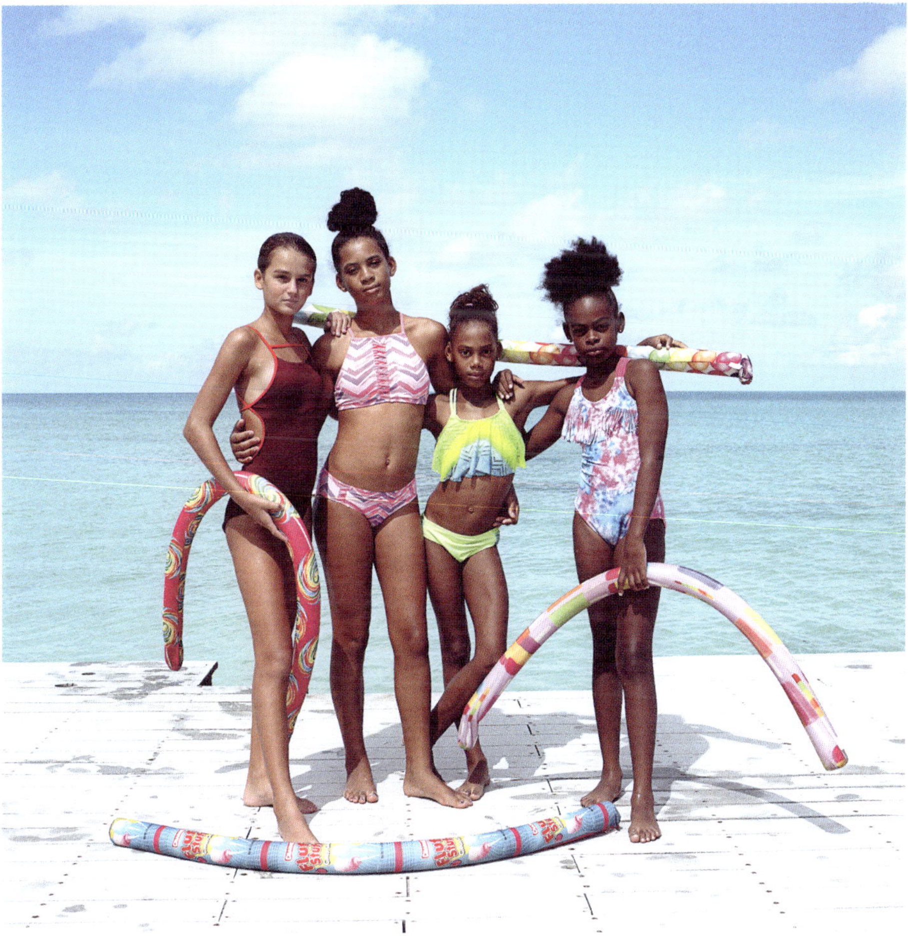

Generation Z

by Nicola Muirhead

Sandys Parish, Bermuda

A group of girls on the cusp of adolescence enjoy an afternoon swim at the abandoned resort of 9 Beaches on the West end of the island, known to locals for its secluded location and empty beaches.

Horse Rider

by Li Wei

Hulunbuir Grasslands, Inner Mongolia, China

A horse rider wearing traditional Mongolian horse racing attire poses in the vast livestock grazing area of northern China's Inner Mongolia Autonomous Region.

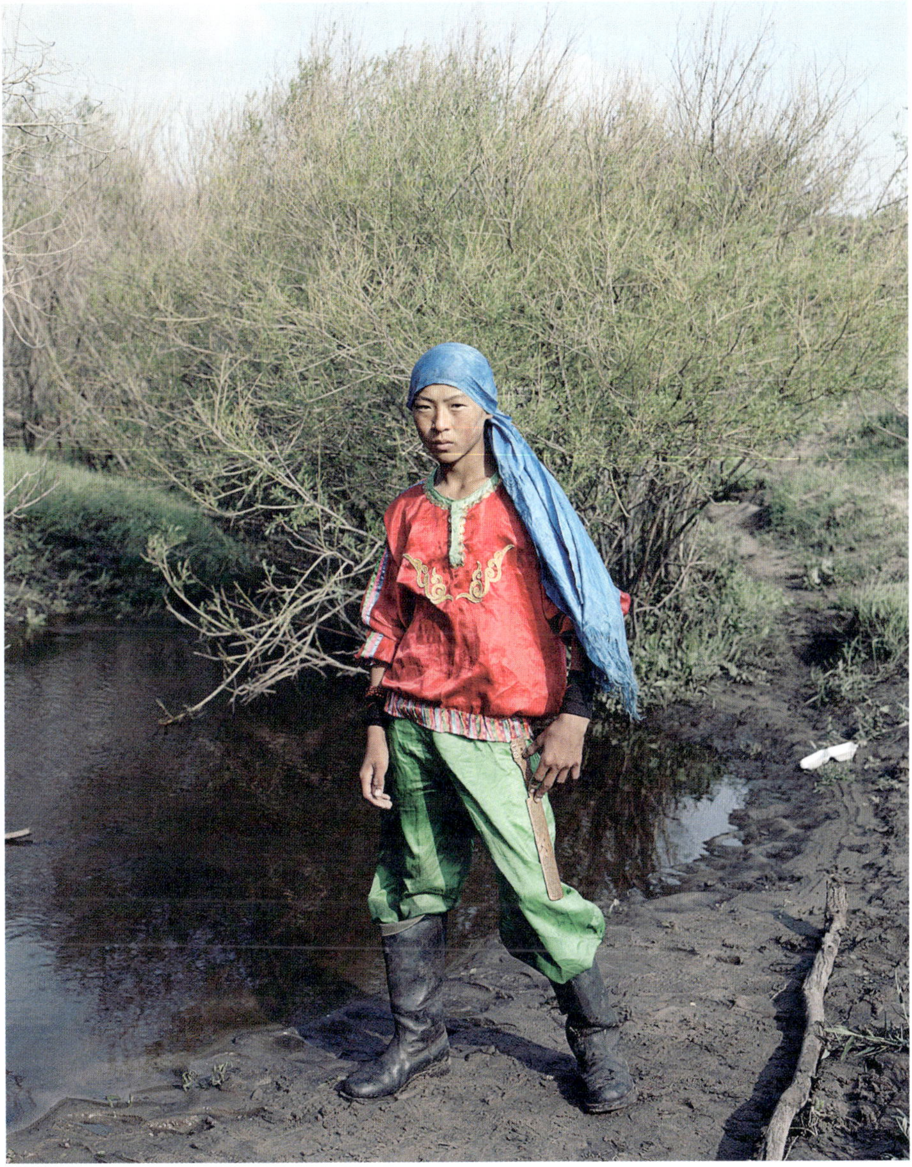

Grace and Roxi the Dog

by Deirdre Brennan
Dublin, Ireland

It was an unusually warm summer day when I saw 10-year-old Grace walking towards me with Roxi. I took this portrait for a project about the people of The Liberties, one of the oldest parts of Dublin.

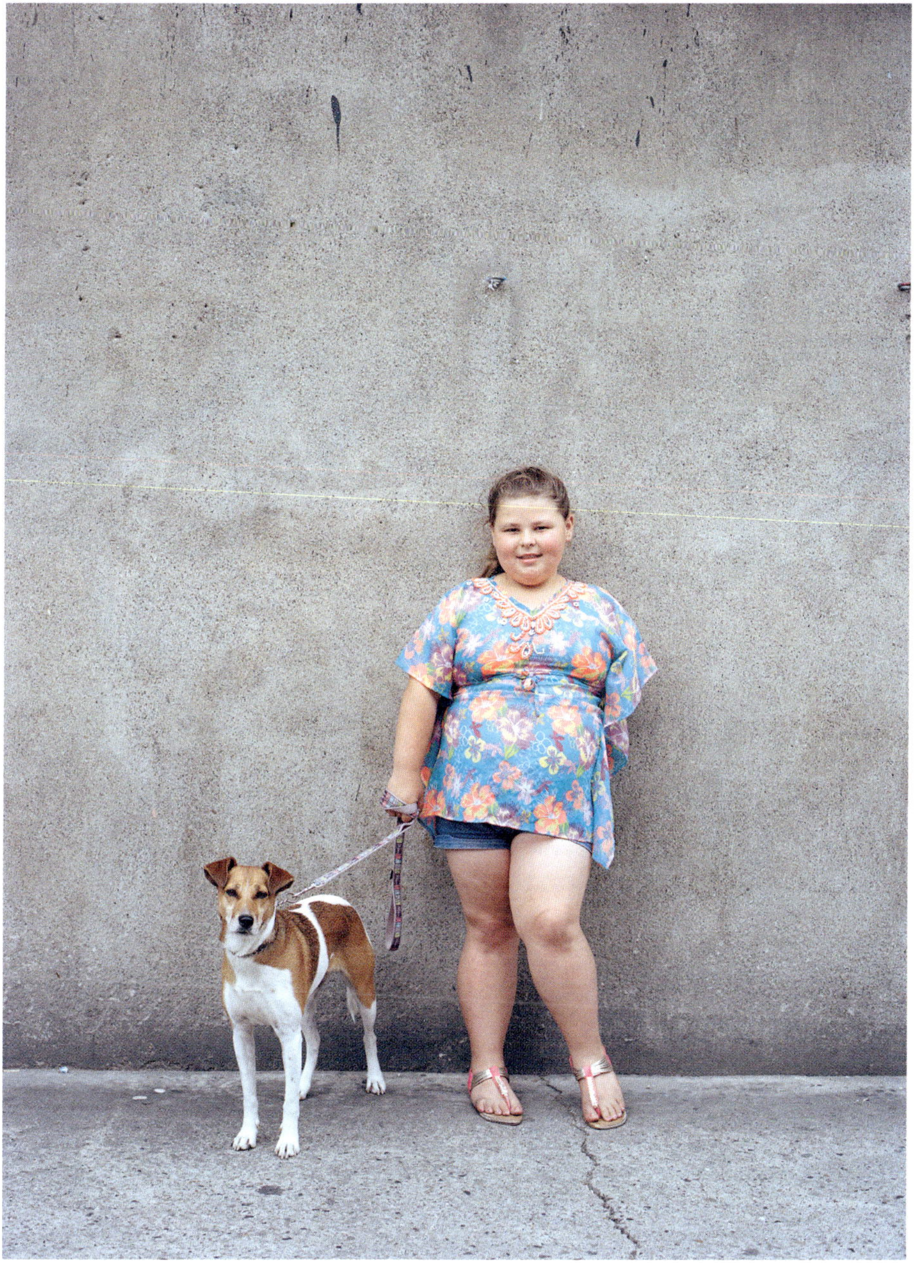

Eye to Eye with Khizra

by Andrea Francolini

Shitindas, Gilgit-Baltistan, Pakistan

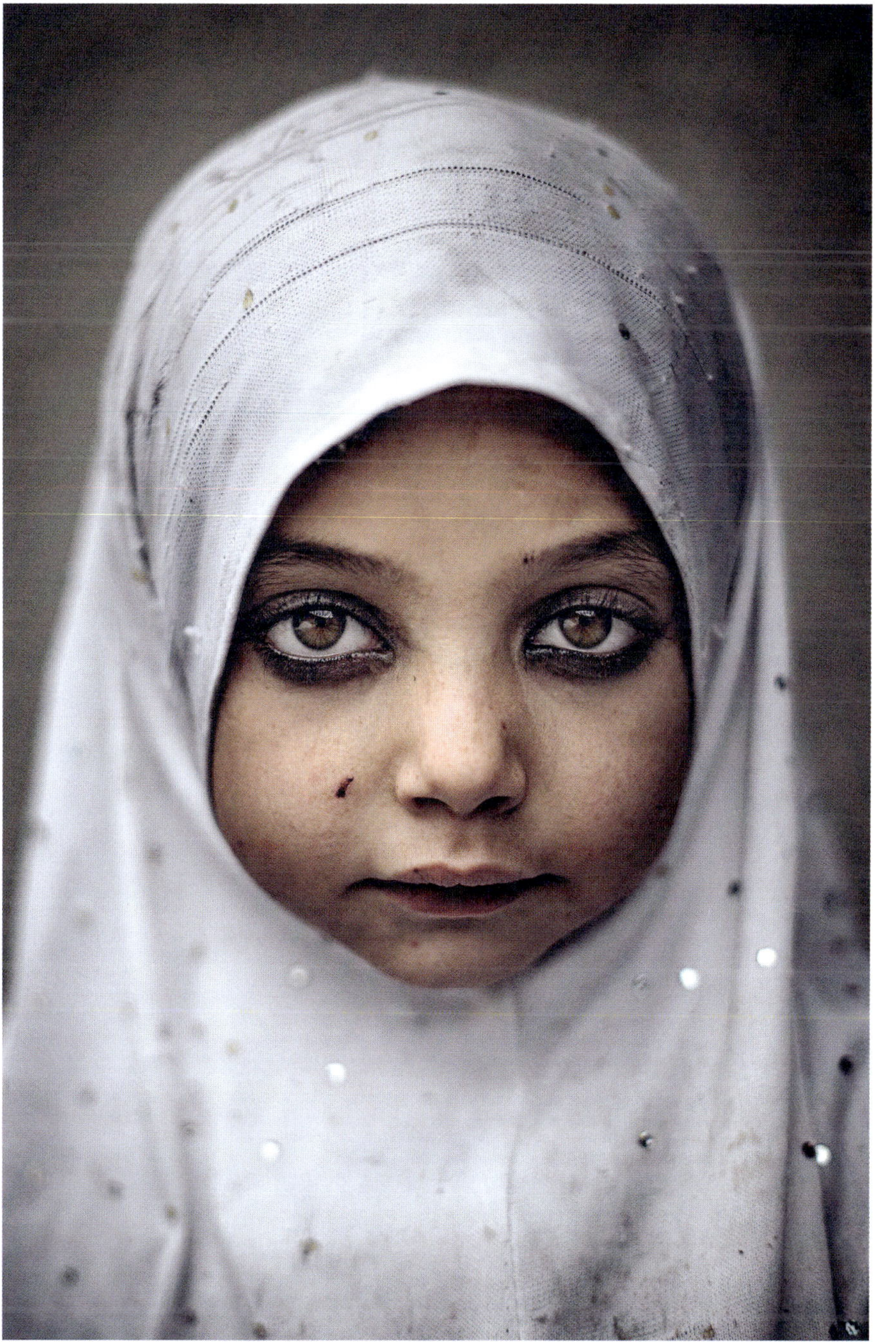

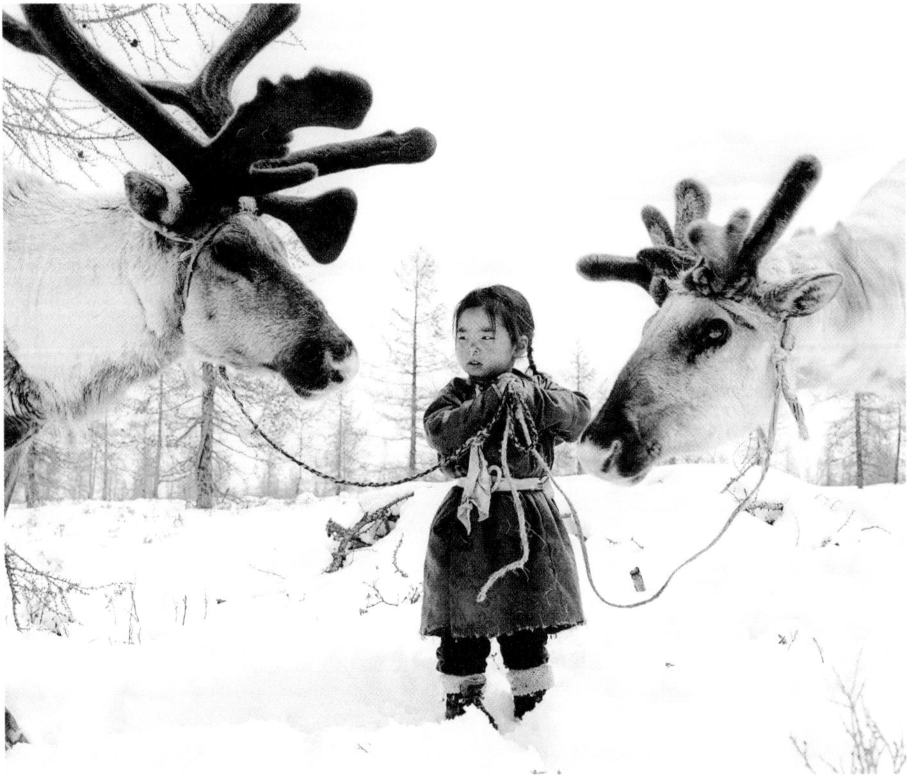

Young Dukha Girl with Reindeer
by Jeroen Toirkens
Taiga, Mongolia

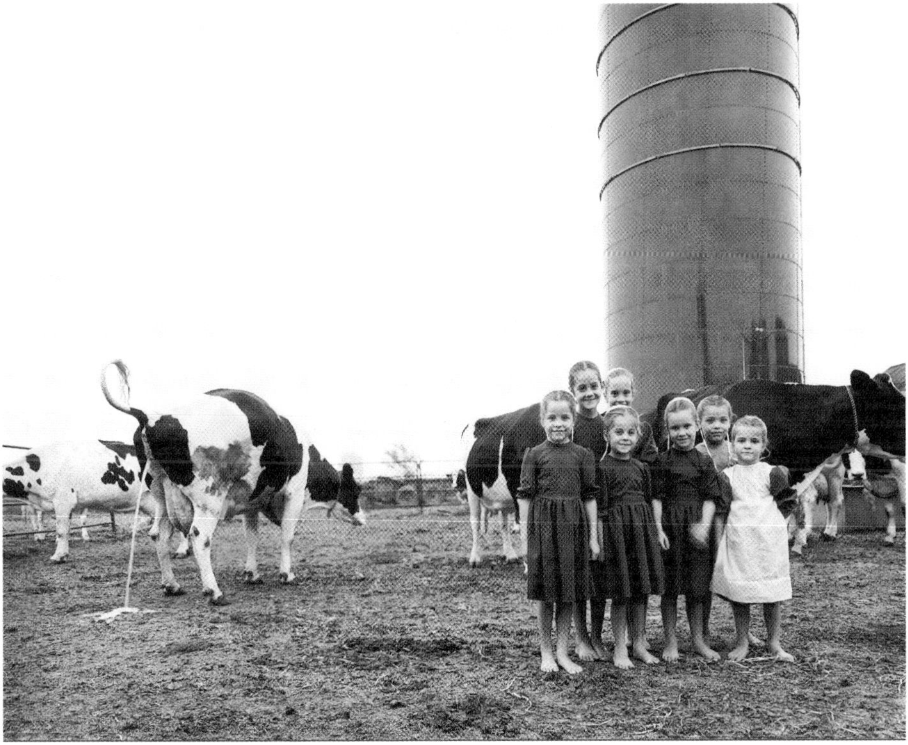

Seven Little Amish Girls and One Cow Peeing

by Martin H.M. Schreiber

Intercourse, Pennsylvania, USA

The girls heard the cow peeing and tried
to hold back their laughter.

Ash Wednesday

by Luke Brossette

New York City, New York, USA

I was outside St Patrick's Cathedral one morning and noticed people leaving the building with ash on their foreheads. This lady passed by me and, drawn to her aura and grace, I ran after her and she kindly agreed to a portrait. Ash Wednesday derives its name from repentance ashes on the forehead of Christians. It also is the first day of Lent, a period of fasting, restraint and abstention.

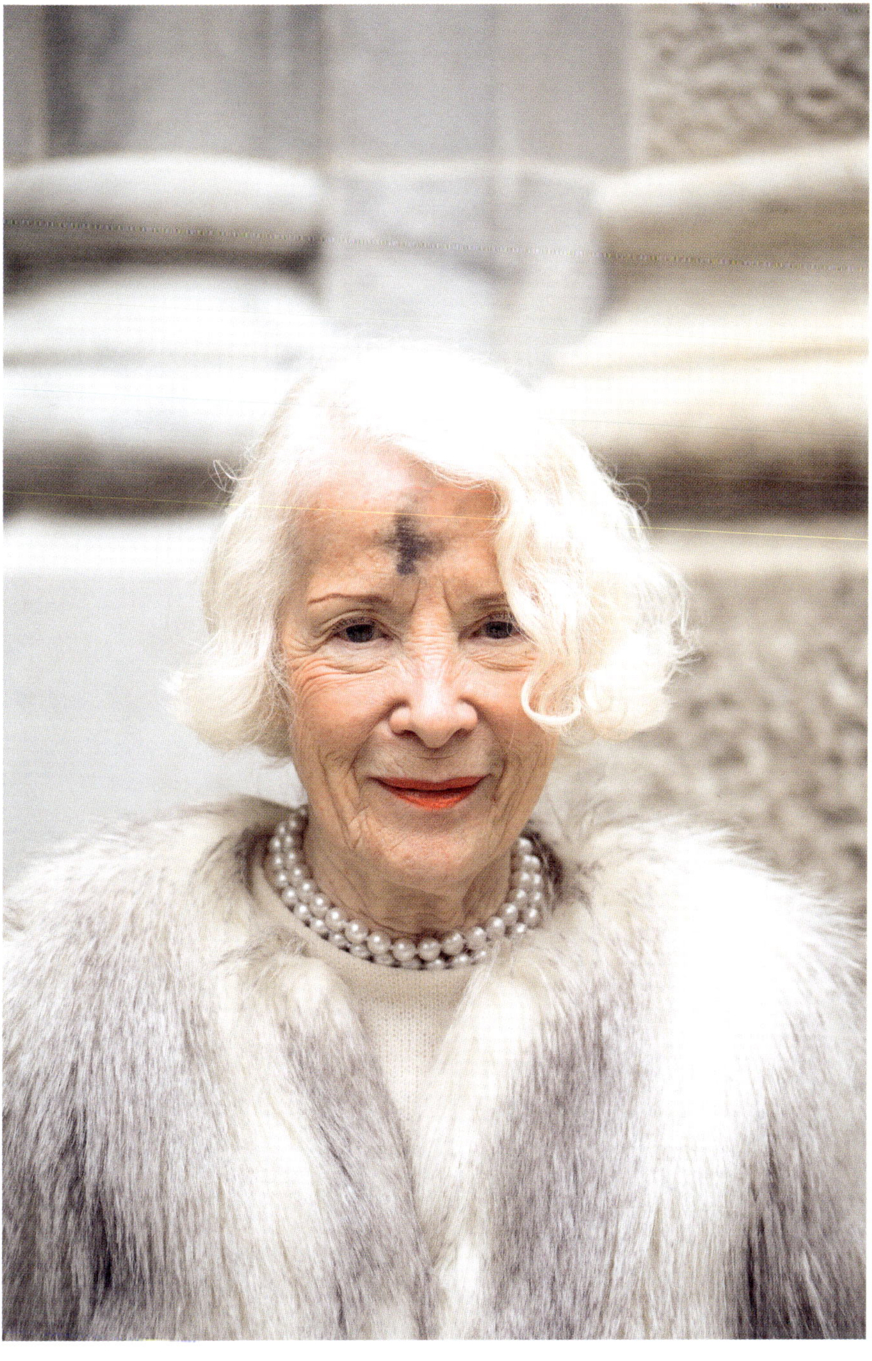

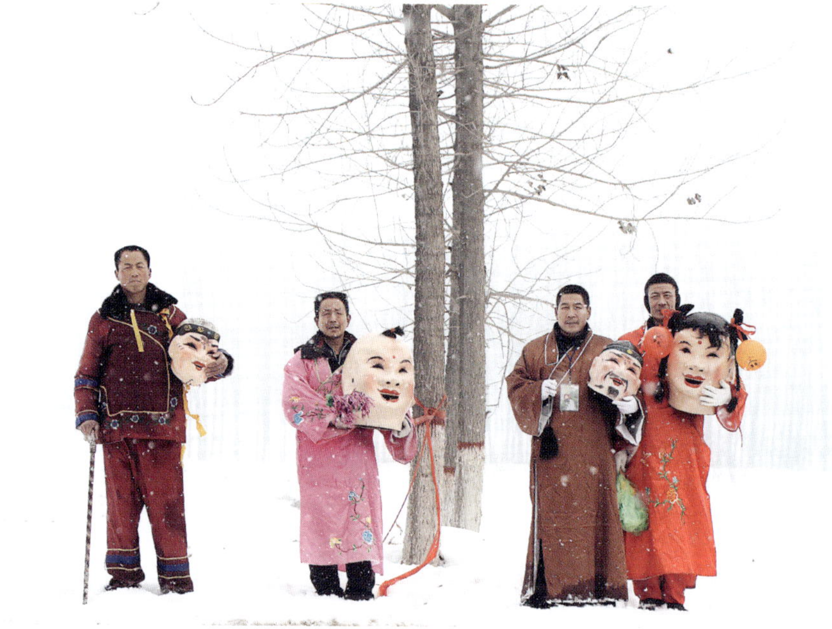

Four Performers

by Qin Xufeng

Qixian, Henan, China

During the Lantern Festival, which takes place on the 15th day of the first Chinese lunar month, people celebrate by dressing up, dancing and singing. It is a time of joy, happiness and peace. I spotted these entertainers as they made their way to a performance.

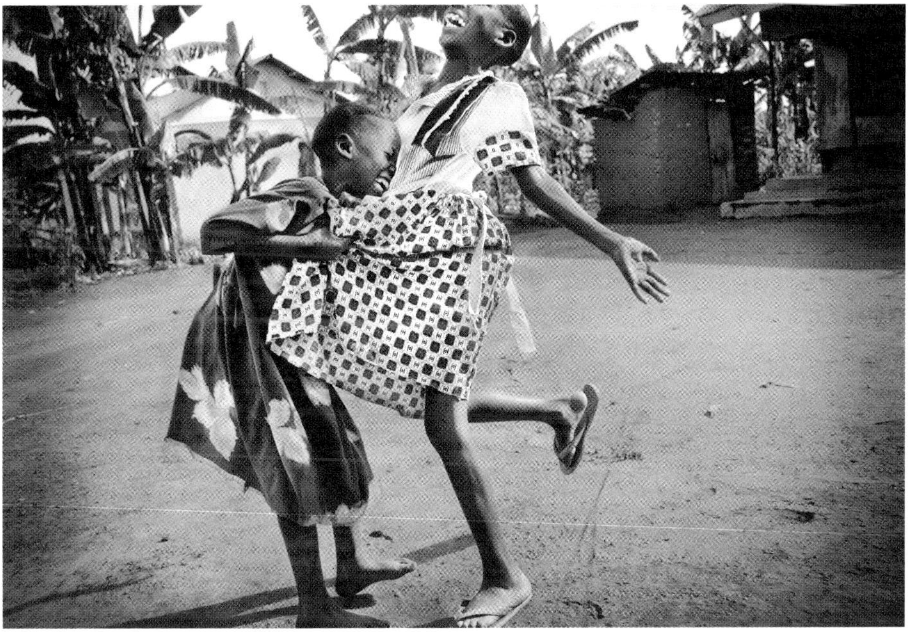

Girls Laughing
by Leslie Alsheimer
Rakai, Uganda

Seeing children at play and witnessing their infectious laughter despite living in an oppressive environment showed me the profound resilience of the human spirit.

Cherry in Her Garden

by Robert Timothy

Cape Town, South Africa

Cherry is a renowned landscape gardener.
I've heard people call her garden 'a sanctuary'.

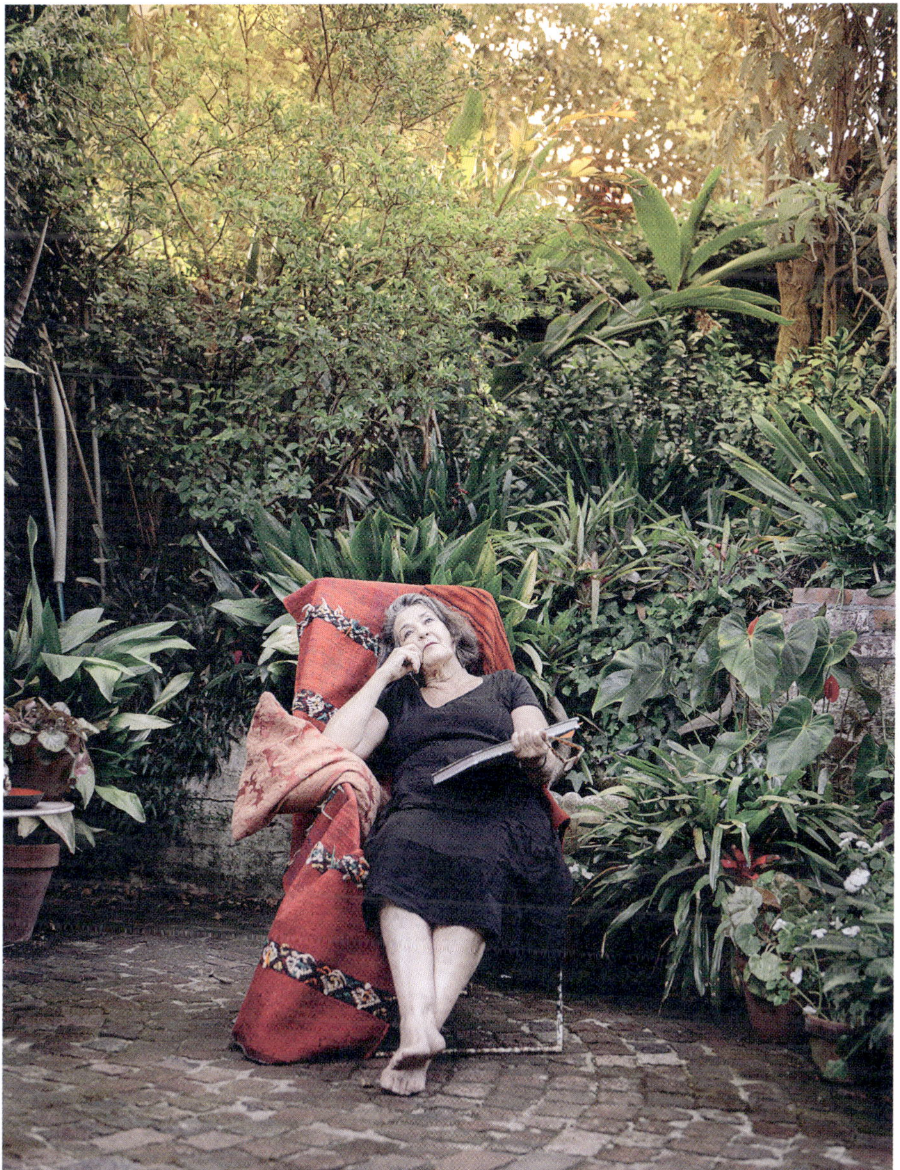

Coco Disturbed Reading

by Sarah Weal
Stroud, UK

This is my friend's 16-year-old daughter Coco Hepner. I was having breakfast and she was reading. I noticed the serendipity of the light on Coco's hair and how it was the same colour as the chair.

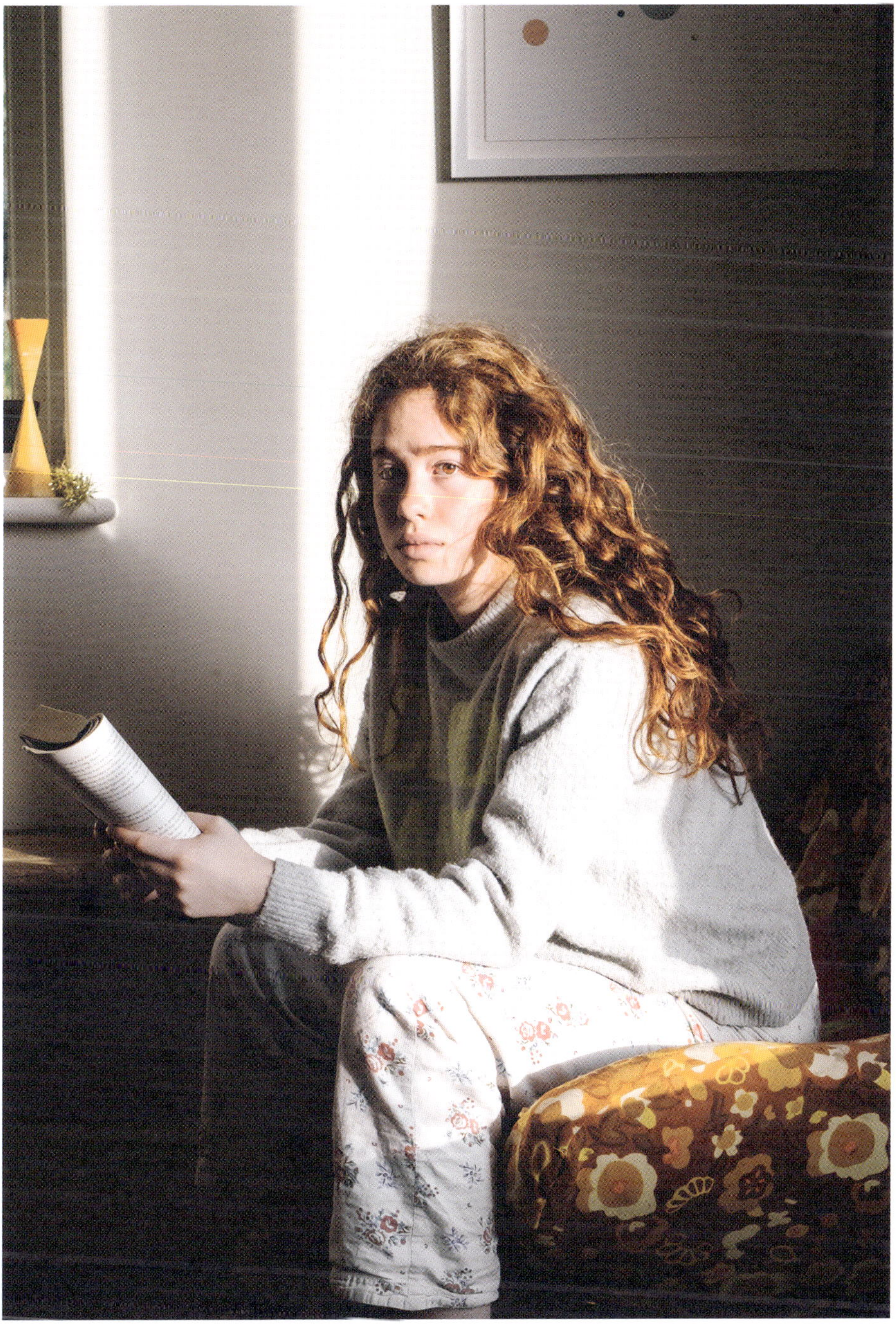

Paul

by Linelle Deunk

Mukono District, Uganda

When I first met Paul and asked him about his childhood he closed his eyes and sang a lullaby. I later learnt that he lost his parents at age 12 and was mistreated in foster care. He has now found a loving family home.

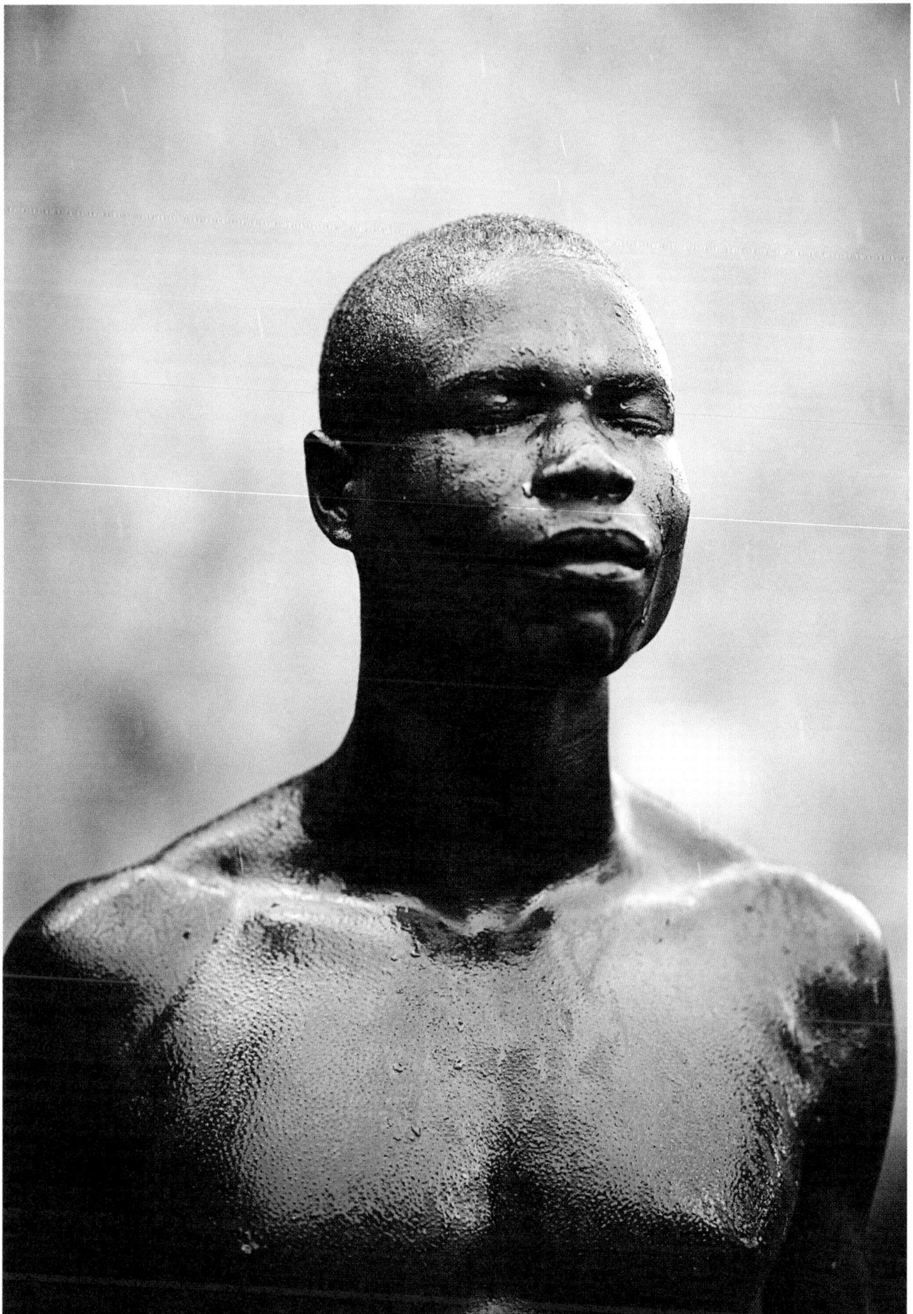

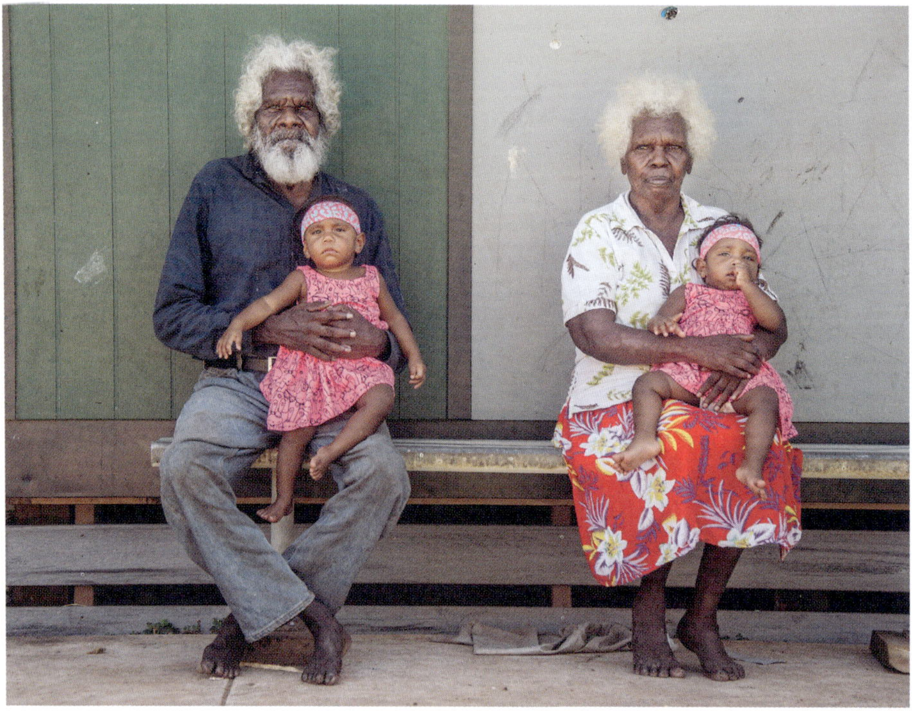

Generations

by Brian Cassey

Aurukun, Australia

Village elders Silas and Rebecca Wolmby pose with their great-grandchildren, twins Shalona and Keola Wolmby, in Cape York Peninsula in a remote part of northern Australia.

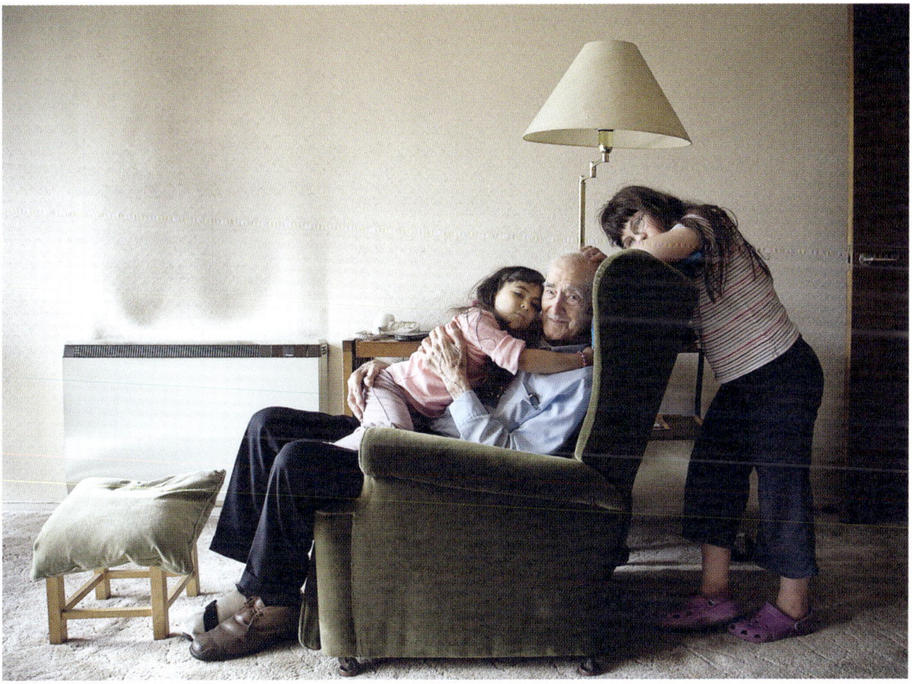

Uncle Tim, Noa and Ophir
by Fiona Yaron-Field
London, UK

Born in 1906, Uncle Tim grew up in an old Jewish community in the north of England, served in the British Army in India, lived through two world wars, saw communism rise and fall and witnessed the technological revolution, yet he appeared untouched and unmoved by change. He barely spoke but his silence filled my imagination with stories of the past.

Summer

by Sem Langendijk

Amsterdam, The Netherlands

For 20 years, the Amsterdamsche Droogdok Maatschappij, or ADM, was home to a squatter community who held festivals in the former shipyard. Summer, who is from the US, visited the site to perform with her band. The community was evicted in January 2019.

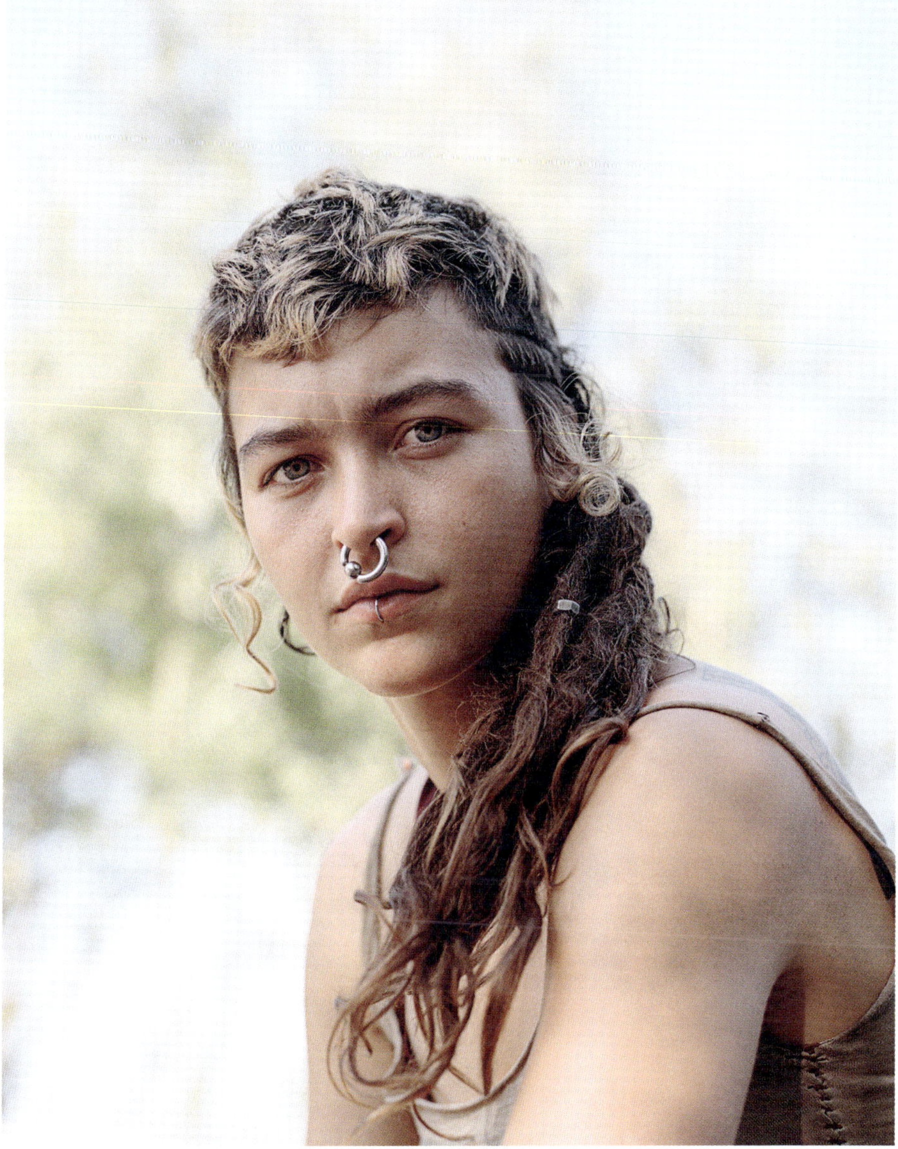

Cora-Allan and her Son, Chaske-Waste

by Kali Spitzer

Banff, Alberta, Canada

This is my good friend Cora-Allan Wickliffe and her son Chaske-Waste Kaitiaki-Twiss. Cora-Allan is Maori-Niuean and her son is Maori-Niuean-Lakota. When I met her at the Banff Centre for Arts and Creativity in Canada she was focusing on reviving traditional arts from her community as part of an Indigenous artist residency.

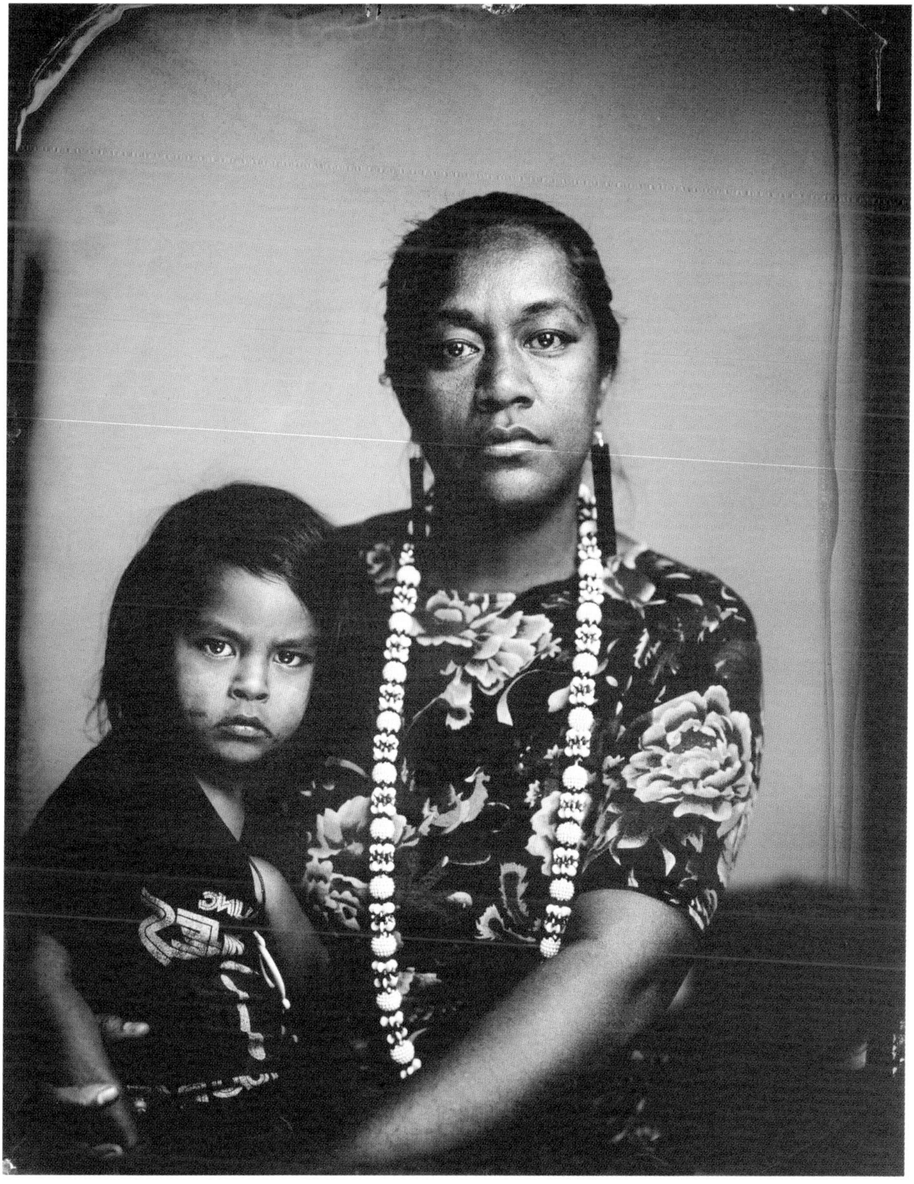

Mary

by Hui Choi

Guangzhou, Guangdong, China

Fifteen-year-old Mary is from Russia. This was the first time she had come to Guangzhou. She is working hard for her supermodel dream.

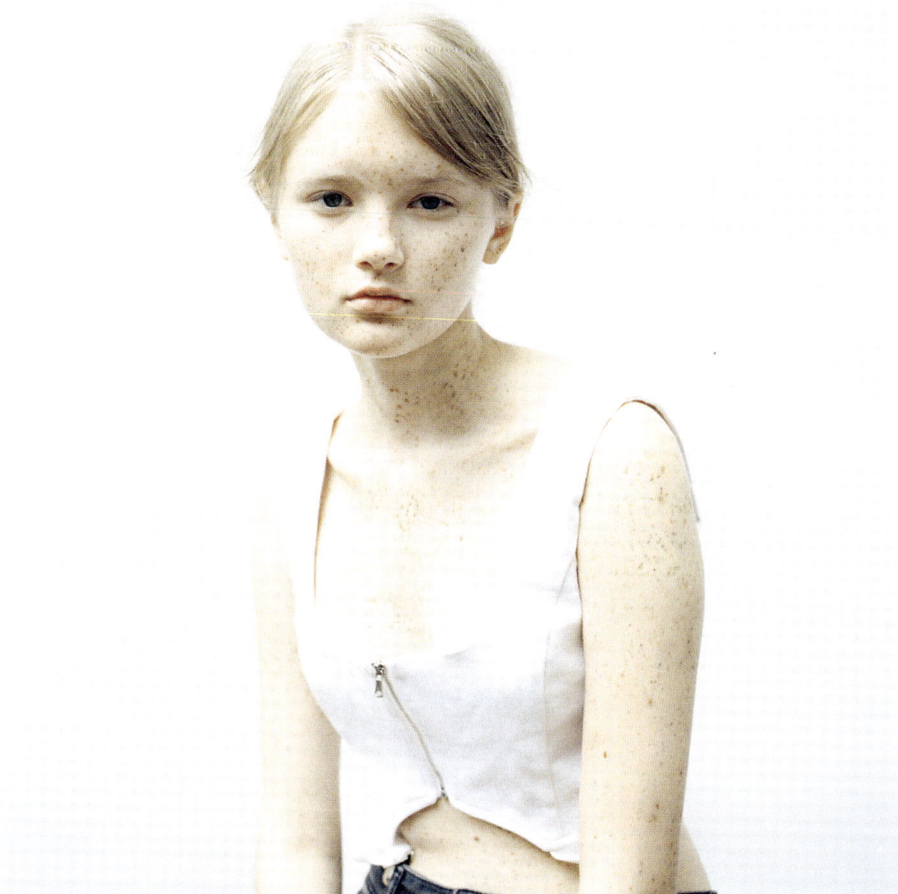

Salum

by Patrick Gries

Dar es Salaam, Tanzania

Eleven-year-old Salum lived in a boarding school run by The Salvation Army. He was extremely shy and wouldn't lift his chin or look up.

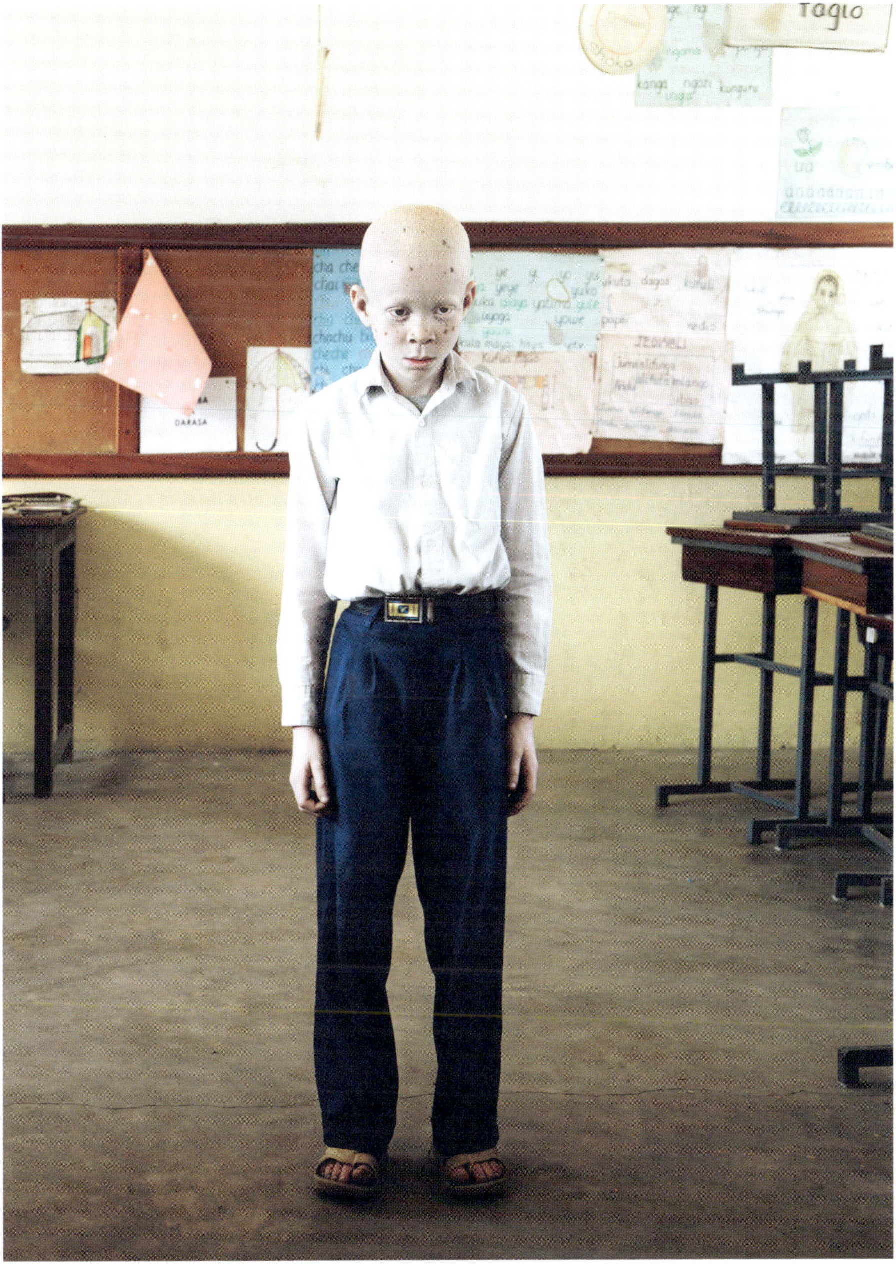
DARASA

Korean War Veteran

by Rami Hyun

Seoul, South Korea

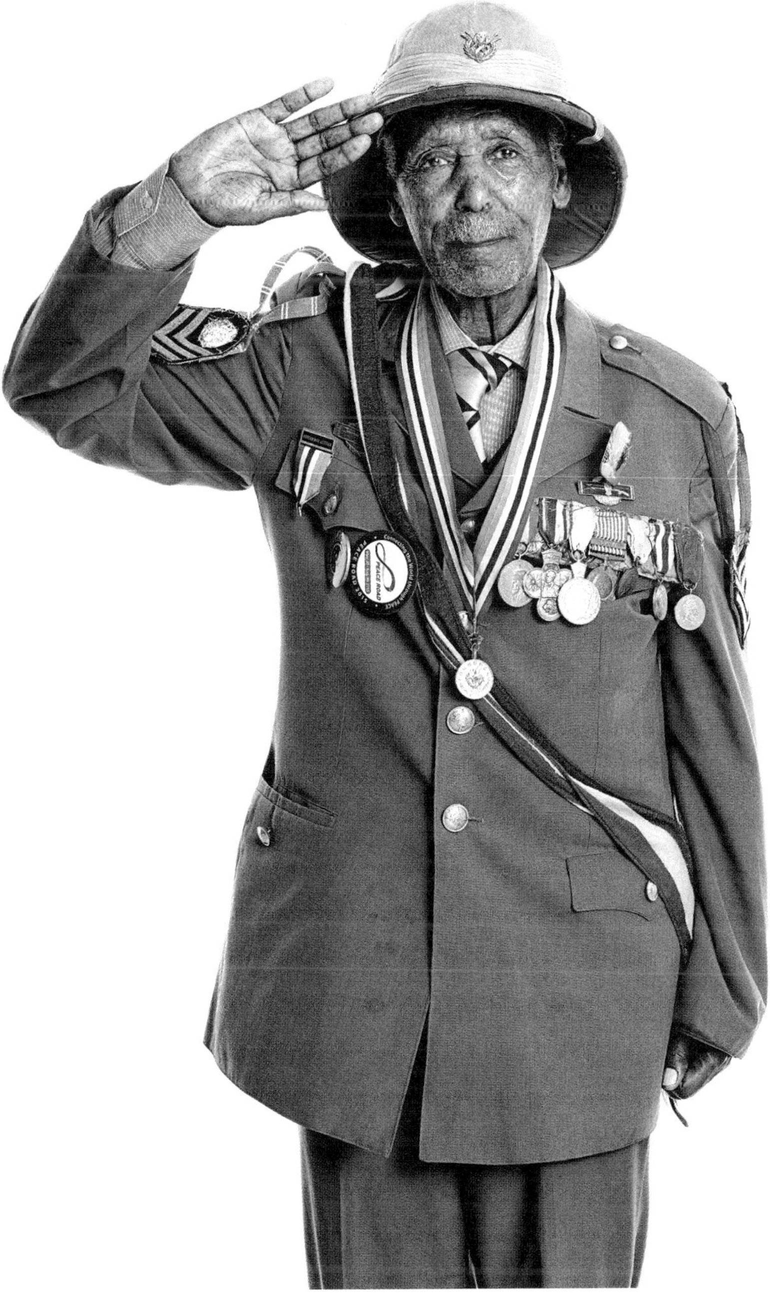

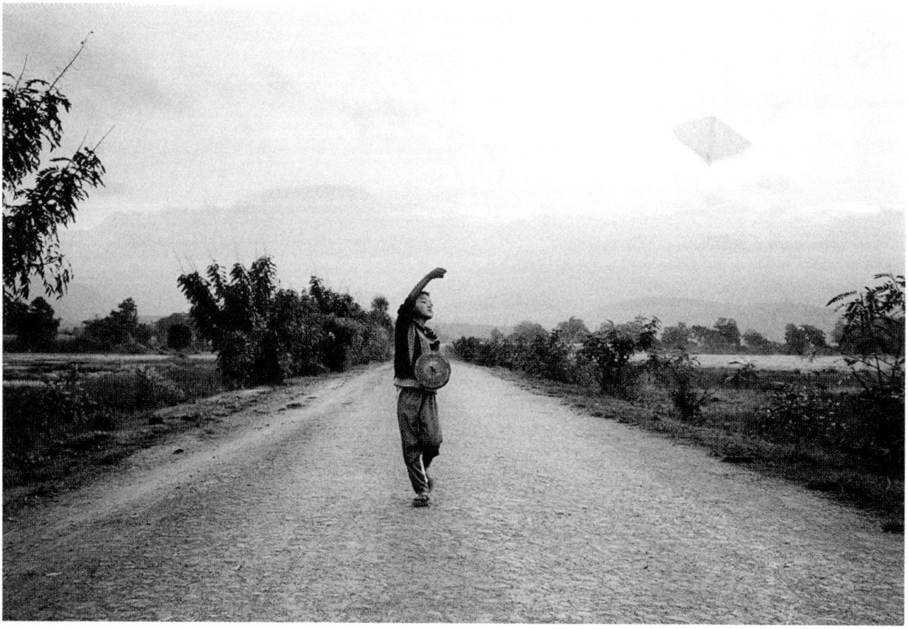

Boy with a Kite

by Lionel Briot

Nyaungshwe, Shan State, Myanmar

I spent a couple of weeks at Inle Lake in the centre of Myanmar. I like taking pictures at dawn when I can observe early morning life around the calm waters. I was walking along the road towards the lake when I saw an approaching silhouette. The boy did not notice me. He was more interested in making his kite fly.

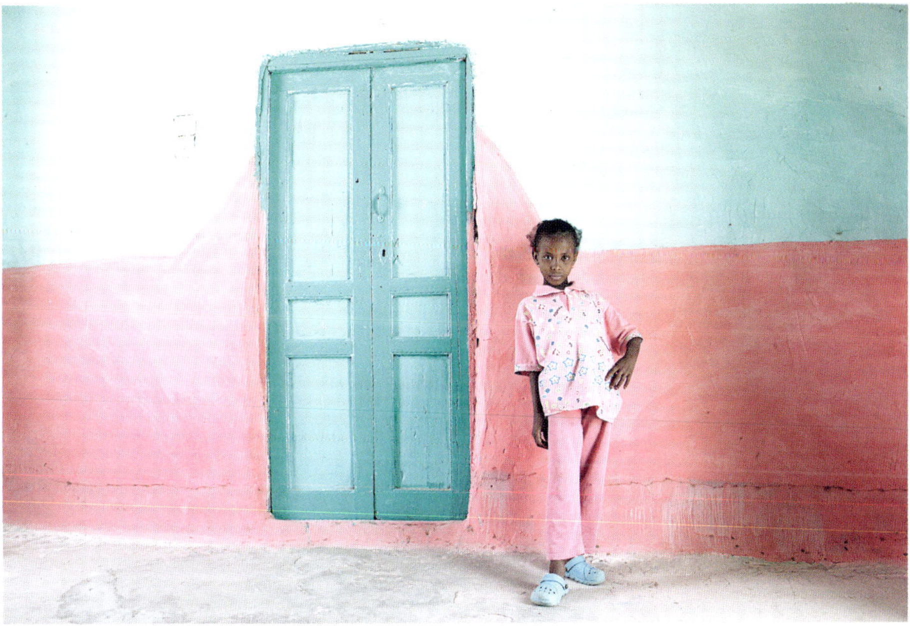

Amna

by Sara Younes

Hesa Island, Aswan, Egypt

Farewell

by Maria Grazia Granati

Higuera de la Sierra, Spain

Matadora María Serra Plasencia after her final fight. She had been pinned to the ground by the bull whose horns tore her jacket and trousers. Despite its death, the bull was still considered to have won; her impresario was not impressed with her performance. María later decided to abandon the bullfighting world she so desperately wanted to be a part of.

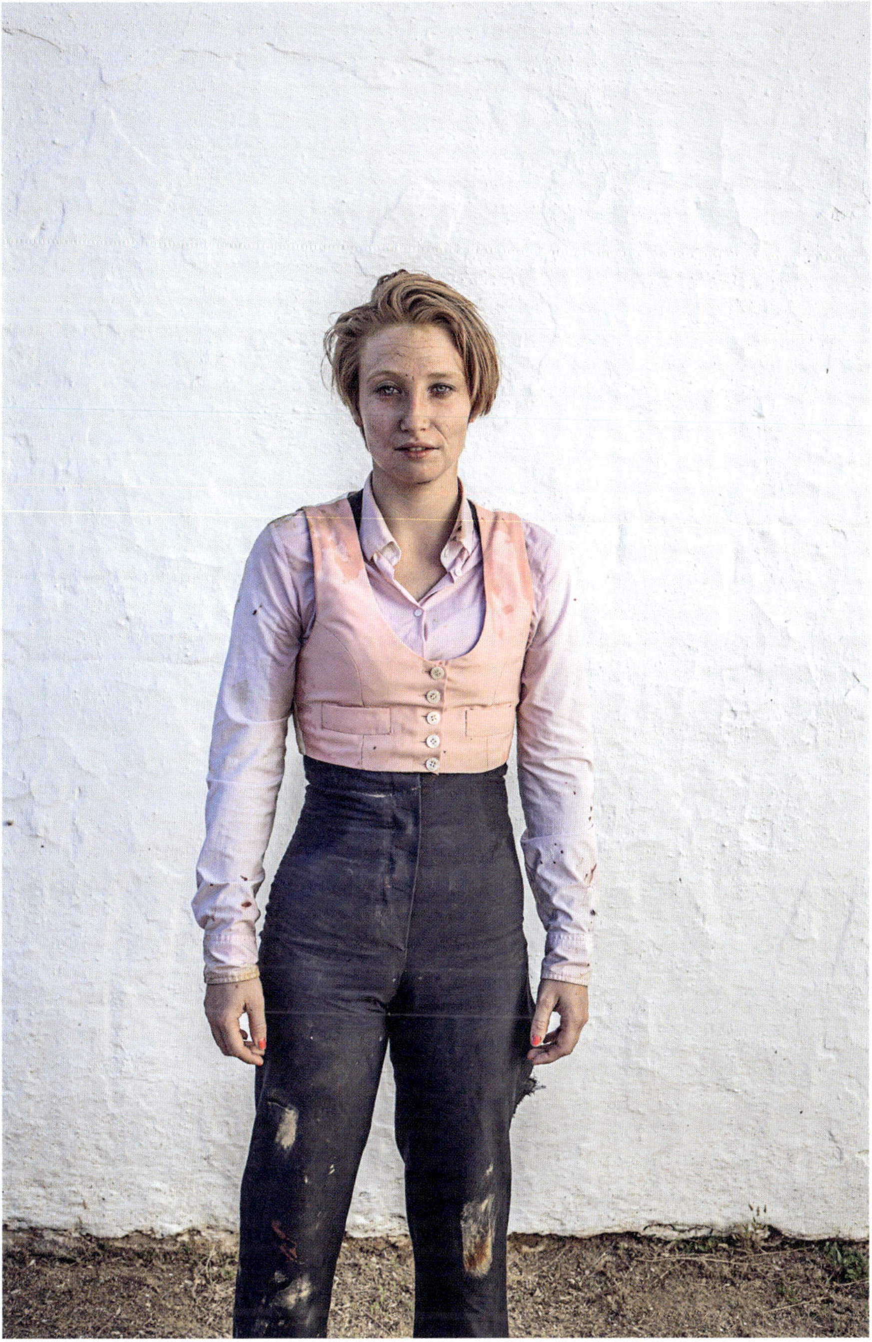

Kpayo

by Perttu Saksa

Comè, Benin

Kpayo, meaning 'leftover', is commonly used to describe cheap petrol sold on the streets. A discarded empty petrol container makes a useful vessel for carrying water, as Edoh discovers.

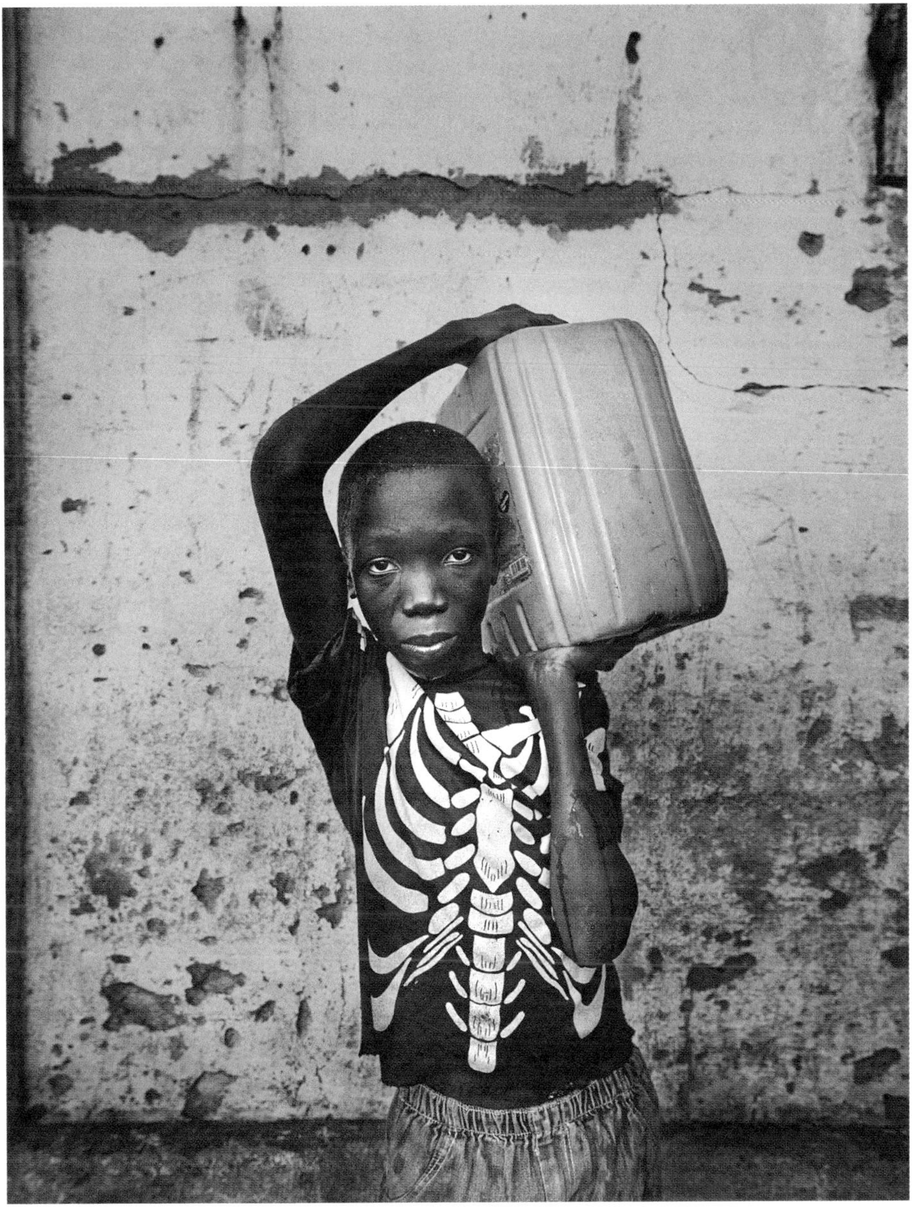

Yolina Invisible

by Erika Blanco

Sosúa, Dominican Republic

Yolina is a Haitian street vendor who sells fruit.
Many woman in Sosúa carry out this job
yet they seem to be invisible to society.

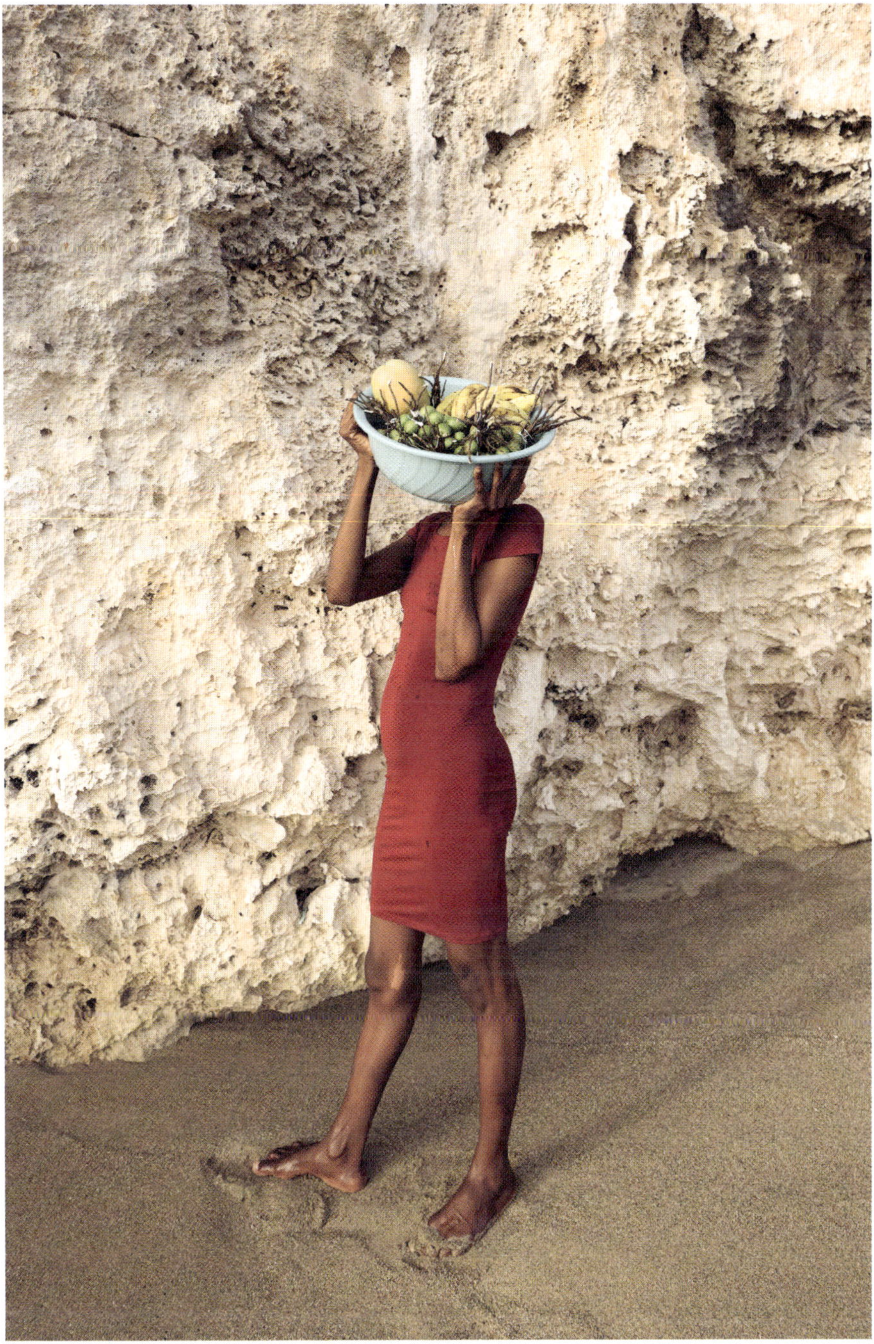

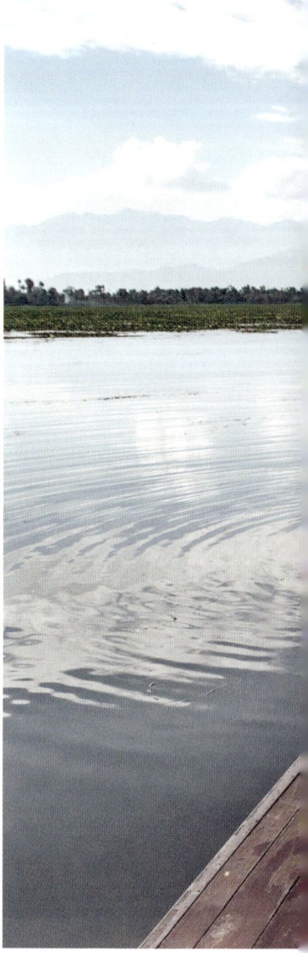

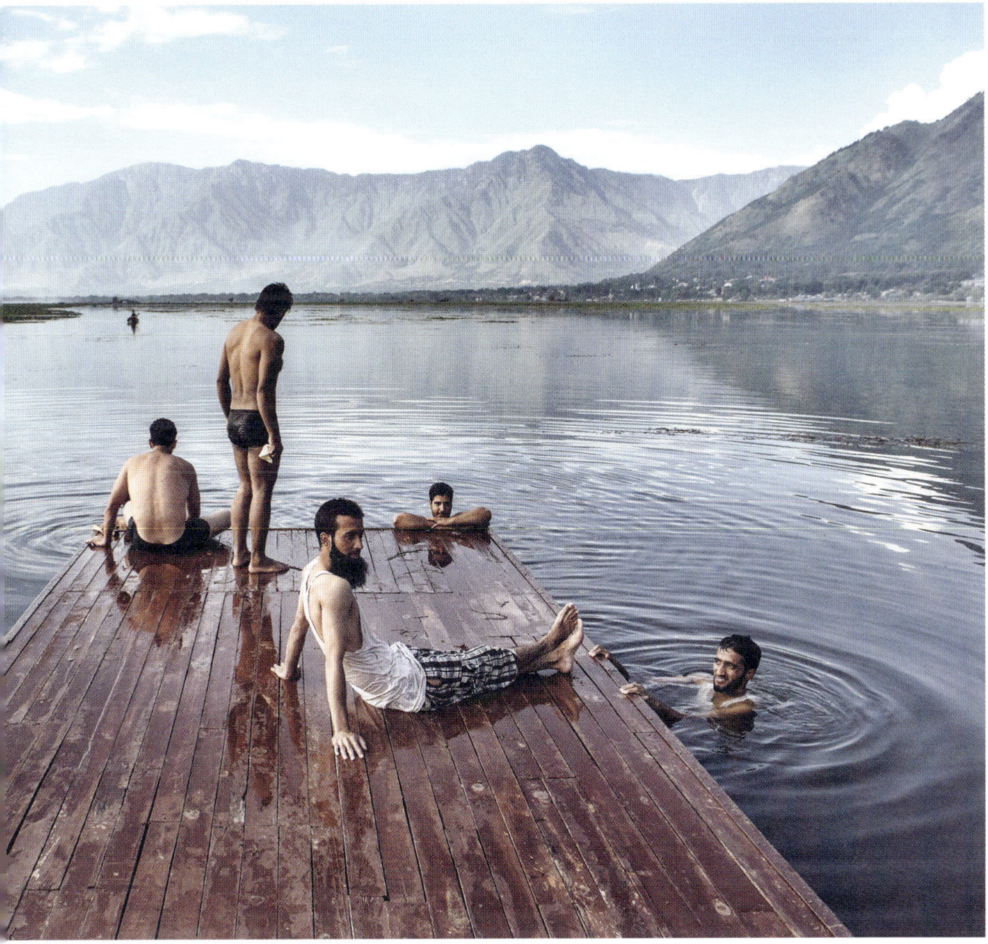

Paradise on Earth

by Camillo Pasquarelli

Srinagar, Kashmir, India

Modern-day Kashmir is one of the most militarised zones in the world, but it was once described by a Persian poet as a paradise on earth. Here, a group of young men enjoy some downtime at Dal Lake.

Buttercup Smoking, Bronx

by Elizabeth Waterman

New York City, New York, USA

Buttercup has been dancing for years and is funny and popular with the crowds and other dancers. I find the women dancers inspiring. To me they embody power, sexuality and athleticism.

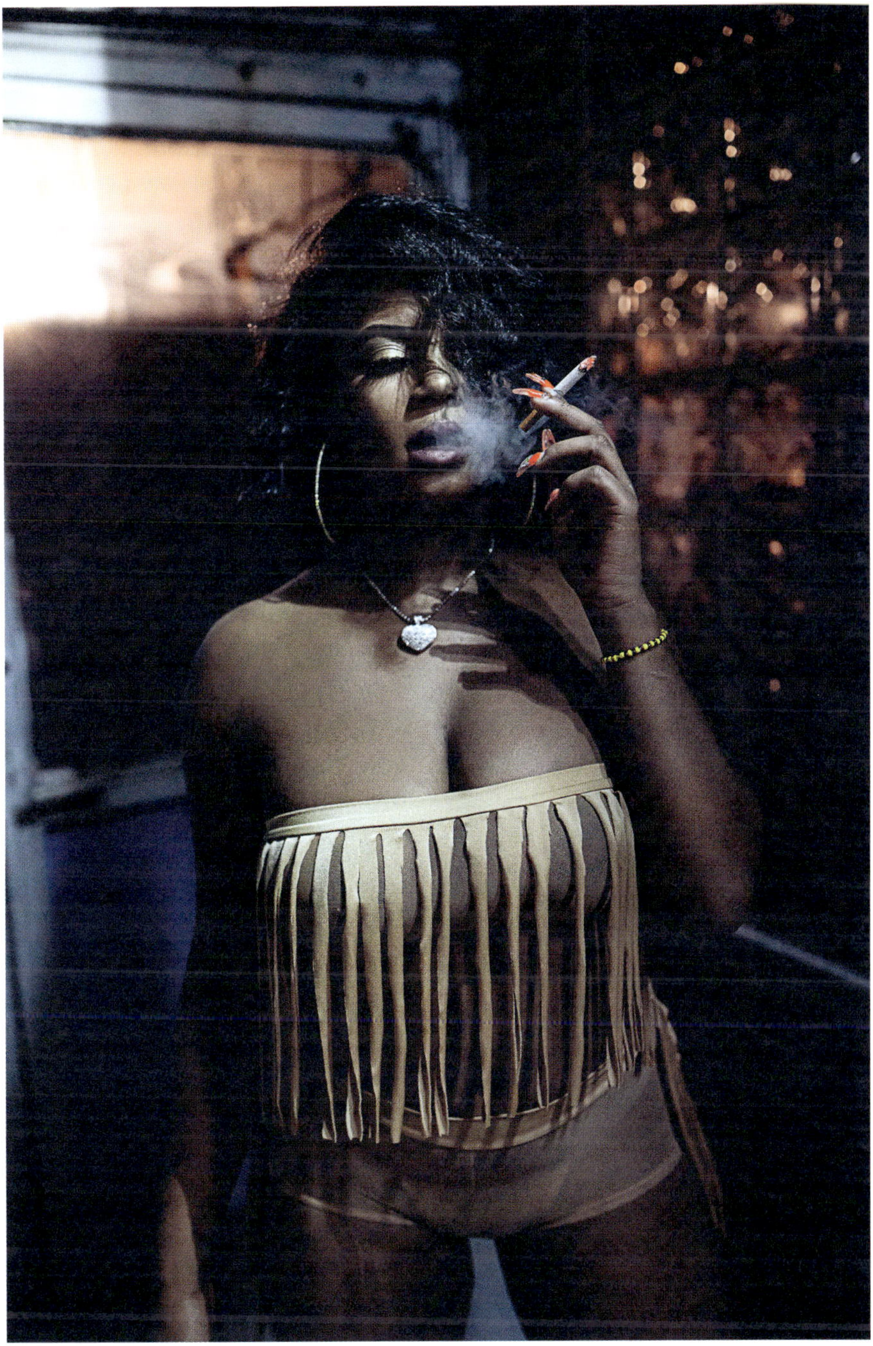

Gillian

by Sipke Visser

London, UK

Gillian is an Irish lady who lives close to my studio. She is very chatty, charming and intelligent.

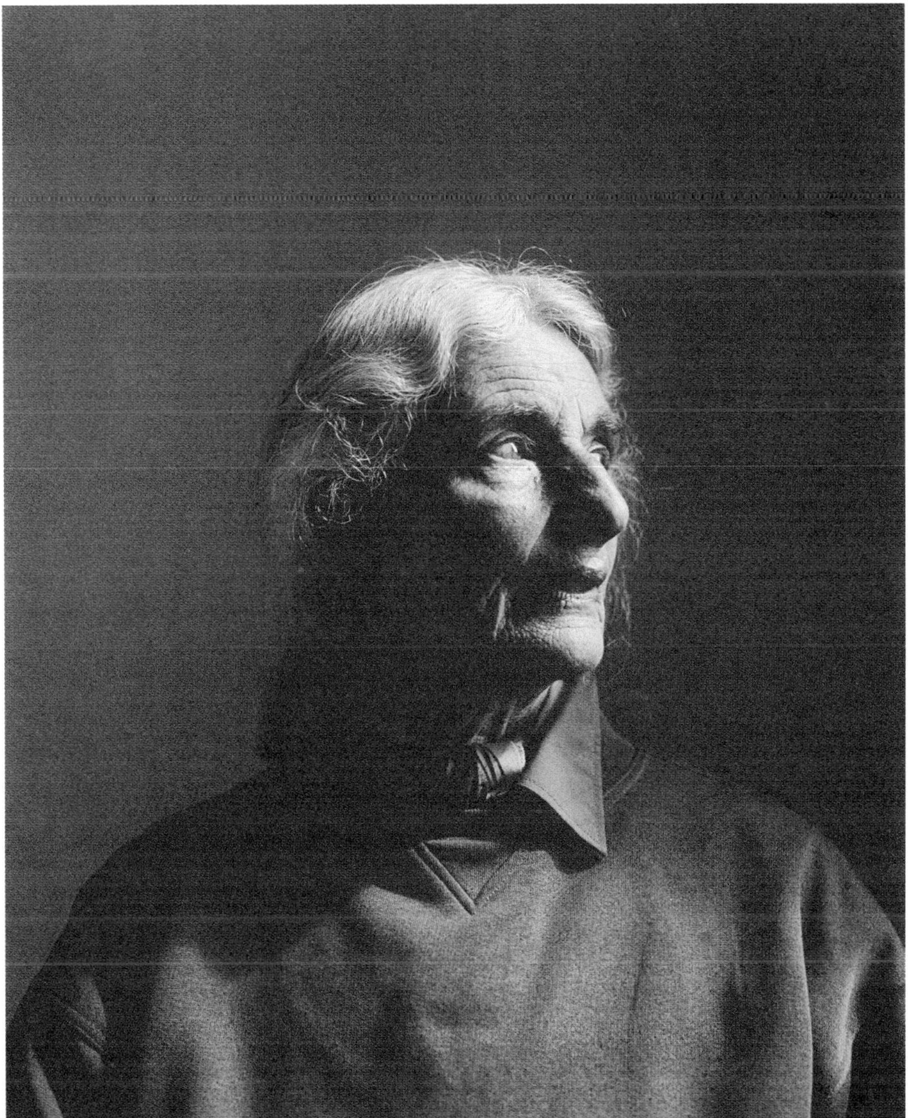

Blue Hour

by Cécile Smetana Baudier

Zealand, Denmark

Nya is a Canadian citizen and the daughter of a Sudanese father and an Ethiopian mother. I took her portrait for a fashion editorial for *Vogue Italia*. It aimed to portray a feeling of vulnerability that is rarely present in fashion photography.

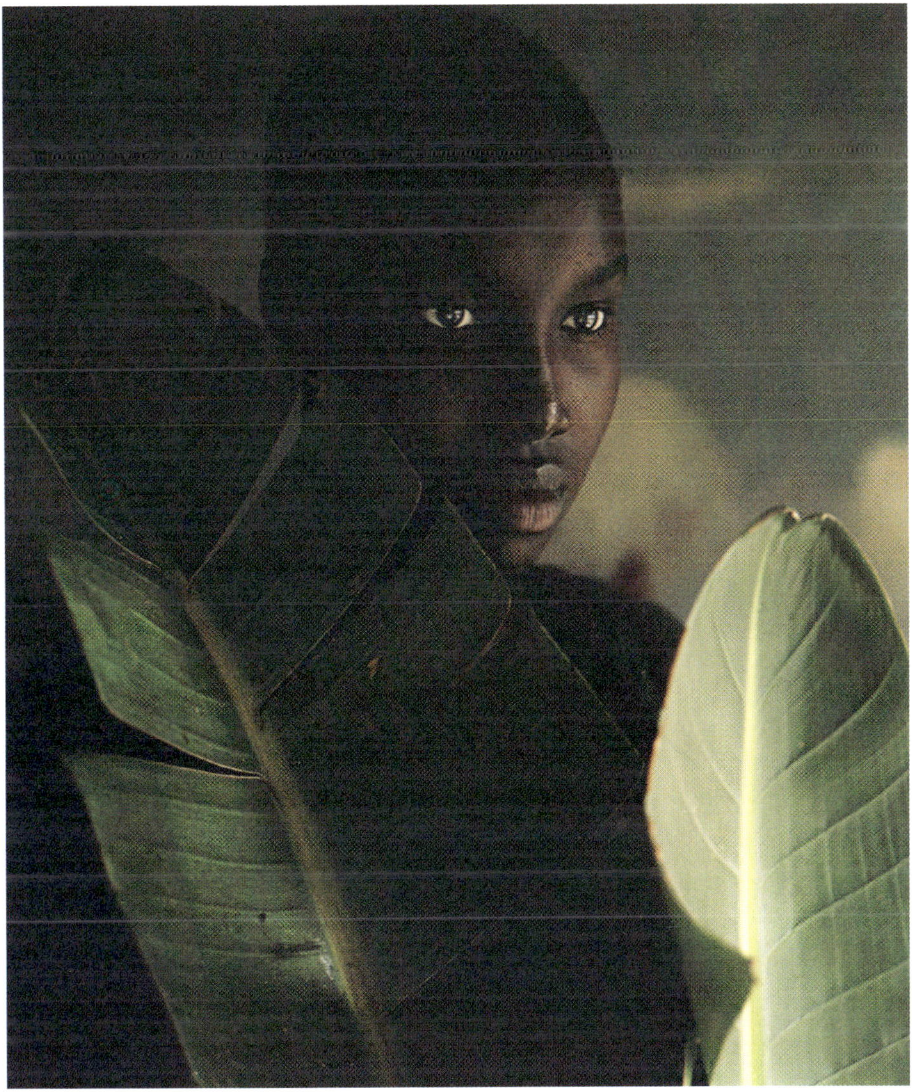

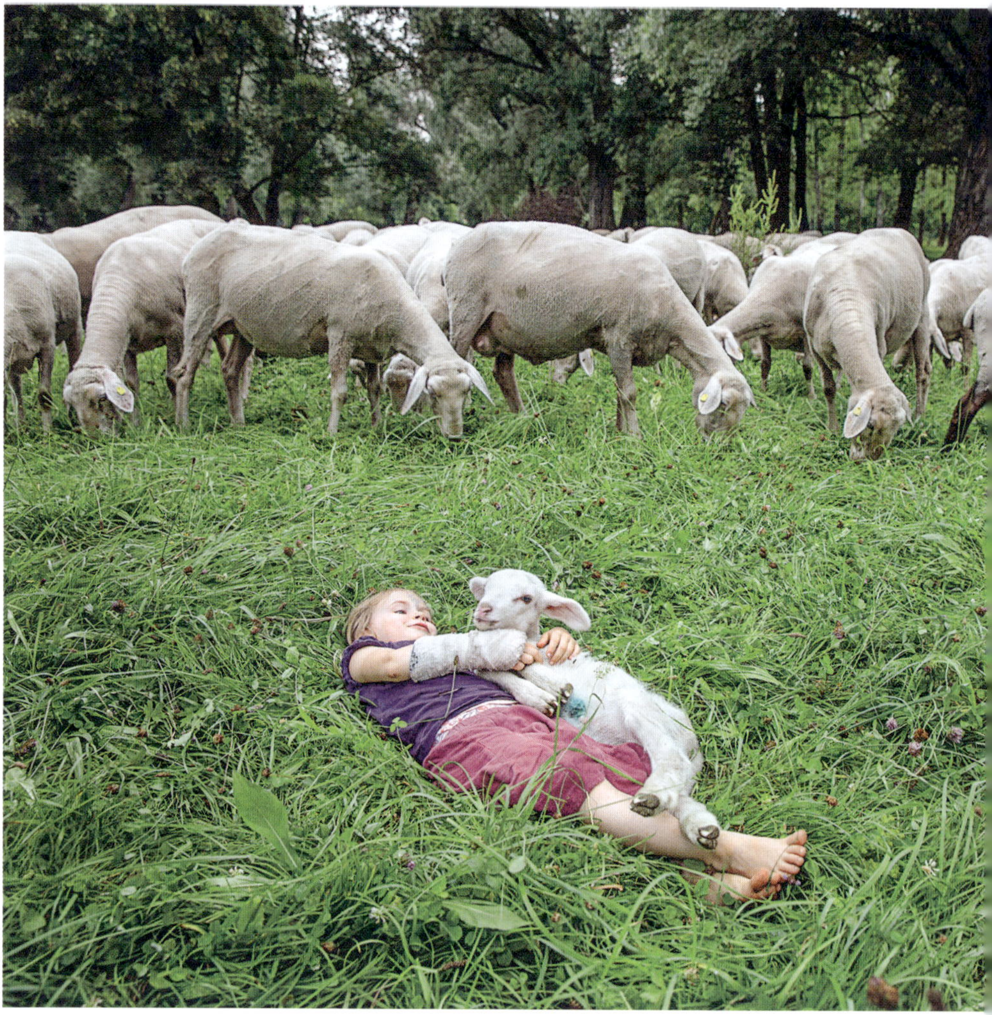

Anabelle's Lamb

by Rui Camilo

Munich, Germany

Anabelle is the daughter of a German shepherdess and is always helping her mother take care of the sheep.

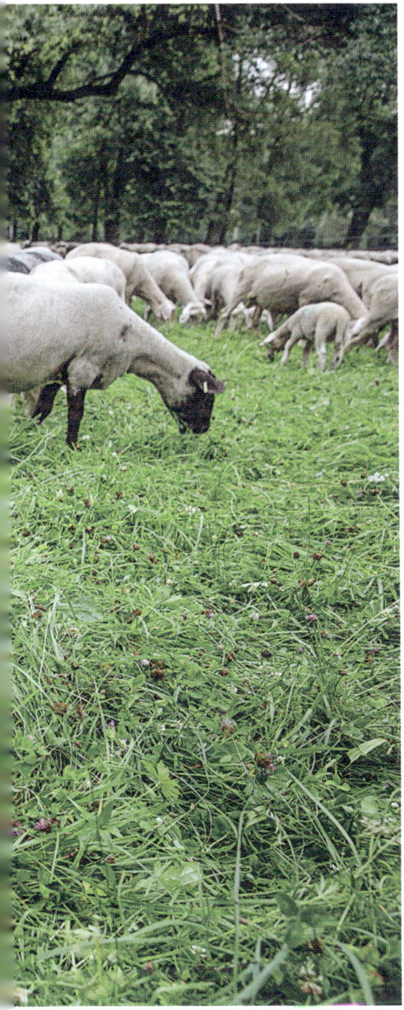

I Can Dream for Us All

by Bevan Agyemang

Jamestown, Accra, Ghana

Velma is the daughter of a fisherman. She dreams of one day leaving her neighbourhood in search of new opportunities.

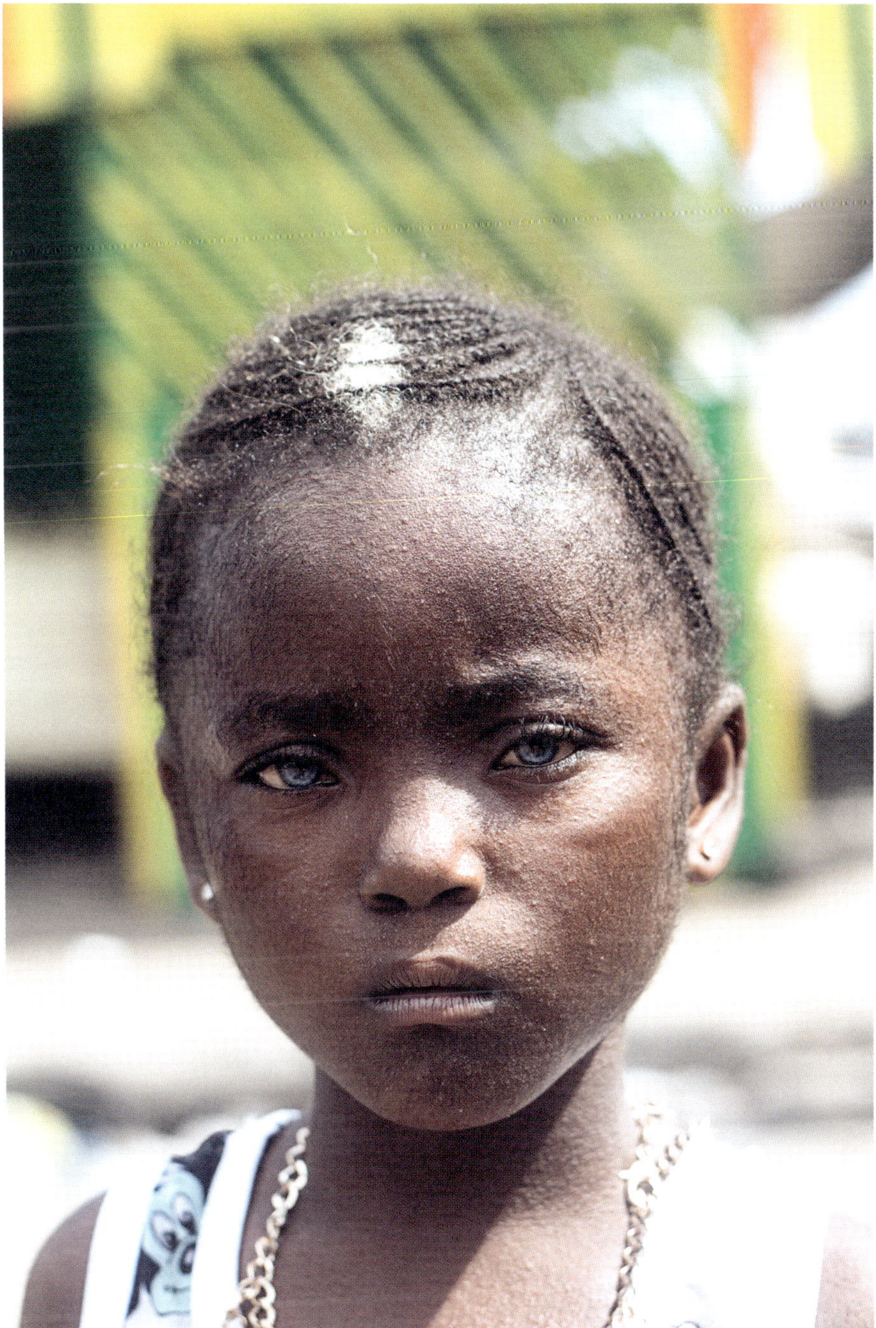

The Mechanic's Daughter

by Douglas Christopher Murray

Tyler, Texas, USA

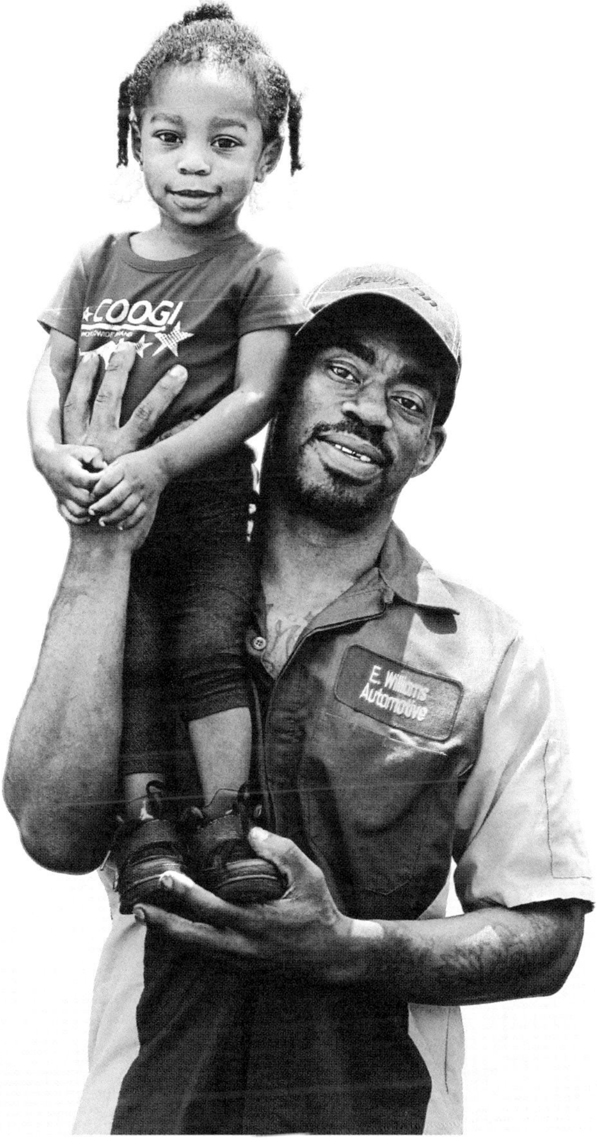
COOGI
E. Williams
Automotive

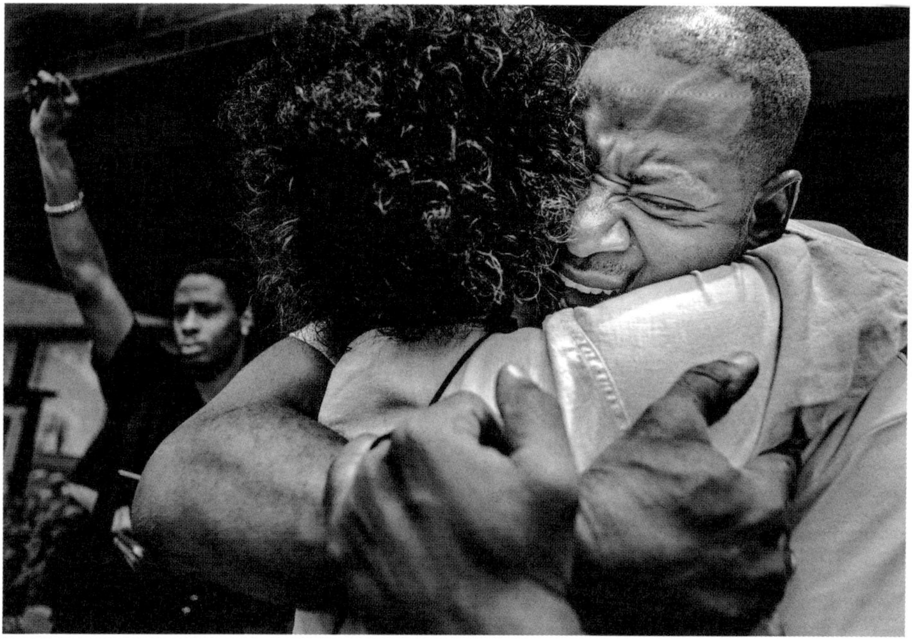

Not My Verdict

by Richard Tsong-Taatarii

Saint Anthony, Minnesota, USA

John Thompson is locked in an embrace after speaking at a memorial rally for his close friend Philando Castile who was killed by police officer Jeronimo Yanez in July 2016. Yanez was acquitted of all charges.

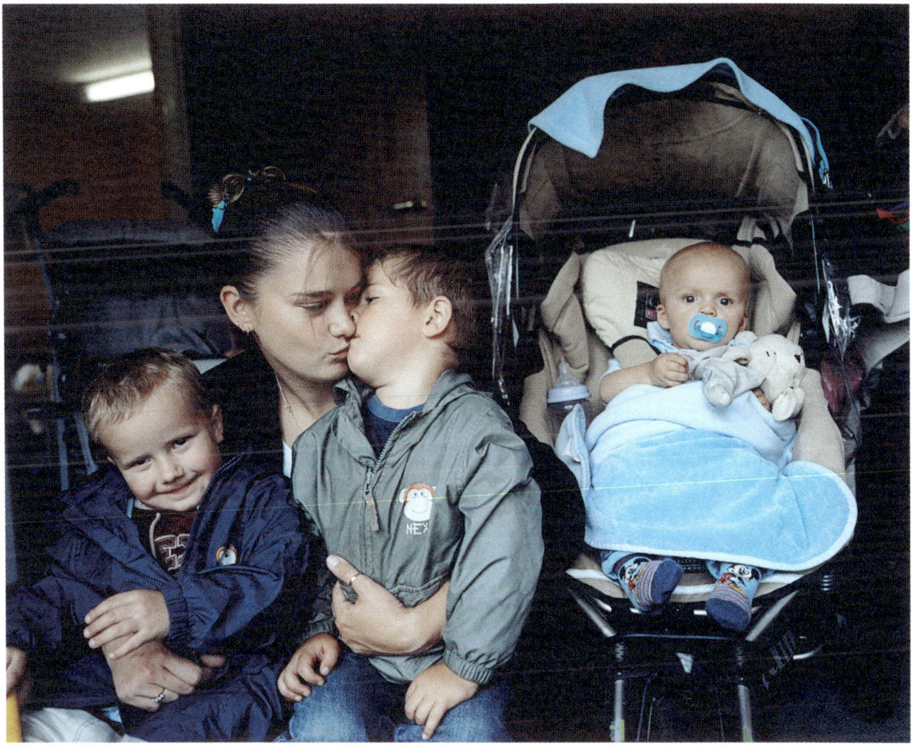

Young Mother with Her Children

by Emma Hardy

March, UK

When photographing at a drop-in centre that supports very young mothers I was struck by this girl's tenderness and the strong bond she had with her children. She came across as calm, practical and committed.

Love

by Mike Chen

San Francisco, California, USA

Elena lies in Zach's lap as he gently strokes her hair. Struggling with heroin addiction, the two support each other and have a positive outlook on their future. 'We're gonna help each other grow out of our habits and get a little house together.'

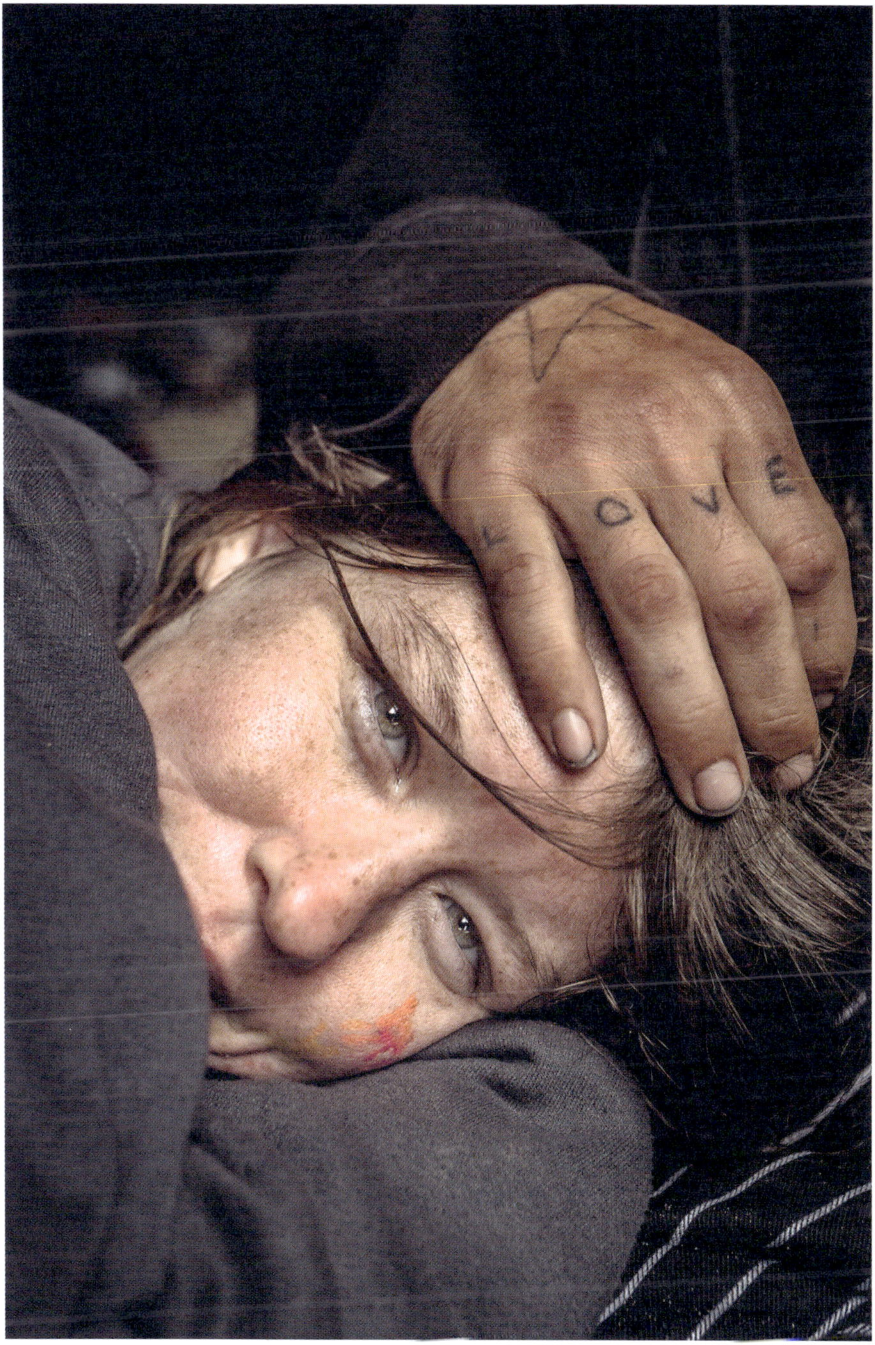

Caro and Dave

by Bastien Deschamps

New York City, New York, USA

Caroline and Dave have been married for 19 years. This photograph, taken in the bedroom of their apartment in Bed Stuy, Brooklyn, is from a series that explores the chemistry between lovers.

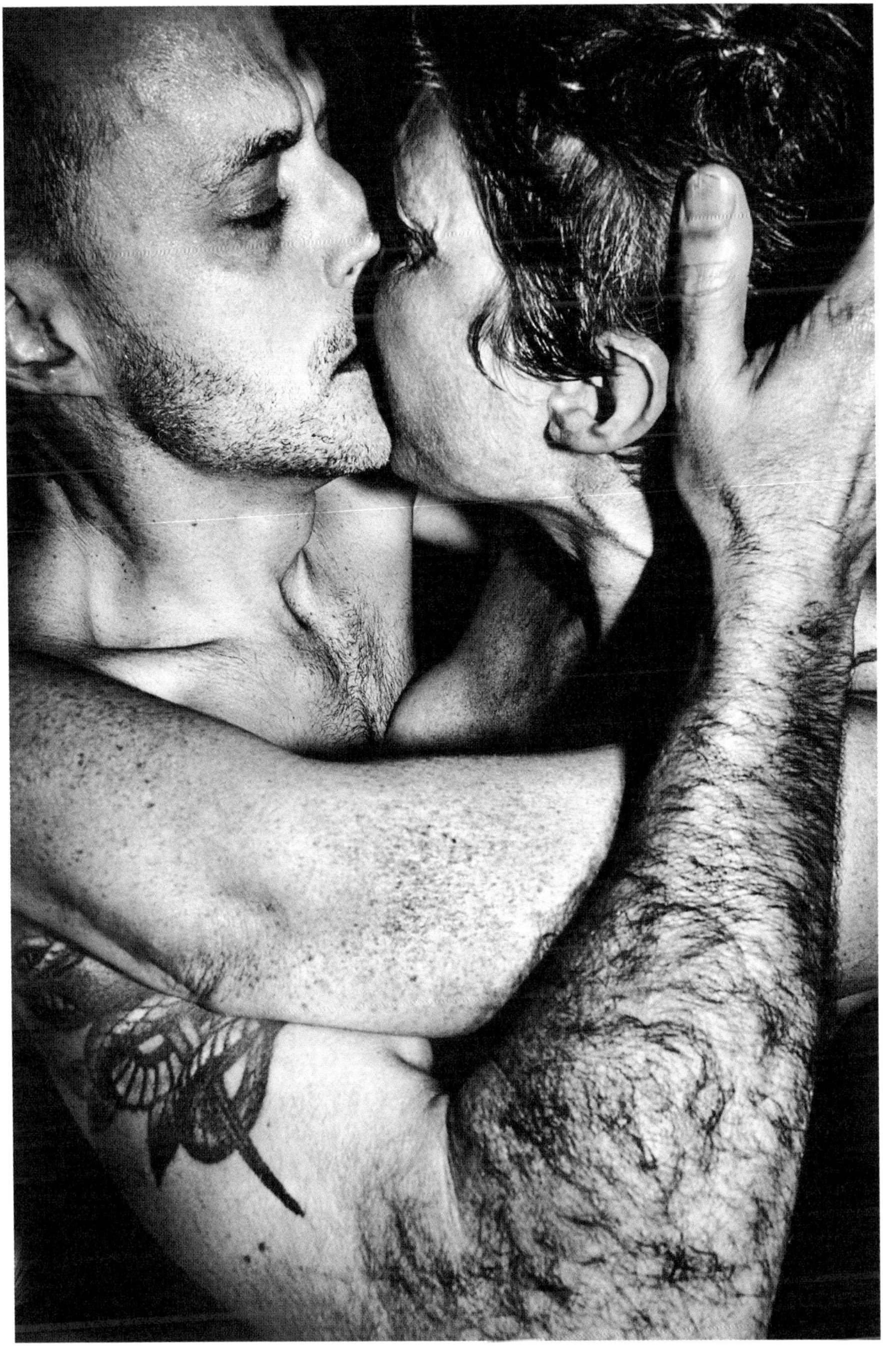

Preserving the Boy in the Man

by Roland Schmid

Karviná, Czech Republic

This is Augustin Drezdowicz, the father of my best friend. Born in 1908, Augustin was a miner, and during World War II he was arrested by the Germans because he helped to source dynamite for partisan forces. He was sent to Zwickau concentration camp and freed by American troops at the end of the war. Although he had a very difficult life he never lost his sense of humour and was the kind of a person everybody loved.

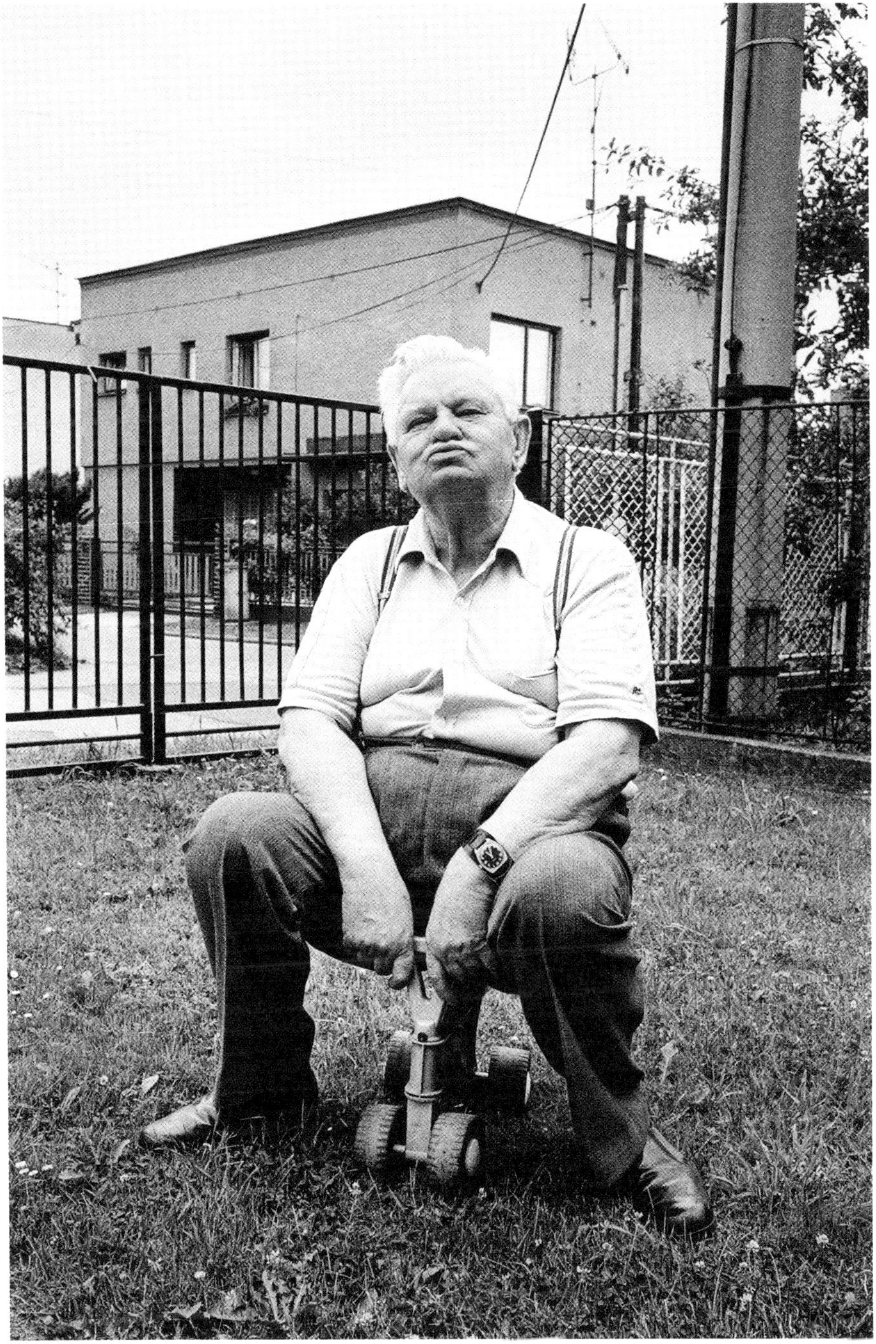

Tilda with Dead Blue Tit

by Danny Burrows

Bellac, France

My five-year-old daughter Tilda and her brother Ernest are fascinated by wildlife. When they found a dead blue tit they wanted to give it a proper burial in the garden of the house where we were staying. Before they committed the bird to the ground they studied it carefully, holding it up to the sky with its wings extended.

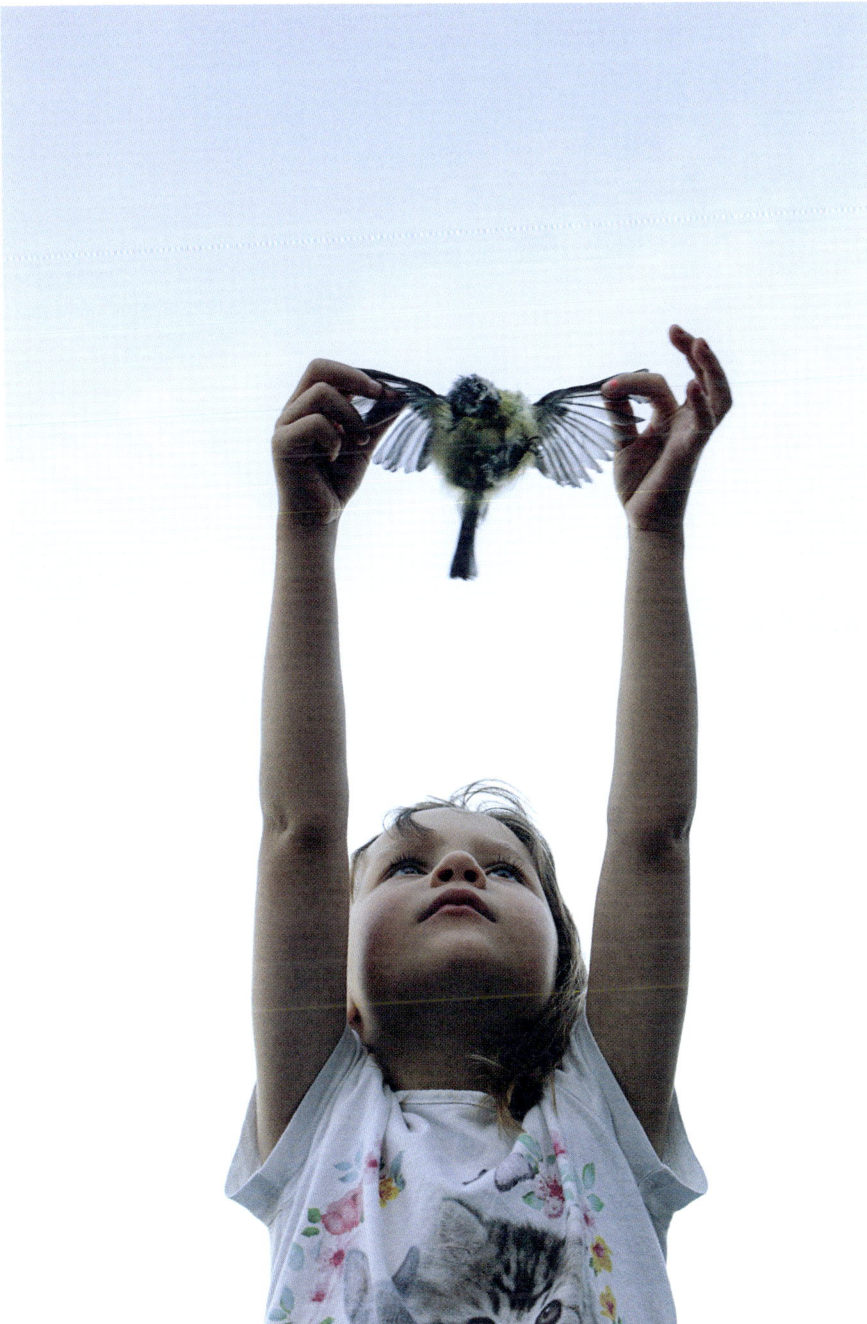

Index